The
Cumbria
Village Book

THE VILLAGES OF BRITAIN SERIES

Other counties in this series include

*Most are published in conjunction with
County Federations of Women's Institutes*

The Cumbria Village Book

Compiled by the Cumbria Federations
of Women's Institutes from notes and illustrations
sent by Institutes in the County

Published jointly by
Countryside Books, Newbury
and
CCFWI, Carlisle
CWFWI, Kendal

First Published 1991
© Cumbria Federation of Women's Institutes 1991
Reprinted 1992

Countryside Books
3 Catherine Road
Newbury, Berkshire

ISBN 1 85306 140 9

Cover Photograph of Buttermere Village
taken by Ted Bowness, Kendal (0539-725880)

County map by Gladys Thompson

Produced through MRM Associates Ltd., Reading
Typeset by Acorn Bookwork, Salisbury
Printed in England by J. W. Arrowsmith Ltd., Bristol

Foreword

Happiness to a Cumbrian is the welcome sight of the hills as you travel north on the M6; stone walls stretching straight up to the skyline and grey farmhouses nestling in the valleys beside rushing streams. The sheep hefted to the hillside for generations, like white dots making a single track to the top of the fells.

Cumbria is steeped in history from pre-historic times, evidence of which is still found in all parts of the county. Cumberland and Westmorland were under the rule of the Scots during the Norman Conquest when the Domesday Book was completed. The feuding and pillaging between the Scots and the English continued for many years, ending with the accession of James VI of Scotland as James I of England in 1603.

The tourist's Lake District gives only a taste of the beauty that abounds. There are many areas off the tourist track where one can find peace and solitude.

We invite you to visit our villages, so widely varied in character, bounded as they are by the Pennines to the east, the Irish sea to the west, Morecambe Bay to the south and the Scottish Border to the north. You will not be disappointed.

Marjorie Morris
County Chairman Cumbria–Cumberland

Doreen Galbraith
County Chairman Cumbria–Westmorland

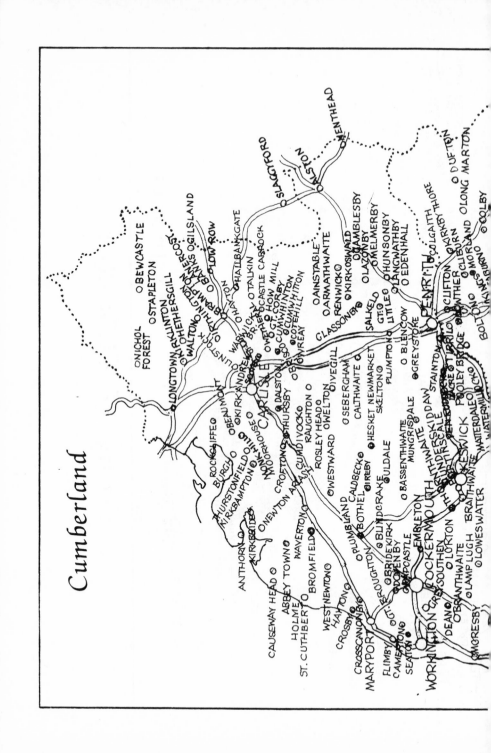

Cumberland

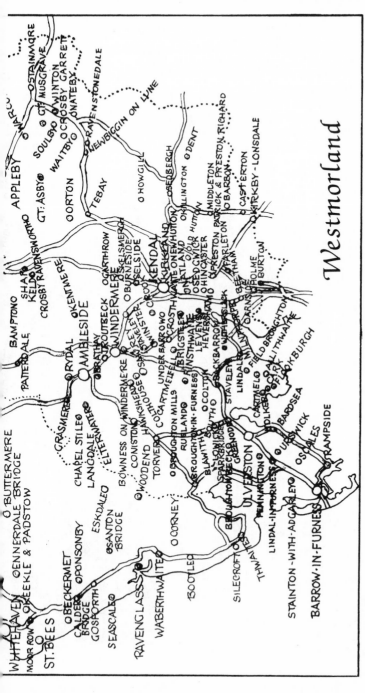

County of CUMBRIA

Westmorland

Acknowledgements

Our thanks to all our members in Cumbria–Cumberland and Cumbria–Westmorland Federations of Women's Institutes for their support, energy and enthusiasm applied to this exciting joint venture.

Especially to Marjorie Morris (Cumbria–Cumberland County Chairman) and Edna Hodgson (Cumbria–Westmorland immediate past Chairman) joint co-ordinators of the project.

Abbey Town ✤

Abbey Town is a crossroads village, centuries ago one of the most important places in the North. It stands on the Solway plain, midway between Wigton and Silloth, in the parish of Holm Cultram. Splendid views of the distant lakeland fells and Skiddaw are enjoyed to the south, and the Solway and Scottish hills to the north.

Its claim to fame is the church of St Mary, known as Holm Cultram Abbey. It was built in the 12th century as a Cistercian monastery, and enjoyed great power for many centuries (entertaining Edward I on two occasions) until the Dissolution in the reign of Henry VIII. It is one of the few monasteries to survive as a parish church, although only a small portion of the original building remains. Many of the buildings associated with the monastery are still inhabited today, one being Mill Grove, once the infirmary. It is being restored to its original state by the present owners. New iron gates, which lead to the abbey, were made by Mr Tommy Wilson, the local blacksmith, in 1959. Cottages belonging to the abbey were transformed into a library and offices. A gift shop was built and an ambulatory connecting these buildings to the church. This work was organised by the vicar, Rev Anthony Miller, mostly with local craftsmen. He also inaugurated an art centre, which enjoyed much success for some years.

Before and after the First World War the village had thriving cricket and tennis clubs, now sadly no more; likewise the bowling green. However, the soccer team has for many years played its matches on the recreation field, bought for village use by public subscription. A popular annual event is the ten-mile, all-comers charity road run, the WI providing over 300 teas for participants and friends.

At one time the village had no less than five public houses, now reduced to one. The Wheatsheaf was built by the State Management Scheme in the 1930s, and is now privately owned. Abbey Town is proud of retaining its post office, but shops are now reduced to two, when once there were many. These included a tailor, draper, cobbler (and clogger), butcher, baker, bicycle shop and co-op. The brewery, flour mill, agricultural implements works and sugaries have long since disappeared. There are now two coal merchants, painters and decorators, a garage, electrician and cabinet maker. Butchers and a fishmonger pay weekly visits. The oldest business is the blacksmith's, which has been in the Wilson family since 1925. It is still thriving in the original smithy.

In the early 1950s a housing estate was built, Friars Garth, followed by 19 pensioners' bungalows, private houses and bungalows, greatly enlarging the village.

The single-line railway which ran between Carlisle and Silloth was built in 1856. Day trips to Carlisle and Silloth were very popular and the closure of the line in 1964 caused dismay. A second station, Abbey

Junction, opened in 1870, running between Aspatria and Annan, but closed after the bridge over the Solway at Port Carlisle was dismantled. It was used by local farmers to attend the market in Annan.

Ainstable 🌿

Ainstable was a Viking settlement and the original name, Einstapli, described the situation – 'a bracken-covered hillside'. The Norsemen cleared much of the birch-scrub east of the river Eden to the fellfoot.

In the Broomrigg Plantation stand two stone circles and a cairn circle. Another ancient stone circle, known as the Grey Youds, was vandalized following the Enclosure Act of 1770 when all but one stone was removed to provide foundations for the drystone walls nearby. (Youd was an ancient Cumbrian word meaning horse). The cost of building the walls was 9d per yard, the work being done by labouring families, men, women and children; most of the walls remain as a monument to their endeavour.

Between Broomrigg and Ainstable, the two west-facing fields above the village are deeply-furrowed and were the highest fields in England ploughed compulsorily to provide corn during the Irish potato famine of 1820. The distance between the furrows was determined by the width of a swath which a man could cut using a six ft long scythe blade. Single-share ploughs were drawn by pairs of horses specially shod to work up the hillside. The work was hard and the local blacksmith had to make replacement shoes every other day.

John Leake, born here in 1729, was known as the 'Man-Midwife'; he wrote many books on childbirth and women's diseases and founded the Westminster Lying-in Hospital near Westminster Bridge. He died in 1792 and was buried in Westminster Abbey.

There has been a church of St Michael at Ainstable, on its present site overlooking the village, for over 900 years. The present building, which succeeded a similar stone one that stood for 100 years, was erected in 1872 at a cost of £2,000. The church, with its 65 ft high tower, striking clock and two bells, was a well-known landmark which could be seen for many miles. Unfortunately, the tower had been poorly built and, after much debate, was dismantled in 1983. A small porch incorporating the old arch entrance was built in its place.

The sandstone school is now a private house, but just picture in the dust-moted sunbeams of the past, the chalky, black-robed master leading the chanting of tables, trying to instil in his scholars the love of literature and the mysteries of the decimal point ('You've made a mullock of it!'). PE was drill marching in the playground. At prayers the master (also the church organist) loudly played the rather sombre hymns, his hands descending on the keys at fractionally differing times so that most of the chords were in two parts! As a result of his teaching at least six girls went on to become teachers and, from one family alone, came a doctor, an aircraft designer with Fairey Aviation and an aeronautical engineer.

In 1706 Rowland and Mary Smith built their sandstone house, which remained thatched until the early 1900s. In 1982 this house became the home of the Eden Valley Woollen Mill, part of the Glen Livet Weavers and the muted sound of the loom was added to the hum of tractors as a background to the village.

Ainstable has grown in recent years, bringing in more people seeking the quiet country village atmosphere as an antidote to city life. This has not, however, weakened the strong community spirit, and, like most country villages, there's always plenty going on!

Allithwaite

The village of Allithwaite, two miles north-west of Grange-over-Sands, was founded by the Vikings. The *Oxford Dictionary of Place Names* translates it as 'Lilifr's Thwaite', 'Thwaite' being the Westmorland word for 'a clearing'.

In the 17th century, Allithwaite boasted a corn mill, and later a brewery, now converted into attractive cottages. Quarrying was an industry which thrived and there is still a prospering wood yard, operated by the Knipe family. The new main door at Cartmel Priory was made by the present owner of the business. A careful look will reveal his trademark, a carved snail.

John Carter, of Cart Lane, whose family had prospered by serving as guides over the treacherous sands of Morecambe Bay, bought

Allithwaite Village centre as it was about 1910

11

Wraysholme Tower in the mid 1700s. The present Queen's guide is Mr Cedric Robinson, who lives at Guides Farm. He can still be seen most weekends during the summer months, guiding parties who wish to cross from Arnside. His is a Royal Appointment, and in 1985 he led a carriage procession, headed by the Duke of Edinburgh, over the sands of the Kent estuary.

St Mary's church and school were built in 1851, with money bequeathed by Miss Mary Lambert who lived at Boarbank. A school house and vicarage was also provided by her. There is a small United Reformed chapel in the village. Boarbank Hall, Miss Lambert's old home, is now a convent, guest house and nursing home run by Augustinian sisters.

Part of the old manor of Allithwaite, lying to the south, is Humphrey Head, interesting for a number of reasons. In the 18th and 19th centuries, visitors flocked to the Holy Well, dedicated to St Agnes, to sample its waters. Miners of Yorkshire and Cumberland thought that illnesses caused by their employment could be healed by the water. Now younger people from Yorkshire come to the Education Centre built on the headland and try their skill in outdoor pursuits. Far more interesting is the legendary fame which comes from the story that the last wolf in England was killed here.

Between Humphrey Head and Kents Bank is a cave where prehistoric and Roman artefacts, including spear heads, pottery, axe heads, rings and coins have been discovered. A more recent landmark is Kirkhead Tower, built on a rise overlooking Morecambe Bay.

Today, the village, a tasteful mix of old and new, has grown. Young families have moved in to enjoy the quiet setting, which is easily accessible for their place of work in Ulverston, Kendal or Barrow. Older people, many who have retired from the stress of business life, have made it their new home, surrounded by the peacefulness of the sandy bay, gentle fells and the Lake District peaks of Coniston Old Man and Helvellyn in the distance.

Alston 🜲

Alston claims to be the highest market settlement in England, standing about 1,000 ft above sea level. It is also remote, being approximately 20 miles from the nearest town. Unquestionably the altitude is high, with the air clear and bracing, and generally gardens here come into bloom about a month later than those closer to sea level.

To approach Alston from any point on the compass is a delight; high on the North Pennines, sheltered in the folds of the fells it drops down to the South Tyne river. For centuries there has been a community here where travellers and drovers met while crossing the Pennines.

Strangers are warmly welcomed, and if they stay are soon accepted. Perhaps this is one reason why it has thrived for so many centuries with only a few fluctuations of fortune. New people bring new ideas. For example the railway was brought to Alston in 1852 and axed in 1976. Later a voluntary group, the South Tyne Railway Preservation Society, was formed, and in 1983 a narrow gauge railway began operating and is expanding, attracting tourists to the area. About the same time the empty Congregational church was bought privately; now known as Gossipgate Gallery, all forms of arts and crafts are exhibited and sold, and at times a musical evening is arranged, all adding to the interest of living in Alston.

In years gone by Alston was a thriving lead mining centre and a great deal of prosperity depended on this activity, now long gone. The mines are currently being researched and part restored by the North Pennines Heritage Trust.

The recreation ground known as Fairhill has activities for all age groups, including a bowling green and adventure playground. In past centuries drovers from the east en route to markets in the Penrith area rested their animals on Fairhill, where a metal ring, still to be seen, was set in a large stone to which the bulls were tethered. During the early 20th century many circuses came here. Once again the bull ring was used, this time to tether the elephants.

There was a dam on Fairhill which fed the millrace. This flowed down through the village and powered machinery for two small grain mills; the wheel house of the High Mill is in the process of being restored. It stands just off the Market Cross, the cross itself a feature of interest.

The size of the three churches in Alston is witness to the fact that the population was once more than double its present size. St Augustine's, St Paul's Methodist chapel and the former Congregational church are all large buildings in terms of present day small congregations. The Roman Catholic church, which is smaller, came later than the others; nevertheless these small congregations of devoted people work hard to keep their churches a living part of the community. The Quakers were also a dominant force in the area, and continue to this day.

When the foundry closed in 1979 a small engineering company set up on the premises. Since then a new factory has commenced manufacturing mountainwear clothing; both these ventures are thriving. For its size Alston has a large number of hotels, restaurants, cafes, excellent bed and breakfast accommodation, and a number of public houses, although their number has diminished over the past hundred years.

Alston streets are cobbled and steep and a menace in icy weather but compensated for by striking views. The stone buildings in and around Alston are mainly 17th century, and give a picture of that era.

Ambleside ༄

Although Ambleside is often referred to as a village, in reality it has been a market town since it received a charter for a weekly market in 1650. It has a resident population of some 3,000 souls and at first sight seems quite a large place for so few people. However, during the summer months the population increases substantially owing to the area's popularity as a holiday resort.

There are many short walks to local beauty spots, one of these being to Stock Ghyll Waterfalls. The falls have a drop of 70 ft and are in woodland under fine trees which have a carpet of daffodils in the spring. In spate the falls are most impressive and for several centuries, from the 14th onward, the force of the waterfall provided power for local industries. There were twelve water mills getting their power from local becks; five of them from Stock Ghyll. There were carding and fulling mills for the extensive woollen trade, a linen mill, bobbin mills whose products were sold worldwide until after the Second World War and, of course, paper, saw and corn mills.

The Romans arrived here in AD 79 on their way to establish a port at Ravenglass. They made their base, which they called Galava, on the flat land to the north of Windermere now called Borrans Field. Their first fort was built of wood and clay; this was replaced some 30 years later with a stone one. This later fort has been excavated on several occasions.

One of Ambleside's landmarks is the tiny 17th century Bridge House on the Rydal Road. This was built as a summer house in the gardens of Ambleside Hall, which is now no more. During its long life it has had many uses; it has seen service as a cobbler's workshop with a pigeon loft in the upper storey, as an antiques shop, and in earlier days was home to a man, his wife and six children. This family also earned their living on the premises by basketmaking. Finally the house was purchased by local people in 1926 for the sum of £450. It was then handed over to the National Trust who opened their very first information office in the house.

In the area east of Rydal Road between Stock Ghyll and the Kirkstone Road lies the oldest inhabited part of Ambleside. On roads such as Smithy Brow and Fairview Road there are many delightful cottages to be seen. They are in a good state of preservation and many date from the 17th century.

Local people and visitors alike enjoy the Rushbearing procession and service which takes place in early July each year. This commemorates the old ceremony of covering the church floor with rushes from the lake in days when church floors were just beaten earth. The main reason for doing this was to make the floor warmer but it was also useful in clearing out a year's dirt when the old rushes were swept out to clear the way for the fresh crop.

Many places have a particular sweetmeat associated with them and Ambleside is no exception. It is not in production today but many older residents remember the tooth-pulling confection, Ambleside 'clag 'em' being made in one of the old cottages in Church Street. Mary Dugdale, known to the children as Mammy Dugdale, was the maker and vendor of the toffee.

Anthorn 🌿

Anthorn is an area of outstanding natural beauty on the shores of Moricambe Bay, an inlet of the Solway Firth.

The village is in two parts, the original part in an agricultural setting dating back to 1279, with a Congregational chapel and manse dated 1869 and a public elementary school built in 1875. The chapel, manse and school are now in use as private dwellings. The residential part was built in the mid 1950s for Naval and later Army personnel use. This became a 'ghost village' in the 1960s, looked after by a Ministry of Defence caretaker, until 1971 when all the houses were bought by the Border Engineering Company and then sold privately.

A NATO radio station opened on the site of the former Royal Naval airstation in 1964, the masts of which still dominate the skyline. During the hours of darkness the red lights on the masts give the impression that Anthorn has a permanent Christmas tree.

The name Anthorn means 'a single thorn bush'. Travelling along the coast road from the village shop towards the NATO station there is a bridge over a small stream; just over the bridge on the left is a very old thorn bush. It is said that freemen of the shire gathered round this thorn to hold important meetings. It is interesting to see that even today this is where visitors to the Bay gather.

To the west of the village about half a mile along the coast road, on the left amongst gorse, almost buried in a mound of soil, is an ancient cross thought to mark the limits of a sanctuary.

Over the coast road opposite the cross stands what is locally known as 'Mary's Tower', which has a window on all sides. There are two stories associated with this tower. The first is that Mary Queen of Scots was held prisoner here for one night in 1568 on her way south to England. The second story is that the tower was built as a studio for an artist named Mary Backhouse in the 1850s. Underground tunnels are said to run from the village to the tower. Moricambe Bay and the original part of the village in days gone by, were said to be frequented by smugglers who used the tunnels and buildings to hide themselves and their contraband tobacco, wines and spirits.

Estuaries like the Solway can be very dangerous places when the tide is coming in. Behind the tidal bore the water can rise very fast and there are many hidden and potentially hazardous channels in the marshes. One can become marooned quite easily, or sink in the shifting sands. A horse and cart has been known to disappear in the shifting sands.

Haaf netting, which is fishing Norwegian-style, can be seen on the Solway. It is a unique method of salmon and sea trout fishing. Fishermen stand in the flood of the rising tide, holding large square nets on poles in which to catch the fish. When a salmon or sea trout swims into the net the fisherman flicks (or heaves) the net over the pole to trap fish (heave is 'haaf' in Norwegian).

Appleby ✍

Appleby, strictly speaking, is more than a village. It developed as the 'county town' of Westmorland after the Norman Conquest, which is an indication of its strategic importance in the Eden valley, and not until the reorganisation of 1974 did it lose the title. But it lies on the eastern edge of mountain land and as the centre of economic activity developed further west, Appleby declined in importance. It remains, however, an attractive little market town with a village atmosphere and a great deal of interest and charm.

The remarkable Lady Anne Clifford, born at Skipton in 1590, devoted much of her life to restoring her neglected estates and castles and the churches at which she worshipped, and in concern for the people she considered her own. The work of her hand is clearly evident in Appleby. The castle stands firm on its hill, and may be visited. St Michael's church, Bongate is redundant as such and is now a private residence, but the 12th century parish church of St Lawrence merits a visit. Both Lady Anne and her mother, Lady Margaret are buried there and are commemorated by splendid tombs. In Lady Anne's time there were many itinerant beggars, and her concern for those who were old women in dire need led her to build the almshouses, the Hospital of St Anne, still in use today.

Appleby's main street, Boroughgate, has been described as one of the finest in England. An avenue of mature lime trees, planted in the 1870s, is flanked by well-kept properties dating from the 17th to the early 20th century. The houses and gardens behind still show the lines of the medieval burgage plots. The warm red sandstone gives the town a mellow appearance and a number of Georgian houses add grace and style. The Moot Hall stands in the lower market area and is still used for council meetings. Though much altered, a plaque above the door is dated 1596 as an indication of the age of the building.

Across the bridge over the Eden is the part of the town known as The Sands. Above The Sands, steep streets of sturdy 19th century terrace houses lead up to the railway station. The line is the famous Settle and Carlisle. Appleby people joined wholeheartedly in the eight-year long fight to keep it open. When the Midland Railway Company in 1869 got permission to build, the church bells rang jubilantly – and would have done so in 1989 when the line was saved, had they not been away for repair!

An institution of some antiquity is now housed in modern buildings to the north of the town. Appleby Grammar School was founded in 1574 by charter from Elizabeth I, but has its roots in a medieval chantry school in the church.

The basis of the local economy is agriculture. The Eden valley is a busy farming area which welcomes and caters well for visitors. It doesn't, however, have too many of the extra 'tourist attractions' which often ruin the very thing which people have come to enjoy. Most local jobs come from work which services farming and tourism. Manufacturing industry is mainly represented by Express Foods, originally set up in the 1930s to send fresh milk to London by rail, but now making a variety of cheeses.

Last, but not least, must be mentioned Appleby New Fair – the biggest gipsy gathering in Britain. The second Wednesday in June is the official date but the travelling people often arrive well before then to give the town a unique and colourful atmosphere.

Armathwaite ✤

Armathwaite nestles by the river Eden – a beautiful village of trees, peace and tranquillity. The name Armathwaite is derived from Hermithwaite, 'thwaite' being the Danish word for clearance – it is believed a hermit once lived in a clearing in Inglewood Forest, near the site of the present castle.

This castle is a four-storey pele tower, built to prevent the Border raiders from penetrating further into Cumberland, and has a Georgian addition. It was owned by the Skelton family and between the reigns of Edward II and Henry VIII members of this family represented the County and City of Carlisle in Parliament. John Skelton was Poet Laureate to Henry VIII. Since 1712, when the castle was sold, it has changed owners and been altered many times.

Armathwaite's church of Christ and Mary was built in 1402 and subsequently fell into disrepair and by the 17th century was being used as a cattle shelter. Richard Skelton of the castle rebuilt it around 1660 and in 1668 endowed it with £100 in his will. The church stands today almost as it was when rebuilt, but with the addition of three beautiful stained glass windows, one of which is pre-Raphaelite and made by the William Morris Workshops in 1926.

Further along the river by the weir, a mill was built for grinding corn at the beginning of the 19th century. This mill was altered to operate electrically in the 1930s and at the same time the village cottages were also given electricity. The generator was somewhat temperamental and in times of flood the power diminished so the local children were sent scudding off to the weir wielding brushes, to clear the generator of its debris! Unfortunately the mill is now derelict.

A beautiful sandstone bridge spans the river. Originally this was a single track bridge but was widened and improved in 1907. As there is no village green or bus shelter, the bridge is a meeting place for locals to have 'a bit of a crack'.

Armathwaite is very proud to own a station on Britain's most scenic railway route, the Carlisle/Settle line. When this line was being built a great number of workers lived in the area, bringing prosperity to the local grocer and publicans (of which there were many) but much trouble for the local constabulary. The line was finally opened in 1870. There are

Cottages at Armathwaite

now six trains each way daily calling at Armathwaite station, which is a great relief to commuters and shoppers since by this time the local bus service had been withdrawn. Fortunately the village shop and the post office continue to flourish, the school remains open and there are two old inns taking visitors and serving meals.

Gone are the days of generations of one family living and working in the same village. Armathwaite has a new housing development to cope with an increased population but almost all of the working population have to commute – even so there are still many benefits to be had from village life.

Arnside ✎

Until the 19th century Arnside was a very small village and part of the parish of Beetham, to which churchyard coffins had to be carried several miles, via Hazelslack and the limestone pavement and up the rock staircase 'Fairy Steps'.

The oldest building, Arnside Tower, now a ruined shell, testifies to the need for defence against pillaging Scots. In the 17th century, to refresh weary travellers and probably to harbour smugglers on occasion, several inns were set up, of which the only one remaining forms part of the Fighting Cocks Hotel and still has the cockpit in its cellars. Saltcoates is Arnside's oldest house and was the centre of a thriving salt industry and there are a few other houses of the 17th and 18th centuries.

It was in the 19th century that Arnside began to be known as a resort as well as a busy little port. Pleasure boats sailed from Morecambe and Fleetwood and passengers came ashore to enjoy the famous salmon and shrimp teas or to take rides by wagonnette up to the Knott. Coal barges unloaded at the jetty and drag horses carried the heavy coal up the hill and returned with limestone from the quarries to be used in such projects as the building of Blackpool Promenade. But it was the coming of the railway in 1857, with the opening of the viaduct, which made Arnside accessible to far more visitors and led to the building of most of the striking stone houses which give it its character. Designated an Area of Natural Beauty, it enjoys one of the loveliest sites on the North West coast.

Behind the village rises the Knott, a rounded hill with woodland walks (where occasionally one may glimpse red squirrels and deer) and from the rocky top may be seen the magnificent panorama of Lakeland hills and the northern Pennines. The Knott is owned by the National Trust.

It is the Kent estuary which commands immediate attention. The incoming tide races over the ebb, creating a bore which dashes against the piers of the viaduct and with high tides and winds can be an awesome sight. This estuary is an ornithologist's delight. The sands may still be crossed, but only with the expert guidance of the sands pilot, whose knowledge of the constantly changing channels and shifting sands is incomparable.

Pleasure boats no longer ply, the river is now not deep enough and the pier is for visitors to sit and fishermen to fish! Not only from the pier but everywhere along the shore, fishermen are to be seen in all weathers, and at low tides, 'treading' for flukes is still widely practised.

Asby

Asby is a scattered parish five miles south of Appleby and derives its name from the old Norse 'askr', an ash, and 'by', a farm or settlement; the name was formerly Askeby. Asby parish contains the villages of Great and Little Asby.

The older of the two villages is Little Asby, about two miles south-south-east of Great Asby. Little Asby is a tiny hamlet which in ancient times had a chapel dedicated to St Leonard, the patron saint of lepers; this may be the reason for its isolation. Nowadays there are very few residents in its one or two farms, while the main area of activity is the caravan park at one of them. Nearby is an ancient earthwork, one of several in the district – a flat platform or court some 80 yards by 20 yards in size surrounded by artificial banks rising to 15 ft. Also near is Sunbiggin Tarn, a well-known nesting site for noisy black-headed gulls – not many years ago their eggs were taken and sold in towns. The adjacent moors abound in wild flowers, in particular the rare primula farinosa.

Great Asby is situated on either side of Asby Gill, which rises on the west side of the village, where the entrance to Pate Hole, a cave extending to 1,000 yards, can be found. The beck is dry for much of the year, and only flows when extremely heavy rainfall causes the 'kettles' higher up Asby Gill to fill and force water down the watercourse. Below the church is St Helen's Well, not a well at all but a strong spring of clear water which gushes out all the year, even in severe drought, filling the beck below. Years ago it is said to have been a meeting place where the village women exchanged gossip. The water was believed to have healing properties, and was taken for medicinal purposes. Close by are St Helen's almshouses, built in 1811 for aged poor widows and widowers. Further down, the beck passes Marble Mill where local limestone was polished into 'marble', some of which can be seen in the church.

The church of St Peter, situated centrally, dominates the village. The original church, referred to first in a charter dated 1160, was deemed in typically Victorian fashion to be in such dire need of repair that it was demolished and completely rebuilt in 1863–6. A painting of the original church shows that the new design was based on the old. It is thought that the studded door of the nearby Three Greyhounds pub came from the old church.

The two most interesting buildings, historically, are the old rectory (now a private house) with its 14th century pele tower, and Asby Hall, a strikingly tall black and white painted farmhouse built in 1694 and once owned by the powerful Musgrave family. The rectory had a door lock which was presented to the rector by the grateful Lady Anne Clifford after she and her retinue were given protection there during a storm. It is now preserved in the church.

When visitors ask what residents of Great Asby do, the answer is usually 'farming' – and this is partly true, although it is a popular place for retirement, and about a fifth of the houses are second homes or holiday homes. The land is unsuitable for crops, so sheep are the main concern, with some dairy and beef cattle. There are no shops now but in the 19th century the village had several shops and many tradespeople – tailors, butchers, shoemakers, weavers etc, and must have been self-sufficient. The village school, endowed in 1688, still survives.

All in all, Asby remains a peaceful rural village well worth a visit. Occasionally it is besieged by sheep and silage trailers, and more and more frequently in the summer by walkers along the Westmorland Way, which is helping to put Asby on the map.

Askerton, Kirkcambeck, Lees Hill & West Hall 🦢

Situated in the north-east corner of Cumbria, only six miles north of the A69, in undulating, unspoilt and uncommercialised countryside, lie the adjoining hamlets of Askerton, Kirkcambeck, Lees Hill and West Hall. They view the northern Pennines rising to the east and the Scottish Border hills to the north and are only 14 miles north of the Border city of Carlisle. At the time of the building of Hadrian's Wall three miles away, this region was situated on the Scottish side of the wall.

Askerton boasts an imposing small castle, first built as a fortified house in the 15th century. The towers were added during the reign of Elizabeth I. Here 'Belted Will' (a Dacre of Naworth Castle) lived when he was Warden of the Marches, supposedly keeping peace between the Scots and the English. From the towers the Jacobites would have been seen riding into England on their ill-fated mission in 1745 with Bonnie Prince

Charlie. Part of the castle is now used as a farmhouse and has been continually dwelt in since its inception. Next to the castle is the Gallows Hill where many men were reputedly hanged for paltry reasons. Local folklore implies that miscreants were buried on land of the neighbouring farm of Gallowberry but nothing has ever been found!

The small church at Kirkcambeck sits perched above the road and the river Cam on the site of the original 11th century church. Sadly, the ancient church was pillaged and destroyed by Scottish raiders at the end of the 13th century. Now only an arched doorway still remains of the ancient church standing in front of the new church.

The primary school at Lees Hill, built in 1876, serves the whole area, with some children travelling many miles to it. The school has one most unusual feature, it also serves as a church.

From the beacon above Gillalees Farm, on a clear day, six of the old counties can be seen (Cumberland, Westmorland, Northumberland, County Durham, Roxburgh and Dumfriesshire). The beacon stands beside the route of a Roman road between the forts of Birdoswald and Bewcastle.

The area once had four public houses, two tile-kilns making drainage tiles from the local clay, two schools, a cornmill (where the wheel may still be seen), a blacksmith and a clogger. Of all these only Lees Hill school and one public house are still used. Farming is the only occupation carried out in the area and, as the need for farm labourers has diminished due to mechanisation, the population dwindled. However, many new people have come to live in the region who commute to Carlisle and neighbouring towns and consequently the population is gradually increasing again.

Ayside

Ayside is a tiny hamlet some three miles from Newby Bridge at the southernmost tip of Lake Windermere. It takes its name from the equally tiny beck which once was plentiful enough to supply the monks of Cartmel Priory with their fish. It is still a pretty place with colourful gardens to cottages, most of which are of stone. It has twice won the prettiest small village competition in recent years. A quite busy road now runs through it where not so long ago only horse-drawn carts and cattle were to be seen, but hedgerows still provide a colourful display of wild flowers.

Once, clogs and shoes were made or repaired in the village, and you could have your washing returned to you within a few days, starched and ironed, on a donkey cart. Near to the main road there is an old farm where once carters and drivers could stop for a rest and a change of horses.

Along the main road, towards High Newton, there is a quarry and here for some years a man lived happily on his own beneath an upturned boat, until he died as quietly as he had lived. It is said that he was an excellent stone-waller who also cut the hedges for busy farmers, taking his own tools and tackle along with him. One day, he was not paid for a walling job so he just knocked it all down again and left. Simple justice.

There is still a splendid family butcher whose business began more than a century ago but whose quality and reputation is as high now as ever it was. He still calls round the local villages twice a week – a real boon for those living far from shops.

Haymaking was a great time for the getting together of friends and neighbours, most of the work being done by hand after cutting – raking into rows before putting into cocks and then forked up to eager hands waiting on a cart. What fun the young ones had, helping with carrying round the 'drinkings' of tea or cider and lemonade or chasing a fleeing rabbit or playing with the farm dogs, who were so much part of the family. And what mammoth feeds the farmer's wife would provide at the end of the day for the tired and dusty workers. Life in the country followed a fixed pattern of sowing and reaping, milking, feeding and lambing, year after year; as it still does. There was always plenty of work to be done and there were more people to do it. It took longer than nowadays, but somehow people seemed to have more time to help one another and to enjoy helping. The question 'But who is my neighbour?' was not one that was often asked.

Backbarrow 🦢

The village of Backbarrow is in the parish of Haverthwaite. Backbarrow was once a tiny hamlet containing very few houses, and on the banks of the swift-flowing river Leven the monks of Cartmel Priory owned a flour mill. This mill has changed many times from its beginning and at one time was one of Blake's 'dark satanic mills' which used very young children – orphans from Liverpool and London. After it closed down it went through various changes until it was taken over by the Lancashire Ultramarine Company and finally by Reckitt and Colman. These last two companies made industrial blue, and this is the foundation of Backbarrow's only legend. It doesn't matter how emphatically visitors are told that the building was not the 'Dolly Blue' factory, they won't believe it. So are legends made.

The furnace where John Wilkinson was once the ironmaster has closed down and is now an untidy ruin, but on the walls is magnificent ivy, which flowers conveniently at Christmastime. The Donkey Field opposite now has sheltered housing, in place of the thistles which delighted the goldfinches.

The number of houses has more than doubled in the past 50 years. The developers who bought the mill property turned the mill building into the Whitewater Hotel, and built a number of timeshare houses, collectively known as The Lakeland Village.

Browedge, up the hill, is where the Victorian school was situated, and a number of septuagenarians can still remember being taught their three 'Rs' there. Higher up the hill was the headmaster's house, which is still known as 'The School House', and further along was once a dame school. Right at the top of the hill is Bigland Hall, home of the onetime squires, and with a chequered history since the 16th century. Henry Bigland in his will, dated 9th December 1689, gave £100 to buy land, half the rent to be given to the school at Browedge and the other half to the poor of the parish. George Bigland had four years earlier also left money for a school at Browedge.

An interesting true story is told of a Mr Robinson, partner in the cotton mill, who, on a cold winter's day in 1799, travelling from Backbarrow to Cartmel, found a poor man lying in the snow. He found someone with a cart and the stranger was taken to a lodging house and attended to by Mr Brockbank, a surgeon. Upon being revived the man complained of poverty and said he was on his way to see his son at Condergreen. A few days later he died. His death was advertised in public journals of the day, but he remained a mystery. On removal of his clothes there were found secreted in them 185 guineas. This money was the source of The Beggar's Breeches Charity.

Bampton ✤

Bampton is a very pleasant village, set in a valley surrounded by hills. Through the valley flows the river Lowther, joined by the Haweswater beck, which is a stream flowing from the beautiful lake of that name. Lying four and a half miles west of Shap and ten miles south-west of Penrith, Bampton enjoys the benefits of a public house, named St Patrick's Well, a garage and primary school.

Until the 19th century, there were many tradespeople in the valley. Tailors, shoemakers, joiners, grocers, butchers, clog makers, master blacksmiths and a miller, all made a good living. The mill was bought by a local lady Mrs A. Preston, who ran the village shop and post office for over 20 years and who was awarded the MBE in 1980 for services to the community. There are no farms left in the village, with many farm buildings such as Bampton Hall being converted into dwellings. Only a few hill farms remain, on the outskirts of the village.

In Bampton Grange stands St Patrick's church, erected in 1726 on the site of an earlier structure, being restored in 1885. Opposite the church stands the vicarage, which houses the famous Tinklar Library, containing many books written in Latin. Indeed, an old saying is that 'they drove the plough in Latin in Bampton'. There is also a Wesleyan chapel built in 1877 and still in use for services. The chapel has its own tea room and Sunday school.

Bampton Grange had many commercial premises. Herbert McCormick, in addition to being a highly skilled blacksmith, killed pigs, cured bacon, swept chimneys, lime-washed the police house, repaired bicycles and clocks and was also the village hairdresser.

There were once four 17th century dwellings with date stones above each door, but only three now remain. Businesses still in operation at Bampton Grange include a hat box maker; a lady who breeds Shetland sheep, whose wool she shears for dyeing, spinning and weaving; and the Crown and Mitre Hotel which caters for local people and tourists. There being no village store, residents of both villages have to rely on mobile shops, or travel to the nearby market town of Penrith.

Hamlets in the parish are Knipe, Bomby, Butterwick and Beckfoot. One and a half miles west of Bampton is Burnbanks village, which was built to accommodate the families of the workforce who built Haweswater Dam for Manchester Corporation. Sixty-six bungalows were provided, along with a mission room, recreation hall and large huts for single workmen. Today, only 20 bungalows remain at Burnbanks and are owned by North West Water Authority. Eleven are still lived in but the remainder are now derelict. A further eight wooden bungalows at Naddle Gate are privately owned.

Barbon 🌿

Barbon is a pleasant village of about 100 dwellings in the Lune valley between Kirkby Lonsdale and Sedbergh.

Past the church, up the steep brow, the fell road winds through Barbondale, with Barbon Manor in the woods on the left. Here by the Barbon beck is a popular picnic area. At nearby Fell House is a pony trekking centre.

Barbon is recorded in the Domesday Book as Brerebrun, and was formerly made up of a few smallholdings and cottages. The nearby hamlet of Beckfoot was, at one time, of more importance than Barbon, having a corn mill, a parsonage, a doctor's surgery and a grocer's shop. The shop book still survives, belonging to Joseph Dixon, Beckfoot, 1st January 1818, and it records tea at seven shillings and nine pence a pound, no doubt a luxury.

St Bartholomew's church was built in 1892/1893 to replace an old church which was believed to date back to the 12th century. Only the porch and vestry of the old church remain and they are used as tool sheds. The oldest part of the churchyard is bordered by yew trees. Look inside the church at the font cover, lectern, organ case, chancel screen and eagle – all were made and carved in Barbon by local craftsmen.

There is a village store, which celebrated its centenary in 1990, where Rob, Isabel, and Thomas Beaumont supply local needs; they also have a sub-post office two mornings a week.

In 1861 the Ingleton to Lowgill branch railway line came through the village, but was closed to passenger trains in 1954 and freight in 1964.

The track was removed in the summer of 1967. The Barbon Creamery which stood alongside the station closed in 1965 after serving the local farming community for many years. The station and creamery site is now a housing estate of modern bungalows.

Sadly the village school which was built in 1867 closed in 1982. The children now attend a new primary school – St Mary's at Kirkby Lonsdale, where the bell from Barbon school hangs. The old school has been converted into a house. The reading room built in 1884 is now a holiday cottage. The village smithy has gone; it was worked by Jack and Harry Tallon, both now dead, and it now houses a clockmaker and repairer – Tom Clapham. There used to be at least three joiners, a cobbler, a coal merchant, a police station and a vicarage.

The Barbon inn is a 17th century coaching inn and the village has, in years long gone, had a couple of ale houses – one was called the Dun Cow Ale House at the head of Beckgate, and the other Hill Top. In the 17th century they used to hold the St Bartholomew Plum Sunday Fair, when booths were set up in the main street for the sale of plums. The fair would go on briskly, but as evening approached they would adjourn to the Dun Cow Ale House.

Bardsea ✤

By the northern shore of Morecambe Bay on the Furness Peninsula nestles the picturesque village of Bardsea. Before road and rail development, the treacherous 'over-sands' route from Lancaster was the main link to this then isolated area of Lancashire, now a part of Cumbria.

On entering the village, Main Street has houses on the right hand side, built on the former site of Bardsea Hall which was demolished in the 1930s. The street rises as it approaches the Ship inn, originally a farm (1750) which offered hospitality to travellers. Opposite is the old school, closed since 1936 and now the church hall. Continuing past the church, the street is lined by carefully preserved limestone cottages. Many of the oldest are in close proximity to the lychgate and one of these incorporates the post office, the only remaining village shop.

At the brow of the hill opposite the Braddylls Arms, the road sweeps left down to the shore with more attractively renovated cottages, formerly the homes of fishermen and farm labourers. Facing the shore is a former water-driven corn mill, now converted to a licensed restaurant. Holy Trinity church, its spire a well-loved local landmark, stands sentinel over the village from its prominent position above Main Street.

On a clear day the views from the churchyard can be breathtaking. To the north, beyond the Crake valley, lie the Lakeland hills and mountains and to the east, across the ever-changing seascape of the bay, the Cartmel fells and the Pennines with the prominent plateau of Ingleborough. Inland to the west, farmland rises to the extensive bracken-covered common land of Birkrigg, which boasts an ancient stone circle and the 17th century Friends' burial ground adjacent to the tiny hamlet of Sunbrick. Here lie 223 Quakers, including Margaret Fell of Swarthmoor Hall. To the south, the dense expanse of Sea Wood sweeps down from Birkrigg to the shore. Its few remaining oaks were amongst those originally planted over 200 years ago to provide timber for sailing ships.

The attractive tree-lined coast road, which was built in the 1930s to provide work for the unemployed, takes most of the through traffic, leaving the village comparatively quiet. Recently, a narrow strip of the shoreline has been designated a Country Park with picnic tables and limited parking, offering a peaceful vista of the bay's shingle and sands. Chapel Island, where in times past monks provided refuge for travellers negotiating the hazardous quicksands and dangerous channels of the bay crossing, seems deceptively close.

Beyond the promontory of Wadhead, the remains of the old shipping jetty can be seen at low tide. Up to the early 19th century, vessels trading between Ulverston and Fleetwood called at Bardsea to unload coal and take on iron ore and corn. Red Lane, the old route to the jetty, was so called because it was stained by the iron ore being transported from the nearby mines at Dalton.

Fishing still plays its part in the life of the village. Tractors, which have replaced horses and carts, can be seen on the sands at low tide, setting nets and bringing in the fish and shrimps — a well-known delicacy of Morecambe Bay.

Bassenthwaite ✺

Some of the earliest known inhabitants of the valley were the 'Cumbri', ancient Britons whose ruins are still visible at Elva Plain and Castle How. The Romans came, and left only their fort at Caermot on Binsey Fell. In the 9th and 10th centuries, marauding Vikings came to the valley, and they stayed to people it. Thus Bassenthwaite came into being.

The village stands in an idyllic setting: nestled at the foot of Skiddaw (3,054 ft high) and Ullock Pike (2,230 ft high), a mile from the lake (old name 'Broadwater') and six miles north of Keswick. The village green is flanked by attractive terraced houses, with an avenue of majestic lime trees, planted to celebrate Queen Victoria's Diamond Jubilee. A chattering stream, Hall's beck, with ford and ducks, flows nearby. Three farms function in the village. The village school still operates, and there is a post office, garage and caravan site with shop. The Sun inn, an 18th century coaching inn, and the Castle inn, cater for locals and visitors.

Occupations in the mid 19th century included farmers, yeomen, millers, blacksmiths, cartwrights, stonemen, shoemakers and tailors. Records show two corn mills, two mines, and several shops and traders. A road through the village is still known as 'Cooper Dub', where barrels were made. Today, there are fewer farmers and labourers, and occupations include employees of public and private authorities, teachers, builders, joiners, forestry and car maintenance workers. The parish population in 1841 was 536, compared with 433 in the 1981 census.

At the Ireby/Robin Hood crossroads, near the boundary, lies Cobblers Hollow where wood was collected for soling clogs. Here, sheep stealers were hanged, and 'the Ghost of Cobblers Hollow' is said to haunt this area.

The parish is served by two churches – the Norman St Bega's, by the lakeshore (probably the most romantically situated church in Cumbria); and St John's church built in 1878 to replace the chapel of ease built in 1470. The Methodist chapel, built in 1865, is situated just off the village green.

Bassenfell Manor, built about 1842 by William Rathbone (shipbuilder and former mayor of Liverpool) is now a Christian holiday centre. North of the lake stands Armathwaite Hall, former home of the Spedding and Vane families. At the end of the 19th century, J. Boustead enlarged the Hall. He built a long, high wall encircling the grounds, and the main road was lowered so that passers-by were not seen from the Hall, thus not spoiling *his* view!

Mirehouse, a family home built in 1666, was acquired by the Speddings in 1802. Situated near St Bega's it is in perfect harmony with its surroundings. It was a literary centre, entertaining such writers as Carlyle, Tennyson, Wordsworth and Southey. In 1835, Tennyson wrote his *Morte d' Arthur*, inspired whilst sitting at the lakeside, near to St Bega's.

Baycliff

During past centuries, the villagers paid tithes to the rector of Aldingham. The barn in the rectory grounds is probably the tithe barn. There was poverty in the village; a workhouse was provided for the older parishioners, and orphan children were put as parish apprentices. Sea Wood Farm was the manor court where grievances were heard and awards and punishments decided.

Apart from farming, quarrying and the mining of iron ore at Stainton and Adgarley provided work. The carts of ore were brought down to the shore at Baycliff, near to the Beanwell, which provided water for the village and the ships in the bay. Flat-bottomed boats took the iron ore to Backbarrow furnace. The soil in the gardens on the shore is still red from the ore. Fishing in the bay developed as the population of the neighbouring town of Ulverston and Barrow increased, so there was a ready market for fish and farm produce.

There are still two inns at Baycliff, and early records show the Farmers Arms was run by John Mount, but for almost 200 years the Porter family were tenants and Eric Porter has only recently retired. John Best had a beer house and grocer's shop about 1849 – the Fisherman's

Arms, a public house until 1936, when the licence was transferred to the new hotel.

There were also stonemasons in the village, as the stone from Baycliff was in great demand, being almost pure white and marble-like. The inferior stone was burned for agricultural purposes, hence the many lime kilns in the area. The stone was also used when the 'new' coast road was built in the 1930s. The stones were broken on the village green with farmers providing horses and carts for transport.

A windmill once stood in a field above the Farmers Arms in about 1901. A reservoir of water was discovered underground and the windmill was used to pump the water to standpipes.

Today there are still many lovely walks in the area, with rights of way clearly marked. The shore is pleasant and a great feeding ground for seabirds.

Beaumont

Beaumont is a small village situated about four miles north-west of Carlisle on the west bank of the river Eden. As its name suggests, the village is set on a hill, on the highest point of which stands the church of St Mary. The line of Hadrian's Wall runs through the village following the bank of the Eden from Kirkandrews to the church, where it turns westward to Burgh-by-Sands. It is likely that a milecastle stood on the site now occupied by the church. Stones from the Wall were used to build the church and local houses. In a garden wall opposite the church is part of an ornamental inscription which was fished out of the river over a hundred years ago.

St Mary's church dates from the 12th century. During the following 300 years of the Border wars, the church and village must have suffered repeated damage and hardship. From outside the church there are fine views in all directions; to the north over the Solway Firth to Scotland, south to the Lake District and east over Carlisle to the Pennines.

A small triangular village green in kept in good order by one of the residents. To commemorate the Queen's Silver Jubilee a tree was planted. It grew well until June 1990 when a freak whirlwind snapped off the top half leaving only a three ft high stump.

Over the past century the population of the village has been halved and now numbers only about 80. Within living memory there have been a great many changes. The village used to support a shop, a public house, (the Lowther Arms), a blacksmith, a shoemaker and a joiner. Before a public water supply was available a windmill pumped water from the river to a tank near the church. This provided a private, tapped supply to three large houses. The rest of the village depended on wells. Rain water was saved in large wooden barrels. St Ann's well, situated at the bottom of a steep part of the river bank, provided very cold water invaluable during hot weather to help to set the butter. Older residents remember that by the time they reached the top of the bank the bucket was less than half full!

In 1823 the Carlisle Canal was opened allowing the passage of shipping of up to 100 tons into the canal basin at Carlisle from Port Carlisle. It must have been a fine sight to see ships sailing through the fields below Beaumont. A lock was built at the west end of the village, and the lock-keeper's cottage still remains. Thirty years later the canal was drained and a railway track laid along the bed. Eventually the line stretched from Silloth to Carlisle and flourished until its closure in 1964. There is still a bus service running through the village from Bowness to Carlisle providing a service for shoppers and commuters.

Beckermet 🥀

A wrought-iron gate between two old stone posts swings in the wind, and sheep clamber over the broken walls on the hillside. The natural mounds here mark the motte of Caernarvon Castle, with views toward Scafell Pike and the Roman fort, Hardknott.

Beckermet has two parish churches. St John's in the village has a lovely interior – sandstone of contrasting colours with terracotta. The old font is now out in the churchyard with a collection of corbels, coffin lids and fragments of eleven crosses. The old church, St Bridget's, between the village and the sea, has four services a year, and the churchyard is still used for burials. Its origins are Norman, and there are two cross-shafts, one on a circular base. Land near here was for the use of the landlord of the Royal Oak to graze five geese.

The old school, now demolished, was near the river and the land is now the village green. Snowdrops and daffodils enhance this area in the spring, and on the opposite side of the river on common land there is an open truck, a relic of Beckermet's iron ore mining days. Five arches of old railway bridges follow the remains of the line which ran from Egremont. A railway engine lies buried in the bog-land it toppled into, down toward 'The Boggles'.

Kirbeck Store is the village shop with year round attractive displays of flowers in their window boxes. On the right of the White Mare were four cottages which have now been converted into one house. Some of the rooms of the White Mare were used as grain stores. Mr Castles, the blacksmith, had his smithy near here and the coalman had to fetch the coals from the old station yard with his horse and cart. The cart was weighed empty, then weighed again with its load of coal.

The other public house, the Royal Oak, run for many years by one family, is opposite the cottage that now serves as the post office. The reading room, cared for and supported by its own committee is used for many public village functions. The new school has pupils from a wide area as the small schools at Haile and Calderbridge have now closed. Village events now include a Lenten lunch, a fete, sports day, a coach trip in the summer, bonfire night celebrations and a Christmas fair and party.

Beetham

Beetham is an attractive village lying in the vale of the river Bela, one and a half miles south of Milnthorpe on the A6 trunk road. The village with its towered church and black and white decorated Wheatsheaf inn, nestles against rising woodlands to the west. With the river flowing at its feet, usually with a gaggle of white geese on its banks, it makes a lovely setting. A fault in the limestone causes the river to fall 16 ft, creating a spectacular waterfall.

The Heron corn mill was founded by the canons of Conishead in 1220. To this day, herons fish there so it is aptly named. The mill is still open to the public, displaying one of the best surviving examples of a water-driven corn mill. On the opposite bank is the important paper-producing plant of Messrs Henry Cooke at Waterhouse Mills, which draws nearly half a million gallons of water daily from the river, and yet hardly disturbs its flow.

The only shop is the post office in Church Street, dated 1881 on the lintel but believed to be 18th century. Passing Ashton House, a road leads upwards to Slackhead. Halfway up on the left, is a lovely little shrine; inside the cell is the figure of St Lioba, in the habit of a Benedictine nun and holding a bell. The parish church was originally dedicated to this Saxon saint, but was changed after the Norman invasion.

On the field in front of Ashton House, 'Beetham Sports' are held on the first Saturday in August: this was started in 1920 by local farmers and is still a popular event.

Further south are the remains of Beetham Hall, now a farm, originally built as a semi-fortified manor house in 1340. The de Beetham family, mentioned in the Domesday Book, held the manor for eleven generations. A Baldwin de Beetham fought at the battle of Hastings. Stories are still told of a ghostly hound who guided the family out of danger on several occasions. In nearby fields many finds have been made, including arrow heads, Roman coins and a Jacobite shoe buckle. Thomas de Beetham was knight of the shire of Westmorland and was granted a charter for a market and fair in the early 14th century, held by the churchyard cross, which was demolished in 1654.

As the river flows west out of the village, it runs through the deer park in front of Dallam Tower. Like Beetham Hall this too was a pele tower in ancient times. The present house was built in 1720 by Daniel Wilson and Dallam Tower still remains in the possession of the family.

In 1834 over 100 silver coins were found in the church. They were chiefly from the reign of William the Conqueror and his son Rufus, but some dated back to Edward the Confessor and even to Canute the Dane.

Bewcastle 🌿

Bewcastle lies 20 miles north-east of Carlisle, close to the England-Scotland border. Because of its position, it figured prominently in the Border struggles and features in many legends and ballads.

The names of farms and cottages evoke memories of the past. Names like Winter-Shields where perhaps there was shelter for people hiding themselves and their stock from the raiders. Pele-o-Hill with its remains of a pele tower, also stirs the imagination, as does Askerton Castle, a well preserved fortified farm. There are echoes of Celts, Saxons, Romans and Vikings, as well as the reivers in Bewcastle. The castle itself, now in ruins, stands on the site of a Roman fort, for Bewcastle lies just north of Hadrian's Wall.

Old lime kilns remain, and a farm called Kilnstown and the Lime Kiln inn are additional evidence of an industry now defunct. Bewcastle was also well known to the drovers bringing their sheep and cattle to the markets in the south; there is an inn called the Drove.

The population still consists of farming families, with names like Noble, Nixon, Forrester, Story, and many more. The farms are mainly sheep and beef cattle, especially the shaggy Galloways, and there are some dairy farms. Forestry has always been a local industry, as is evident in names like Forrester and Forster. Family names are all recorded in the local churchyard, and their descendants proudly continue to play prominent parts in Bewcastle.

There is no lack of talent in Bewcastle. The traditional fiddle and accordion are still popular, as are singing and poetry. Other talents are also encouraged, eg leek growers enthusiastically compete with each other, holding an annual show in September.

There are few amenities of the sort townsfolk take for granted. No shop or policeman, no mains sewers, no gas except in tanks or bottles, and many residents still rely on spring water for domestic use. The post office opens part time, and there is no public transport. Bewcastle has one primary school, no secondary school, and the nearest doctors are eleven miles away!

When travelling to Bewcastle, follow the signs to Roadhead. Bewcastle itself is a parish. Nearing Roadhead there are signs to Bewcastle Church, or Bewcastle Cross. The local people are justly proud of the Cross which is a rare example of early Celtic carving. It stands in the churchyard. Nearby is a small museum exhibiting items of Bewcastle history.

Visitors to Bewcastle, beware the elements! It can rain so hard one can hardly see! The clear river becomes a muddy torrent. When all is calm, however, how lovely it is. The sunrises and the sunsets are glorious, the starry nights are breathtaking.

Bewcastle Bailey

Bewcastle Bailey stands at the Border crossroads and boasts a lofty range of crags stretching to where Cumberland, Scotland and Northumberland unite. The scars of limestone quarries are like memorials to the past. Music, fiddles and folklore are rife and many tales are told down the generations, like that of Lizzy Baty.

Lizzy Baty was a wise woman of Cumberland who obtained great notoriety in her day. She died at Bleach House, now known as Low Beckside, in Brampton in 1817 aged 88 years. Old Lizzy was known as the Brampton Witch. She is described as a canny old body who usually wore a red cloak trimmed with white fur. On one occasion she gave a short account of her life. She was born and brought up at Castle Douglas, and eloped by escaping down a ladder from her bedroom window on a snowy night with John Baty, a local schoolmaster. They journeyed to Bewcastle Fell, where they settled, and lived by fortune telling. A song about her goes like this –

> 'An lang the lasses leave to tell
> To neighbours and to kin
> How Lizy with her witchery
> He'd gard them dance and grin.'

Blackhall Low & Blackhall High

A quiet stroll at the beginning of the 20th century, leaving Carlisle by its natural south-west boundary, over Wire Mire beck, would have brought the walker to the hamlet of Blackhall Low – a gathering of farms, cottages and residences encapsulating most of the history of Carlisle from 1700.

Pleasantly situated on high ground overlooking Carlisle City, the river Caldew and the West Coast Railway, the area was a gathering point for revellers from miles around who were drawn to the single storey pub called T'Theekt Cott, for here were held the 'Bleckell Murry Neets' made famous by Anderson in his lengthy ballad of that name.

The Theekt Cott was demolished in April 1904 and replaced by the present day White Ox, using slate from Newfoundland to roof it – almost unique in the area. It was intended as a much larger hotel to accommodate racegoers who attended meetings at the adjacent race course, which was moved to Blackhall from the Swifts in 1905.

Moving further out the walker would have come to Blackhall Hall (now the racecourse house) which commanded clear views over the south-west of the city and the river Caldew and was chosen by Prince Charles Edward Stewart as his haven for the night on Sunday 10th November 1745. On the ground floor, in what was known as Bonnie Prince Charlie's room, was an antique oak cupboard which concealed a sandy passage leading down to the river by a subterranean route. From this room the Young Pretender sent a demand to the Mayor of Carlisle for the surrender of the city, giving him two hours in which to reply. The answer was a barrage of guns from the battlements! The next morning the Prince marched with his army to Brampton by way of Warwick Bridge.

As the walker continued south past the race course he would enter the hamlet of Blackhall High, which at the turn of the century was just as 'murry' as Blackhall Low, having three public houses in its very small area: the old Black Lion (which stood on the opposite corner to the modern inn), the Red Cat and the White Quey.

The walker would also encounter another regular meeting place for the lads of the area – the blacksmith's forge from where Tom Hetherington the smith could be seen at eleven o'clock every morning crossing the road for his pint at the Black Lion.

Life was not all merry making! Education played an important part so there were two schools in the same small area. Several trusts existed to ensure that poor children were taught free of charge; from these each child was also given a shilling and an orange at Easter. These trusts still exist in the form of St John's Educational Trust, the interest from which is given to Stoneraise school, being the only one remaining today. The fir wood around Stoneraise school harboured many red squirrels which often found their way into the cloakroom and ate the boys' lunch!

Should the present day walker wish to retrace this route, the Blackhall Low and Blackhall High of yesteryear are today known as Blackwell, Durdar and Stoneraise.

Blawith 🌿

The location of the village of Blawith is scenic, being situated at the head of the Crake valley and extending to the south-western shores of Coniston Water.

To the north, set among trees by the lakeside, lies Brown Howe estate. The mansion house, originally built by a Victorian industrialist, has been converted into flats, along with its adjacent stable blocks. Nearby, standing high above the road, is Lake Bank which is also converted into flats, but holding memories of a much more elegant past as an hotel, very popular with Victorian and Edwardian holidaymakers, and also as a charabanc halt for excursions on the two steamers sailing on Lake Coniston.

A little further south, lies the village of Water Yeat. The old water cornmill carried out its trade until the turn of the century. Its origins are lost in the mists of time, but it was said to have an unending source of water from Beacon beck, where a dam was constructed to regulate its flow. The village also boasted a smithy and another corn mill (which was converted into a schoolhouse and shoemaker's in 1753). The building now forms three dwellings. In 1852 a pillbox mill was opened, but the venture failed in 1870.

About half a mile down the road past the old vicarage, the traveller will reach the village of Blawith. The hamlet consists of about a dozen houses situated alongside the road and several farmsteads in close proximity. The church, dedicated to St John, is now closed. It was built in 1883 to replace the earlier chapel, which was in existence prior to 1577 and whose ruins can still be found half way up the hill leading south out of the village. Even in those early times, finance for the chapel must have been a problem for, according to a rhyme – 'Blawith poor people, an auld church and a new steeple, as poor as hell, they had to sell a bit of fell to buy a bell – Blawith poor people'. The land sold was Blea Brows on the west shore of the lake, the money buying one of the two bells in its 18th century turret.

The school, now closed and converted to a house, was rebuilt in 1859 and there are indications that it was supported by several local landowners as early as 1772. It is interesting to note that one of its former teachers, a Mr Wilson, was well respected as both teacher and disciplinarian, despite the handicap of having lost both his hands.

Blencow 🦌

One might be forgiven for not visiting Blencow as it is situated between the main road to Keswick and the main road to Wigton, about four miles west of Penrith. It is a small village, quite pretty in the centre, with a village green and the river Petteril running through under a hump-back bridge. The river divides the village, Little Blencow to the north in Greystoke parish and Great Blencow to the south in Dacre parish. The hamlet of Laithes is close by; both communities join together for many occasions.

Blencow Hall, a most imposing building, is situated about a quarter of a mile out of Blencow on the Greystoke road. The north tower is the oldest part and is thought to have been built at the beginning of the 16th century as a pele tower.

Another noted building is the old Blencow grammar school where pupils attended from a wide area. This was first built in 1577 and later rebuilt in 1795. The school bell tower is still intact. The old school is now named Burbank House and home of Major Tim Riley, a descendant of the Rileys who in 1881 purchased Ennim from the Troutbeck family and owned most of Blencow in the 19th century. A lot of the inhabitants of Blencow at that time were employees of the Rileys, ie butlers, gamekeepers, dressmakers, etc. Ennim is one of the most attractive country houses in the county, and now the home of Viscount and Viscountess Whitelaw, one time local Member of Parliament and Deputy Prime Minister.

Many stone quarries, now defunct, are to be found in and around Blencow. Stone from these quarries was used to build part of Keswick. Blencow station, before it was closed in 1972, was kept very busy dispatching the stone.

For many years Blencow was one of the few villages with a resident blacksmith; the ring of the anvil could be heard up to the middle 1970s, struck with an iron grip by Mr Harold Simpson, continuing until his 70th birthday. The original blacksmith's shop was on the site where the chapel, built in 1877, now stands. Can you imagine the wealth of folk lore and local gossip exchanged amid the whirring bellows and roar of the furnace? A standing joke remains if someone doesn't want to disclose the source of a rumour, 'I heard it down at t'smiddy'.

Laithes is about a mile away by road, and has been extended greatly over recent years. There is still a timber mill working. Originally a grain mill, it was renovated by a Mr Heelis from Appleby, who installed home-made machinery to fashion heels for the shoe industry. The present owners deal with any wooden products for the joinery trade.

In the centre of Laithes, where the river Petteril flows, is the place where local farmers took their cows to be watered and also a communal sheep dipping place. Six farms made up the village, now there is only one.

Blindcrake

Blindcrake is a small village of around 100 inhabitants to the north-east of Cockermouth, built on the site of an old British settlement.

The village has always been a rural backwater; the main road from Cockermouth to Carlisle does not trouble Blindcrake and only local traffic and farm vehicles and animals frequent its one straggly road and offshoot down to Isel. Mains water and drainage came to the village in 1936/37 but electricity only came in 1954. Before the advent of these modern conveniences water was carried from the village well which is to the rear of Blindcrake Hall, the most imposing house in the village with an elegant Georgian facade, and the Town Well which is behind the wall near the telephone box. Most houses also had their own well or pump. The village pump used to be where the memorial tablet now stands by the wall of Easter Cottage.

As with many villages there is a village green, but this one started life as a pond called Mortar Dub. It was used for watering stock and washing horses' legs after ploughing. The villagers had been long troubled by recurring fevers and the pond was blamed for this, so eventually it was drained around 1900 by Cockermouth RDC in spite of opposition by local farmers. After this was done the fevers subsided. The four drinking troughs were placed by the wall at the north side of the green after the pond was drained.

Blindcrake had a rather unusual custom of burying its dead horses in the village instead of having them taken away. In the south-east corner of the village is an area where several horses are buried. One, with a gravestone marked 'Marmaduke 1900', used to belong to the then vicar of Isel, Rev W. A. Sharpe.

Blindcrake has provided a few colourful characters, the most famous of recent times being Adam Slee, an octagenarian who died in 1988. He lived at Woodlands, or rather in a colourful caravan to the rear of the house. He had a flair for painting which he displayed on his house walls. Years ago the outside walls were beautifully painted with ornate designs incorporating colourful trees and flowers as well as all the walls and ceilings inside. Coach parties used to stop to admire the murals. He was a very gentle man and could regularly be seen riding his painted bicycle, sporting his waxed moustache and wearing one of his hats.

Blindcrake is basically a farming village – there are seven farms, which are family concerns, approximately one fifth of the population being employed in agriculture. Farming is mainly mixed with dairy, suckler beef and sheep. There are four dairy herds averaging 60 head, the milk being made into cheese at nearby Aspatria.

Blindcrake does not have a shop now or a pub since the Ghyll Yeat, which was one of Britain's smallest public houses, closed its doors a year or so ago. However, Laal Moota on the Carlisle road is not far away and mobile shops supply us with many items several days a week.

Bolton &

The village of Bolton lies four miles to the north-west of Appleby-in-Westmorland. It is situated on rising ground above the flood plain of the river Eden, a mile from the main Penrith to Scotch Corner road (A66).

There is evidence that there was a settlement in Bolton about 1,200 years ago, but Bolton was a chapelry in the parish of Morland until 1868. However, the church of All Saints goes back much further than that. The nave and the former west tower are said to date back to the second half of the 12th century. The church's most unusual treasure is found outside above a 17th century door in the north wall. It is a stone relief of two knights jousting. There are believed to be only two such in the country; the other is in Dorset and is dated 1110. Beside it is an inscription 'St Lawrence de Vere gives to the men of Bolton . . .' but what he gave and when he gave it we do not know.

Within the parish boundaries is Bewley Castle which dates back to 1250. Its name is derived from the French 'beau lieu' – beautiful place. It became the residence of the Bishops of Carlisle. Its remains are largely of the 14th century.

Bolton has seen many changes. It is recorded that the village had a teacher in 1600. It is still a centre for education, the new school opened in the 1960s, replacing one built in 1856 which is now a house. In former times the occupations of Boltonians were as farmers, farm labourers, cycle maker, woodman, publican, blacksmith, miller, tailor, even woollen knitters. Over the last 60 years ten farms have ceased to exist as complete farms; there are only two farm labourers in the village today. The farms left are run by families. A major employer is Eden Grove School, which has occupied the Elizabethan style mansion at Eden Grove since 1954.

Bolton Memorial Hall is a fine solid structure, erected on the site of the former Mid-Town Farm buildings between 1922/24 as a war memorial. No alcohol is served in keeping with the Methodist tradition in the village, where there is a Methodist chapel, built in 1818 and refurbished in 1926. Many of the older people meet in the Memorial Hall for dominoes and carpet bowls on a Thursday. Many others meet in the New Crown inn to enjoy each other's company and the ale. Bolton is certainly changing, but it is still a good place to be, and its people still grand folk to be with.

Bootle ❧

An ancient settlement, the earliest record is a mesolithic site at Eskmeals; numerous Stone Age tools have been found in the parish, plus remains of a large Bronze Age settlement. It was a market town lying to the north-west of Blackcombe, at the confluence of two mountain becks, which now assume the name of the river Annas. The market charter was granted in 1347, and it was once said to be the smallest market town in England. Owing to the increased prosperity of Millom it has lost the dignity of a market town but the market cross still stands. It is now a quiet country village.

The parish extends to 6,780 acres. The parish church of St Michael and All Angels (parts of which date back to Norman times) was originally an oblong building which was extended in 1837. The tower was completed in 1882. About a mile to the north of the church, lie the remains of the nunnery of Seaton, a Benedictine foundation dating back to before 1227, dedicated to St Leonard.

In the village there is a resident doctor and surgery, a rector and until recently a policeman. There is a grocer-cum-post office, hairdresser, butcher, petrol filling station, two banks and a public house. The chapel was built in 1780. There is also a fire station and one of the firemen, Mr Harry Wilson was honoured with the MBE in 1990. An Abbeyfield

House, Alexander House, has been built recently. Several of the older properties in the village have now been demolished for road improvements etc, but new properties have been built, viz Summerhill estate and 14 senior citizen's bungalows.

The railway station serving the village is one and a quarter miles away at the small hamlet of Bootle Station. Here there is a post office/general store, a public house, a depot of the West Cumberland Farmers, a coal merchant's and a school (the 18th century Hycemoor school). Towards the beach there is an estate, Hycemoor Way, built on the site of Bootle ammunition factory. In 1944 a munitions train blew up just outside Bootle Station. The driver was killed going back to uncouple a wagon that had caught fire.

Today there are between 20 and 30 farms in the parish, mostly family farms. The majority of the working population travel to work, some to Sellafield Atomic Energy Establishment and some to Eskmeals gun range further along the coast.

With the help of donations and a lot of fund raising the people of Bootle have built a sports and social club, which has a new pavilion, football pitch, fitness track and a superb crown bowling green. Bootle has always had a football team, which in the 1920s included three Knowles brothers, who were also the World Champion Cumberland and Westmorland wrestlers.

Bothel 🪴

Bothel, which means a dwelling or dwelling place, is situated on high ground and during medieval times the inhabitants were required to perform a service called 'seawake' or seawatch, which entailed lighting fires as warnings which could be seen for many miles and across the Solway. During the reign of Charles II (1660–1685) a horse race was run along a three mile course which stretched from Craggs above Bothel to Moota Hill. The last part of the course was so steep that the horses were forced to walk the last stage of it!

Today Bothel is separated from Torpenhow by the busy A595 road but the two villages remain inextricably linked by the parish church of St Michael at Torpenhow. This Norman church which was built in 1120 (probably on a Saxon site) is still the focal point of Anglican worship. Bothel has two Methodist chapels, one of which is still in use, supported by a small but enduringly faithful congregation.

Sixty or more years ago some of the buildings had very different uses from those of today. The farm known as Bothel Parks had its own water wheel which was used to grind the grain it produced. The grinding stones from the mill are now made into a feature of the farm's garden. The village had a clogger who lived in Mid Town House, which is situated to the side of Woodford House (until recently used as Bothel's post office).

Woodford House has had many uses in its time, being a general store and a pork butcher's. The pork sausages from this shop were enjoyed by discerning folk as far away as London.

Next to Woodford House was a building which housed the local blacksmith. Sadly, this was demolished but it was a thriving business for many years run by Mr Garnet Hope. A tailor with the amusing nick-name of 'Pricky Three Thumbs' used to live in a cottage down what is now School Lane and the village reading rooms were part of a modern house called Barn Walls situated next to Hope House.

St Bathan's Lodge, Park View Farm and Greenfell Cottage and House were all at one time or another village pubs. The present and only remaining pub is the Greyhound which lies at the junction of the A595; it gleans its clientele from the villagers and from travellers on the main road.

Prior to 1920 the limestone quarry on the Aspatria Road provided employment for local people, and also at Moota Quarry where Bothel bricks were made.

Bothel's seat of learning has been established for more than 300 years, though the new St Michael's school was officially opened by George, Bishop of Penrith, in November 1989. The school sports day which takes place in July still has a tradition which links the children of yesterday with those of today. They run a long distance race 'Round the Jockey Stone'. This stone is believed to be a boulder left behind when a glacier melted but there are also amusing mythical tales abouts its origin.

Bouth ❧

Bouth, whose name is of old Norse origin, is a village of great antiquity in the parish of Colton, in Furness.

In its earlier days, Bouth had six farms (three of which still remain) and was the centre of a busy agricultural district. A weekly market was held there, and it also had two fairs during the year, one at Whitsuntide and one in October, where the great feature was the wrestling matches. Bouth wrestlers were famous all over the north.

After farming, coppice products supplied wood for bobbins, barrel hoops and staves and ship's fenders. Oak bark was also used for tanning leather and Bouth has its Bark House today. There are also some Kiln Cottages and in existence today are old pint pots bearing the Bouth stamp so this important village must have had its own kiln. Horses were kept adjacent to Bouth House to pull the coppice wood up the hill for storage. This is still called Horses Hill.

In the middle of the 19th century many were also employed in the Black Beck Gunpowder Works of Messrs F. C. Dickson which suffered two explosions, after the second of which, in 1929, the works closed.

In structure, Bouth suggests a square, built as a protection against

The Village of Bouth, with the White Hart Inn

Border raiders. The square is guarded by deliberately narrow and easily defended exits. Bouth was called the capital of Colton (a very large parish) and Colton church, standing on a hill, serves Bouth and three hamlets.

Bouth has an excellent village green, designed in the late 1960s and early 1970s, the work done by villagers themselves. For several years Bouth has won the prize for the Best Kept Small Village in South Lakeland. Many villagers take great pride in their garden and the beds in front of the cottages are ablaze with blooms which strike the eye. As Bouth is a village where the main street is on a hill, the wealth of colour is dazzling.

Adjacent to the village green stands the hostelry, the White Hart, which has a remarkable inn sign – a white hart, couchant, wearing a golden crown round its neck like a collar, tethered to the ground by a golden chain. In olden days the White Hart was a well-known coaching inn on the road north from Dalton, the capital of Furness, which passed through Bouth on its way to Kendal.

Bowness-on-Windermere

Bowness is situated on the east shore of Lake Windermere, within the Lake District National Park. It is a tourist resort, attracting walkers, boating and fishing enthusiasts and those who just like to potter around.

Bowness dates back to the 11th century when the Vikings settled there. It is said that Vinand, a Viking chief, named the lake 'Vinand's Mere'. Bowness was little more than a settlement with a few cottages and fishermen's huts but with the coming of the railway in the 19th century, it grew into a sizeable village consisting of a number of shops, cottages and a few hotels, together with a large number of lodging houses built to cater for the influx of visitors from the Lancashire and Yorkshire industrial towns. Wealthy industrialists came to live in the area, employing local builders to build palatial dwellings where they enjoyed a high standard of gracious living.

One such residence was the Belsfield (now a hotel) built in 1845. In 1869 it was bought by Mr H. W. Schneider, the Barrow iron magnate, who had a special pier built at Bowness Bay for his own private use. Each morning he would walk down to the pier, preceded by the butler carrying breakfast on a silver tray. He would then board his private steam yacht *Esperance* to make the journey across the lake to Lakeside railway station at the south end of the lake, breakfasting on the way. There he would board a special train (he owned the railway) accompanied by his secretary who had already picked up the morning's mail which would be dealt with during the journey to his office in Barrow. This same pier is now used by pleasure boats and visitors can enjoy a trip on the lake. The steam launch *Esperance* can be seen at the Windermere Steamboat Museum, which was opened in 1977 by the Prince of Wales.

The church, dedicated to St Martin, was built in 1483, replacing a previous church which was destroyed by fire. In 1870 it was restored and enlarged. Under the chancel is the mass grave of 47 people who were drowned in 1635, when the ferry on which they were travelling capsized as they were returning from a wedding in Hawkshead.

The oldest part of Bowness is behind St Martin's church and is known as Lowside and here is a jumble of narrow streets and cottages reminiscent of old Bowness. Here is to be found the New Hall inn, more commonly known as Hole Int' Wall, due to the ale being served through a hole in the wall into the adjoining smithy. In 1857, the landlord was a Thomas Longmire – a famous Cumberland wrestler. Charles Dickens, an admirer of Longmire, stayed at the inn and there is a plaque to note the occasion.

Bowness Bay and the lake feature in the life of the village and tales are told of how the local boatmen would go out in their boats hunting for the fabulous creature known as the Twizzie-Whizie, which was reputed to be found around dusk in the bay near the pier. The hunting, by the visitors, of this elusive creature – said to be a cross between a hedgehog and a bird with a squirrel's tail – was encouraged by the local boatmen as a means of promoting their boat-hire service. There were many 'sightings' but the creature always got away!

Bowness is today an extremely busy village as more and more tourists swell the local population. Yet despite the growth of tourism, second homes and time-share development, Bowness still retains its local village community.

Braithwaite 🌿

The village of Braithwaite nestles at the foot of the Whinlatter Pass with a magnificent backdrop of the mountains of Grisedale, Causey Pike, High Stile and Barrow, forming the famous Coledale Horseshoe as it curves round the head of Coledale Hause. Coledale beck winds its way down the valley and enters a narrow gorge before tumbling and rushing through the village where it is crossed by two humped-backed bridges – aptly named High Bridge and Low Bridge.

Low Bridge and the nearby village shop are at the hub of the village. From the bridge, it is interesting to look up the old village streets with evocative names of Duck Street, The Puddle, and The Island, and visualise the whitewashed cottages as the small farms of bygone days. There were also the woollen and pencil mills which provided the inhabitants with a livelihood, and a flour mill on the common. The clogs of the miners, on their way to Force Crag or Barrow mines, would be heard clattering over the bridges at 5.30 am and the last ones returning at 10.30 pm.

The population of Braithwaite is about 400, having been at 1,000 early in the 20th century. At that time, the village was well served by tradespeople – builders, butcher, tailor, baker, at one time four blacksmiths, joiner, grocer and shoemaker. The last shoemaker died in 1970. He had a shed below the bridge and was an expert craftsman, specialising in shepherd's boots 'of a substantial kind'. The character of the village has changed completely since then, and now only a handful of people are employed locally and are associated with the farming or holiday industry.

It is the people, not the buildings or the breathtaking scenery that make a village, and there is a marvellous community spirit and caring feeling, to which many people can testify. Some community activities are based at St Herbert's church situated next to Braithwaite school. The school is actively involved in village life, inviting residents to join them for Bonfire Night, Sports Day and services in church. The village institute, built by villagers after the First World War, provides excellent facilities.

Happily some old customs survive, and the custom of Candlemas tea, dating from the Civil War in the 17th century, is one. Income from a piece of land is used annually to provide a tea at the local Royal Oak for the widows of the village after they have attended a special church service. Originally the tea consisted of beer served with the meal, but the beer was discontinued!

The Blencathra Hunt appears in the village from time to time at the request of the local sheep farmers. The red-coated Master of the Hunt is on foot and the hunting horn can be heard echoing across the fells. In summer, hound-trailing – an old Cumbrian tradition – can be seen. Aniseed trails are laid across the fells and the hounds bay as they wait for the starting signal.

Brampton 🐚

Brampton, with a population of approximately 4,000, is built of local sandstone, and is situated in a hollow formed by glacial action which took place during the Ice Age. 'Kames' (gravel ridges, as a result of sand and gravel washed out from the ice) form part of the surrounding countryside, thus enabling the town to be hidden from sight until you approach it more closely. The character of the town has changed very little during the past 150 years, and still retains its 'cobbles', which gives the town a charm all of its own.

Great expansion took place during the late 1950s when Spadeadam Rocket Establishment opened employing hundreds of people, including scientists and engineers from all over the country, as well as many local people. A large number of houses were built for personnel and the impact upon the quiet community was tremendous. When Spadeadam closed, many of its employees chose to remain here, and ex-employees have retired to this area because of the impact the town and its surrounding beauty had on them, whilst working here.

In the centre of the town stands a fine octagonal building, the Moot Hall, built originally in 1648, but the present building dates from 1817. It has an external staircase, and on the outside wall is a plaque to the memory of a local poet, Peter Burn. Below the steps are the stocks and a bull ring, a reminder of bull baiting. The parish council meet in the Moot Hall, which is also the venue for the Tourist Information Centre. On Wednesdays throughout the year there is a thriving market in and around the area of the hall.

In High Cross Street stands a building which was Bonnie Prince Charlie's headquarters in 1745. After his defeat at Culloden, six of his supporters were hanged from the Capon Tree, a spot where in ancient times the judges who came from Newcastle to Carlisle rested. The tree is no longer there but a monument erected on the site gives the names of those who supported the Stuart cause.

Brampton's old parish church, which is situated on the outskirts of the town overlooking the Vale of Irthing, was built by the Normans with stone from Hadrian's Wall. Worship was conducted here until 1788 when, on the site of Brampton Hospital, the present church was built.

The old church remained closed until recent years, when Brampton Preservation Trust renovated it.

Brampton is surrounded by many attractive footpaths. For fine views of the surrounding area, climb to the top of the wooded Mote and along the Ridge, accessible from Main Street, and delight in the rolling country-side below. Nearby Gelt Woods is a delightful walk and also an RSPB reserve. About 50 ft above the river Gelt, which runs through the reserve, is a rock with an inscription carved by a Roman soldier in the 3rd century.

Bridekirk 🦋

Bridekirk is a small village three miles north of the A66, which is one of the main routes into Cumbria.

The name Bridekirk comes from the 6th century Irish St Bride and the Norman church, which is a dominant feature of the village. The church is called St Bridget's and has many interesting features, in particular the font which experts date back to the 12th century.

Originally, the village consisted of farms, the church, the vicarage, Bridekirk House and half a dozen cottages. On the outskirts of the village was another residence, Wood Hall, which stood in acres of beautiful parkland. The parkland remains but the Hall was dismantled and the outbuildings converted into a house and cottages.

The main occupation was of course farming and that is still important today. Now it is fully mechanised and though there are horses in the village, they are thoroughbred race horses, belonging to a local permit holder, not farm horses. During the First World War there was a cheese factory at Home Farm.

Water for the villagers came from a well at the bottom of a field in the middle of the village, called Well Close. That area is now called Spring-well.

The Bridekirk of today has a population of 155, many living in new houses and bungalows built by those who work in the town but choose to live in the country. Bridekirk House was bought by developers and demolished to make way for an estate of bungalows.

Although most residents have to travel to work there is no bus service, and there are no shops or post office either, although some travelling shops visit the village each week. The surrounding woods are used for organised shoots and a gamekeeper is employed to manage the Wood Hall estate. This is a picturesque and peaceful place to live. There are some lovely walks around the village, with footpaths maintained by the parish council. Despite all the changes one thing which has remained constant is the community spirit in the village.

Brigsteer & Helsington 🦢

Brigsteer is more a hamlet than a village, between the parishes of Helsington and Levens and about three miles from Kendal.

Most of the houses in Brigsteer are snugly settled under the limestone escarpment of Scout Scar and overlooking the one-time drained mosses, once a forested area. A further development of the drainage system was undertaken in the valley during the years 1980/90, aided by an EEC grant and, to a certain extent, flooding has been contained. There is evidence that early settlements were there in pre-Norse times and farming and peat cutting was carried out for hundreds of years, each villager having an allotted strip.

The earliest permanent houses in Brigsteer date from the 16th and 17th centuries and include a mill with buildings, now houses. The Wheatsheaf inn, now Wheatsheaf Hotel, had a smithy until the turn of the century. There are still three working farms in the village. Since the late 1940s several bungalows and houses have been built, mostly infilling, and in the early 1960s a small estate covered a field in the centre of Brigsteer. Later new housing includes alteration of stone barns. Village life has survived, centred round the village hall built in 1958 to replace the old Sunday school, and the Wheatsheaf. There is no longer a shop or post office nor any public transport in Brigsteer.

The climate of Brigsteer is milder than Helsington and many nearby villages, shown by the fine early flowering gardens and the prolific daffodils, early orchids, lily of the valley and other wild flowers, especially in Brigsteer Wood.

St John's church, which serves Brigsteer and Helsington, is in the parish of Helsington and is sited at the top of the steep hill out of Brigsteer off the road to Kendal. It was founded in 1726, consecrated in 1745 and rebuilt in 1845, when a school was built alongside. This school closed in 1965, at which time it had only four pupils. It is now used occasionally for local events and has been leased in the past by Bury grammar school and by Bramley parish, Leeds. There are some five or six working family farms in Helsington.

In Helsington the manor house of the parish was Helsington Laithes and it is on record that in 1341 it belonged to William of Thweng. Parts of the present house may be of the 15th century. This is not the oldest house in the parish as Sizergh Castle, though perhaps geographically in Levens, is in fact in the parish of Helsington.

Brisco 🦢

The village of Brisco lies three miles to the south of Carlisle in the parish of St Cuthbert Without. It forms a ribbon of dwellings between Upperby and Wreay. The early name for the village was Birksceugh, meaning birch-wood. Most of Brisco used to be part of the Woodside estate whose main house stood half-way between Brisco and Wreay. The estate was owned by the Losh family at one time (Sarah Losh built Wreay church) and the last owner was Andrew Gibson, a wealthy Liverpool merchant. Following his death in 1934, the estate was sold and tenants were given the opportunity to buy their farms.

Prior to this sale, Brisco consisted of a collection of small farms, cottages, and a few larger houses. It had a post office, general store, pub, blacksmith's shop, joiner and cartwright, shoemaker, police house and, for six years only, a railway station. The latter was found to be unviable and was closed in favour of the one at Wreay. Various cottages housed the estate workers, such as the joiner and gamekeeper.

Following the sale, the family who were the tenants at Brisco Hall Farm became the owners thereof and have since acquired land from four other farms, so that they now own most of the agricultural land in and around Brisco.

St Ninian's Well is of historical interest. It is believed that Christians were baptized here by St Ninian around AD 400. The notable property known as The Cottage was one of the few properties in Brisco which was not part of the former Woodside estate. The main front door is studded and heavy and was used as protection in the times of siege during the Border wars; a similar one exists at Brisco Hall. Next to the former post office is Wooden Walls, with the date 1681 clearly visible on the front. Formerly a pub called the Ship, this was also a victualler's.

Brisco today has no focal point (no post office or pub) and, when so much travel is by car, villagers can go for many weeks or even months without meeting each other. A small common exists and is provided with a telephone booth. There are distant views of the Northern Fells from here.

Opposite the common stand two flat-roofed houses. These were experimental houses built by local builders Laings, in the 1950s. Nearby is a lane leading to the brickworks, brainchild of Sir John Laing. Apart from farming, the brickworks is the only source of employment in Brisco, although no villagers work there today. The brickworks was the subject of a management buy-out in 1989 and is now under group management. At the northern end of Brisco another lane leads past High and Low Woodbank farms. Near here, between the railway and the river Petteril, is the site where the ironworks firm of Cowans Sheldon was started.

Bromfield 🌿

The village of Bromfield is situated between the Solway Coast and the Lake District and within easy travelling distance of Wigton and Aspatria. Bromfield parish comprises the villages of Blencogo and Langrigg and the hamlets of Crookdake and Scales.

The sources of employment are many and varied – agriculture plays a large part as does the UCB Sidac Ltd at Wigton (producing wrapping film), the Sealy Sleep Products (bed manufacturers) and Larma (clothing) factories and the Milk Marketing Board (cheese and butter) at Aspatria.

The parish church is dedicated to St Mungo (St Kentigern), where the nave and chancel still remain after 800 years. The oldest relic is an ancient British cross carved in white sandstone, believed to date from about AD 400. St Mungo's Well lies about 300 yards north of the church and until mains water was laid on in 1929 most villagers drew their water from it.

The Greyhound inn was built in 1720 and has the sign of a greyhound over the door lintel. The back of the inn joins the garden of the old vicarage (now a private house) and rumour has it that in days of yore the vicar could avail himself of the inn's hospitality without the parishioners' knowledge!

The Gill Farm is on the outskirts of Bromfield village and is owned by the Reay family. The lands were granted to them by William the Lion, King of Scotland, in the 12th century. It seems that The Gill is the oldest entailed property in England – over 800 years – and, of course, is reputed to be haunted!

In comparison to the ancient history of St Mungo's Well, a big new water extraction scheme was undertaken by the North West Water Authority at Low Scales at a cost of £1.2m. The project was started in 1983 and was fully operational in 1990. There are two pumping stations and when working to capacity two million gallons of water per day are being pumped up to the recently established water treatment plant at Boltongate, seven miles away.

At the old smithy in Langrigg horses are still being shod, but the windmill fell into disuse a hundred years ago and has now been converted into a quaint cottage.

Brougham 🌿

Just beyond Eamont Bridge and the large field used for the yearly Penrith Show and numerous fell and pony club events, the road winds up to the tree-crowned site of the ancient village demolished to make way for Brougham Hall, now in ruins. In spite of the fourth Lord Brougham (he of the song) having twice broken the bank at Monte Carlo, he was forced to sell his home known as 'The Windsor of the North' for demolition. A charitable trust has begun an ambitious restoration of the Hall, providing work units for local craftsmen and capturing the imagination of all who visit this picturesque place.

Across the road from the Hall and connected to it by a narrow stone bridge is a churchyard with a sandstone chapel, well known for its exceptional carved woodwork. Its most famous possession, a magnificent Flemish triptych, is now on permanent loan to Carlisle Cathedral.

Brougham, pronounced 'Broom', is now an area of scattered dwellings. Down the road from the Hall the majestic ruins of Brougham Castle tower above the river forded by the Romans. Here they built their fort, Brocavum (hill of the badgers) from which the name Brougham evolved. The castle was the 16th century home of the remarkable Lady Anne Clifford, daughter of the Earl of Cumberland.

Annually on the 2nd April curious motorists speeding along the A66 can see the local vicar with a group of parishioners standing beside the Countess's Pillar on a small rise by the busy road, taking part in the dole ceremony. This was inaugurated by Lady Anne to distribute £4 to the poor of the parish, in memory of her last parting from her mother before rejoining her husband, the Earl of Pembroke, in London.

The Village of Broughton Beck

Further east along the A66, the old Roman route from York to Hadrian's Wall, there is a walk across the fields to the river Eamont where in an attractive and secluded spot stands the old sandstone church of St Ninian, known locally as Ninekirks, barely changed since being rebuilt by Lady Anne. Now redundant, its door is still open to visitors who cannot but be impressed by its simplicity, with its stone flagged floor, whitewashed walls and old box pews.

Broughton Beck 🌿

Tucked away on a Furness hillside can be found the tiny village of Broughton Beck, in the rural parish of Osmotherley. It lies near the main road which leads from the old market town of Ulverston, about three miles away, into the former county of Cumberland.

The village was once a self-contained agricultural community. Older inhabitants can remember when there were three farms in the village itself, a water mill, a smith and joiner, a little general shop, a sickle-maker and an inn. One of the ladies ran a small tea-shop which was very

popular; her patrons, who had to book in advance, often coming from some miles distant. Later on there was a petrol station.

The beck, which gives the village its name and which provided the power for the water mill, flows down the hill and across the fields lying below the grassy slopes of the hills opposite, known in the area as 'The Alps'.

Across the beck, at nearby Oak Bank, were housed the kennels for the pack of hounds used in the local hunt, where huntsmen follow the dogs on foot. Flan Sports, held on the first Monday in August, catered for others who had outdoor interests and the children, shod in clogs, played 'whip and top', hopscotch, 'hoop and stick' and guinea pig throughout the year.

In the 1920s the water mill ceased to grind corn and became the village hall – the Mill Room. Until a few years ago the miller's daughter, now in her nineties, took an active interest in the Mill Room and when she was 84 she gave a lively demonstration of a clog dance to her fellow WI members.

A school was built in 1770 about half a mile out of the village, on the road to Netherhouses, where it stood in isolation surrounded by fields. For many years church services took place in the school which possessed portable altar rails, brought out for use on Sunday.

In 1873 a church was built on ground next to the school and St John's, chapel of ease to the parish church of St Mary, Ulverston was consecrated by the Bishop of Carlisle in 1874. Looking ahead from the church door is a distant view of Coniston Old Man.

At the beginning of the 20th century a fine house for the schoolmaster was built on the other side of the church. In the garden wall there is a stone slab carved with figures and the letters of the alphabet; this was the test piece of a stonemason's apprentice.

The school was closed in 1927 and later sold. The money from the sale was invested in an educational foundation from which grants are made annually to help meet educational needs of the children of Osmotherley and Mansriggs. The school, made into an attractive bungalow, and the schoolmaster's house are now privately owned.

Broughton-in-Furness 🦢

Broughton nestles in a hollow between wooded hills midway between Barrow-in-Furness and Millom, just off the A595. It is of ancient origin; it was mentioned in the Domesday Book, and the two important buildings, castle and church, are Norman in foundation, but strangely they each stand a quarter of a mile outside the village. Broughton Tower, many times altered in succeeding centuries, is now a special school; the church was largely rebuilt in Victorian times, and has a ring of ten bells –

most unusual for such a small place (the population of the whole parish is about 1,000).

Many of the houses are Georgian, including those in the elegant square, set out by the lord of the manor to resemble a London square. The big horse chestnut trees, and the obelisk commemorating the golden jubilee of George III in 1810, are close to the fish slabs once used for the sale of fish caught in the nearby river Duddon and its broad estuary. Here too is the 'Town Hall', once a market hall with lock-up shops but now housing the Tourist Information office.

In Elizabethan times a charter was granted giving permission to hold fairs, and thus on 1st August each year the ceremony of Reading the Charter is carried out at noon; councillors walk in procession to the obelisk steps and throw new pennies to the children, and there are refreshments for the burghers at the expense of the lord of the manor (currently Cumbria County Council).

Broughton was once a centre of the wool trade and of the manufacture of the oak baskets called swills, and a livestock market is still held in alternate weeks. Many tradesmen once carried on their work in the narrow streets and yards – millers, tanners, cobblers and saddlers, blacksmiths, hatters, dressmakers and carriers. Fewer trades flourish today, and many of the householders have turned to the bed-and-breakfast trade, since Broughton is a good centre from which to explore the Lake District.

High Cross inn on the rim of the hill taking the road out to Millom was a carriers' pub when transportation was by horse and cart. The animals must have needed a rest after the steep climb from the ford over the river Duddon. More centrally situated is the Old King's Head – an old coaching inn, now catering for tourist coaches instead of the horse-drawn ones which used to ply between Ulverston and Whitehaven. Like many of the older buildings it has nooks and crannies tucked away. There are several yards leading between the old buildings of Broughton with strange restrictions placed upon them, because of the rights of way once necessary to reach the wells which supplied the water.

Broughton Mills 🐚

Broughton Mills is a hamlet about three miles from Broughton-in-Furness. Quite a large area is comprised of scattered farms. Some farms and cottages cluster at the centre of the hamlet – situated in the valley of the river Lickle. This river joins the river Duddon, before entering the sea in the Duddon estuary.

In the past the river provided natural power for the mills. There was first a woollen mill, which later became a bobbin mill – providing bobbins, shafts for brooms and implements etc. The corn mill ground the farmers' corn and made oatmeal.

A row of cottages is still called 'Shuttle Street', these were occupied by weavers. There are remains of old kilns where lime was made for the land and building. Also kilns were used to burn bracken in order to make potash – necessary to clean the wool. On the surrounding fells there were slate quarries and coppice woods, these produced wood for the local basket makers in Broughton.

The old inn, the Blacksmiths Arms, dates from the 18th century. This still has its old beams and fireplaces. There is no bar – just a shelf. Visitors and local inhabitants sit on benches around a big table before an open fire. Many walkers and tourists enjoy the hospitality in the summer months.

Two roads meeting near a narrow bridge, lead to the Duddon valley and Coniston. Here there is a small church dedicated to the memory of the Holy Innocents, consecrated in 1888. Before this people had gathered in a barn for worship.

Broughton Mills is still quiet and unspoiled – the hope is that it will remain so.

Burgh-by-Sands 🦜

Burgh-by-Sands is situated five miles north-west of Carlisle where the river Eden runs into the Solway Firth, and is on the site of Hadrian's Wall.

About a mile from the village, on Burgh Marsh, Edward I died whilst preparing for war against the Scots on 7th July 1307. A monument was erected here in 1685 by Henry, Duke of Norfolk, and when it fell into decay the Earl of Lonsdale erected another in 1803.

The parish church, dedicated to St Michael, was built mainly with stones from the Roman fort on the site of which the church stands. The church was restored in 1883, with the exception of the old tower which has walls six to eight ft thick. The entrance from the nave of the church to the ground chamber is guarded by a cross-barred door, six ft eight inches in height, which is made of hammered iron. A stone staircase leads to an upper chamber and there are arrow slits for defences and light. This tower was probably used as a place of refuge during the Border wars.

In earlier days many of the houses were 'clay daubins' (this being the local form of building where clay was plentiful) with very thick walls and small windows so that the rooms were warm in winter. The thatched roofs were supported by branches of oak trees with a natural bend conforming to the shape of the roof and braced together in pairs with wooden pins, and with cross beams. These were often built in a day with the help of neighbours. Large boulder-type stones were generally used for the foundations, and in some cases these were left partly visible. There are three original clay daubin cottages left in the village – Leigh Cottage (which now has a corrugated iron roof), Edna's Cottage and Lamonby Farm which have been recently re-thatched. There are also six clay daubin terrace houses at White Row which have been modernised and have slate roofs.

Tatie-Pot Alley gets its name from the fact that there was a public bakehouse on waste land abutting this lane, where people could take their tatie-pots and bread to be baked for a small charge. The bakehouse was heated mainly with old thorn roots which gave great heat so the cost of fuel was therefore negligible. This property was demolished many years ago. An automatic telephone exchange has been erected near the site.

In one of the older houses, John Stagg, known as 'Blin' Stagg the Fiddler, was born in 1770. He was the son of the village tailor and was educated for the Church, but an accident deprived him of his sight. This did not prevent him seeing the humorous side of life as well as the nobler one, and he was much in demand at 'merrie-meets' when he played his fiddle and sang a good song, and might be regarded as the Robbie Burns of Cumberland.

The pond at Amberfield has been filled in, but the pond still remains at The Hill, and now has an island in the middle. This site has recently been cleared and fenced off by the parish council. Canada Geese have made their home here and it is a regular haunt of wildlife.

Burneside 🦢

The village of Burneside nestles in that part of Cumbria once known as Strathclyde. There have been settlements here since the Stone Age, as is reflected by the remains of a stone circle on Potter Fell.

By the 15th century Burneside was a settled agricultural area. A rich variety of mills sprang up along the river Sprint – fulling, corn, wool, cotton, bobbin and the original rag paper mill at Cowan Head. The use of this natural resource meant that Burneside and area prospered with agriculture and industry working in harmony, side by side.

At the top of the hill is a monolith erected by one John Bateman. The original inscriptions were never placed – they said 'In honour of William Pitt, the pilot who weathered the storm'. This referred to Napoleon's eventual defeat, but Bateman lost heart when Napoleon escaped from Elba, and left the monolith bare.

In the 19th century one of our most famous families moved into the area. James Winstanley Cropper bought the paper mills at Cowan Head and Burneside and so began rapid industrialisation. The family motto of 'Love all men, fear no man' can be seen on a memorial to Charles Cropper in Abbott Hall Park, Kendal. Constant reminders of the Cropper heritage can be seen on the local buildings of this time, Winstanley Place, Charles Court, houses built for the many workers now needed in the area. More palatial homes were built at Ellergreen and Halhead, now both divided into flats.

The present church was built in 1801, having moved to a site less liable to flooding. Near to the church is the post office, originally one of the first Co-ops in the North West. Then there is the pub, the Jolly Anglers, originally sited next to the smithy when it was on the main Kendal to Cockermouth coaching route. Steeles Row no longer reflects its history of a dame school and reading rooms, but it does have a bakery where a sweet shop used to be.

At the back of the churchyard is the old school house. A long dedication can be seen over the door to one Allen Fisher. Besides bequeathing foundation scholarships to local children, this worthy also bequeathed a library, a fact which caused great difficulties when a new school was built as Mr Fisher's will stated that the books must never leave the building!

At the opposite end of the village lies the Bryce Institute, originally housing the public baths. Today it hosts most of the village societies, including the WI. Behind the Institute is the original telegraph and post office, one of the first in the North West. The railway station is now a trivial halt but once was a bustling goods yard, and a private tram line, connecting the three mills, thrived. Parts of the rails are still there. Sadly, the mills at Bowston and Cowan Head have gone and the Burneside Mill is now immense compared to its humble beginnings. They supply 'poppy' paper for Remembrance Day, map making paper and post office supplies.

Burrells

Burrells, originally spelt Burrels, is a small hamlet one and a half miles south-west of Appleby, astride the B6260 road to Orton. There is a little dispute over the origins of the name; some historians claim that it indicates the position of the old walls of Appleby, others that it derives from a word meaning burial place. Certainly, prior to 1884 the boundaries of Appleby did extend to include the hamlet.

Burrells is a living, thriving community. There are two farms and all the houses are occupied by people who live in them permanently. The most notable recent development is the row of houses on the Ormside road, known officially as Pennine View, and locally as the 'Camp'. Built in the 1950s as council houses, they have a spectacular view of the Pennines at their most dramatic point. In the Second World War the site was a prisoner of war camp, occupied at first by Germans and later by Italians. All that remains of the original development is the short stretch of concrete road.

The seat adjacent to the telephone kiosk commemorates the Coronation of Elizabeth II in 1953 and the notice board behind, the wedding of The Prince of Wales in 1981.

Burton-in-Kendal 🍃

Burton is ten miles south of Kendal and ten miles north of Lancaster, just within the southern boundaries of the old county of Westmorland.

Burton became a market town by charter in the 17th century and came to possess one of the busiest corn markets in the south of the county by 1818. The Lancaster-Kendal canal was opened in 1819 and the wharf and weighbridge where the coal was brought to the area are to be seen half a mile to the west of the village. The canal is not now in use, being blocked three miles to the south when the building of the M6 motorway took place. Of the many inns that were in the village the Kings Arms and the Royal remain, still serving visitors as they have done since coaching days. Cromwell and Keats are reputed to have stayed therein.

In the village square, the cross of limestone in the form of a Doric column was once used as stocks. The remains of leg shackles may still be seen.

Cocking Yard off the main street is paved with stone setts and is where at one time the blacksmith worked. Many other trades were carried on in Burton, including wheelwright, ironmonger, shoemaker, cobbler, miller and flour merchant. There were five grocers, a milliner, a photographer, a draper and a laundress, and there are still today a baker, butcher, general store and post office. A remnant of past history is the tannery, now a private dwelling near which are two 17th century houses, Burton Hall and the Old Hall.

The parish church of St James has a Norman tower built in the 12th century and was added to in the 14th and 16th centuries. It has a private chapel for the Hornby family of Dalton Hall. The interior is unusually bright and clean in its lines due no doubt to careful maintenance which is carried out to this day.

In 1818 premises were licensed for a Quaker meeting house; this is now a private dwelling. There is evidence on a stone plaque in Hilderstone Lane of a Quaker family residing there and a piece of ground was enclosed in 1687 for the interment of his family, and descendants, the last being in 1844.

The population of the village has multiplied since it was at its lowest in 1938 for 130 years. It has grown past 1,000 in recent years with the building of numerous new houses on the outskirts of the main village. It is still a thriving friendly community with the M6 motorway making it a popular commuter spot.

Buttermere

Buttermere is a small village surrounded by some of the higher mountains of the Lake District, which roll down to the lake and the meadow land. The western side of the lake is wooded partly with coniferous and partly deciduous trees. There are two significant waterfalls in the area. Lakeland's highest waterfall, Scale Force, flows over stony terrain into Crummock Water, whilst from Blea-berry tarn high on the fellside Sour-milk Gill cascades down into Buttermere Lake.

It is accessible from the south-east either by the pastoral Newlands Pass or the more austere Honister, on the summit of which stands the Buttermere Slate Quarry. At the foot of Honister Pass stands Gatesgarth which is one of the biggest farms in the area, farmed by the Nelson family until the mid 1930s. They raised a flock of Herdwicks sometimes considered to be beyond competition. Wilkinsyke, Syke, Croft and Cragg Farms form the group of farms in the centre of the village, whilst Rannerdale is situated on the shores of Crummock Water. Rannerdale, Cragg and Wilkinsyke are all owned by the National Trust.

There are about 50 inhabitants living in the village; most of them subsist upon two revenues, one from sheep (which have not profited them much latterly), the other from visitors.

The village school closed in 1950, and the children are transported to schools in Lorton and Cockermouth. The building is now in the care of the vicar and parochial church council.

The church of St James is the smallest in the United Benefice of Lorton with Loweswater and Buttermere. The present building dates from 1846 and has an attractive interior, furnished with oak and the sanctuary and aisle paved with Honister slate. A wrought iron gate depicting a shepherd and sheep is hung at the entrance to the porch.

The social highlight of the year is the annual show which is held towards the end of October. This is largely a show for sheep and dogs and open to the local farmers. Herdwicks and Swaledales are the main feature, other attractions include senior and junior fell races, and there is always a good display of horn-handled walking sticks. Hound trails always draw a large crowd and the tug of war is a test of strength and stamina. The day is rounded off with hallowing, hornblowing and singing competitions.

Caldbeck
& Hesket-New-Market 🍃

The fell villages of Caldbeck and Hesket-New-Market lie on the northern fringe of the Lake District and at the southern limit of the medieval Inglewood Forest.

The dedication of Caldbeck's parish church to St Kentigern (or Mungo) and the nearby Mungo's Well suggest a missionary visit by that saint, who was Bishop of Glasgow in the 6th century.

Mining in the fells above the villages began in the 13th century – the most important minerals were lead, copper and barytes; the last mine closed in the 1960s. The Cald beck and its tributaries provided water power for the industrial development of the 17th and 18th centuries: corn, woollen and bobbin mills, a paper mill and a brewery flourished. Priests Mill, built in 1702 as a corn mill, was latterly in use as a saw mill. It has now been restored to provide craft workshops, a mining museum, gift shop, restaurant and tourist information centre.

The village has claims to fame out of all proportion to its size. The churchyard is the resting place of Mary Harrison (the 'beauty of Buttermere') and of John Peel, the famous huntsman. Mary, wife of farmer Richard Harrison, had been the innocent victim of a scandal of the early 19th century through her 'marriage' to John Hatfield the bigamist (he was hanged in Carlisle in 1803, not for bigamy but for forgery). John Peel (1776–1854) was made famous by the song written by mill-manager John Woodcock Graves, at whose Caldbeck mill the 'hodden grey' of Peel's coat was woven.

Hesket-New-Market, one and a half miles east of Caldbeck, still has its market cross and bull ring, though the market, established in 1751 for sheep and cattle, was discontinued by the mid 19th century. The annual agricultural show has been held on different sites near the village since 1877.

Old customs, common to other parts of Cumbria, such as the barring of the road to newly-married couples until they have thrown coins to the waiting children (the Scrowmally), are still current. A Kern Supper, formerly held in the old Fellside school, now forms part of the Caldbeck harvest celebrations. A recently revived custom is the Blessing of the Plough on Plough Sunday, when an old horse plough, decorated by members of the Young Farmers Club, is brought into Caldbeck church. Although Tatie Pot, rum butter and herb pudding are made by Cumbrian cooks everywhere, there is one delicious product unique to the district – Caldbeck Rolled Gingerbread, which mystified a Scottish judge when faced with exhibits at a WI show!

Calderbridge & Ponsonby

Calderbridge is situated on the A595. The river Calder runs through the village. The river has some good stretches of fishing and there is a local angling club. Calderbridge has changed from a mainly agricultural community with various shops and services to a quieter village with a post office, garage, two public houses and a sawmill. Many of the people living within the parish boundaries are involved with agriculture but since the coming of British Nuclear Fuels on the Sellafield site in 1952 and Calder Hall in 1956 many people in the village work there.

Calder Abbey is situated out of the village and was founded as a Cistercian abbey. It is now a ruin but the manor house is still lived in.

The church, St Bridget's, is in the centre of the village. It was built in 1842 by Thomas Irwin of Calder Abbey. When the vicar retired in 1978 the parish was joined with Beckermet. The vicarage was sold and an extension was built on and made into flats for the elderly and other people of the parish. The old school has also been turned into four flats for elderly people.

Calderbridge has a large village hall which was built in 1958 with money raised by parishioners. Annually the Calderbridge Picnic and Sports are held in the field behind the hall, on the third Saturday in June. The village has two public houses, the Stanley Arms and the Golden Fleece. Both have been trading for many years.

Ponsonby parish has been a united benefice with Calderbridge since 1957 and is now served by the vicar of Beckermet. Ponsonby church stands in the park of Pelham House, which used to be Ponsonby Hall. It has a ha-ha round it to keep livestock out. The tower and spire were built by the Stanley family in 1840.

Ponsonby is a small community of farms, houses and a joinery and furniture business. Ponsonby Old Hall is farmed by the Stanley family. This farm has recently diversified and it now has a Farm Park which is open from Easter until September.

Newmill, which is on the A595 to Gosforth, is included in the ecclesiastical parish of Ponsonby. Newmill consists of a farm, a smithy and a few houses on the road-side. The smithy up until a few years ago was worked by the Gainford family who had been there for several generations. It has recently been sold and is now an undertaker's and carpenter's shop.

Calthwaite 🐏

'Calthwaite? Oh yes', Cumbrians say. 'Yoghurt and Jersey cows!' But there is more to Calthwaite than the dairy which for many years was the main source of local employment.

Calthwaite has a church, a school, a pub and a post office (where you can obtain anything from stamps to Cumberland sausage). Visitors will notice that many of the buildings are of local red sandstone and dates above doorways tell that much building was done between 1880 and 1900 when Calthwaite Hall estate rebuilt many old properties, particularly farmhouses.

The church, also of sandstone, was built in 1913 and many local functions helped to finance this. To the south of Calthwaite is Plumpton Back Street Methodist chapel which incorporates two foundation stones, one belonging to an earlier chapel which was sited nearby.

In the village, 'Reading Room Cottage' reminds us that here was a building where lads could go for warmth, to read the newspapers or play billiards. The story goes that a certain elderly gentleman hogged the fire nightly and was eventually transported to the back of the room, chair and all!

The Globe inn is an old coaching inn and is noted for its hospitality, good food and fund raising events. Adjacent to the inn is the old village smithy where two generations of Reays shoed horses, re-rimmed cart-wheels and repaired farm implements. The area in front of the Globe was the green with a duckpond until Calthwaite Hall estate drained the pond and built cottages there.

A traditional Calthwaite event which is over 100 years old is the annual Christmas Party held about three days after Christmas and financed by various functions over the year. All local children receive a gift from Father Christmas, have a free tea and entertainment. Everyone is invited. Another annual get-together is Sports Day, held in the field next to the church.

This was the Royal Forest of Inglewood and many local names bear this out – Aikbank Farm, Low Wool Oaks, High Oaks, Inglewood House, all have their origins in the forest. Calthwaite's parish is Hesket-in-the-Forest and nearby is Hutton-in-the-Forest, Lord Inglewood's home. Roe deer are still seen in the woods or crossing from plantation to plantation. Thiefside, east of Calthwaite, was the site of the gallows where unfortunate poachers and sheep stealers were hanged.

Before there was a graveyard at Hesket-in-the-Forest, corpses were carried from the Petteril valley via a path over Lazonby Fell to Kirkoswald in the Eden valley. Almost at the summit of Lazonby Fell is a coffin stone where bearers rested the coffin before proceeding.

Before 1987 very little new building took place in Calthwaite. Now an area of derelict barns and farm buildings has been developed. About half the houses are owner-occupied, tenanted houses mostly belong to Brackenburgh estate which grew out of the original Calthwaite Hall estate.

Camerton 🖋️

Camerton is a small village in a hollow, with three main roads leading into it, each consisting of a steep hill. Many years ago, it was thriving with industry, the main places of employment being the brickworks and the drift mines. Clay was also found at Camerton, and this was in great demand by brickworks both locally and nationally, much of it being transported by the local railway. During the Second World War, the old drift mines (by then out of productivity) were used to store armaments for the Royal Naval Armaments Depot at nearby Broughton Moor.

Camerton Hall is a very large house on the outskirts of the village, and has been designated as a building of historic and architectural value. Said to have been designed by Inigo Jones, it is built on the site of a pele tower of about the 14th century, and is a well known local landmark.

Without doubt, Camerton's best known building is the parish church of St Peter, which dates back to the 11th century, though it is firmly believed that there was a church standing on the same site many years before that. St Peter's stands in a lonely place about half a mile from the village, amid beautiful scenery, and is set in a loop of the lovely river Derwent, which flows on three sides of the church. A more idyllic setting would be difficult to find. There is no actual road to St Peter's, just a path across the fields.

Inside the church there lies a sandstone effigy of a warrior painted black, known locally as 'Black Tom of the North'. Many tales and legends have been told and written about Black Tom, and it is difficult to separate fact from fiction, but it is known that he was a direct descendant of the Curwen family, of Curwen Hall at Workington. He was a smuggler, leading a Robin Hood type of life, stealing from the rich to give to the poor. He died in about 1500 and even today his exploits are still discussed by local historians, and not least by the customers at Camerton's only public house, which used to be called the Derwent Arms, but in 1987 was renamed the Black Tom inn.

Near to St Peter's is a grassy field, known locally as 'Camerton Church Hill' which, in years gone by, was a favourite place for pasche-egg rolling. Pasche-eggs are ordinary hen eggs which have been wrapped in newspaper containing gorse flowers, daffodil leaves, primroses, coffee beans etc, or any dye, then boiled for half an hour. When unwrapped, they are beautifully patterned, and coloured. Whilst still warm, butter is rubbed into the shell to make it shine. The eggs are then left to go cold.

This same grassy field has a bridge at one end, which connects Camerton to the village burial ground. When the bridge was first built no-one could think of an appropriate name for it, so the council decided to name the bridge after the first person to be carried over it, en route to burial in the cemetery. This was a man called Joseph Parkin, who died in the year 1800. He had a reputation for hoarding money, and was known to be a miser. Thus the bridge is always known as 'Miser's Bridge'.

On the outskirts of the village stands Seat House Farm, where the Conway brothers bred their well-known strain of Clydesdale horses. They travelled many miles, usually walking, with their stallions at stud, visiting many Cumbrian farms.

Cark-in-Cartmel 🐚

From Flookburgh the road leads northwards towards Cark, a small village which, it is said, takes its name from the Celtic word 'carrec', meaning rock.

Cark Hall was built by Thomas Pickering (he was married in Cartmel in 1571) and passed by marriage to the Curwens of Myreside Hall, Flookburgh, then later to the Rawlinsons. The Hall has mullioned windows and a magnificent entrance with Ionic columns supporting a large arch. On the western side a wing was added, probably in the 17th century.

In the early 17th century the paper mill was built, whilst in 1782 it was decided to build lower down the village a large cotton mill with a considerable number of attendant cottages. The top and bottom of three rows – known as High Row and Low Row – survive, but the Middle Row was largely demolished.

The mill was one of the first cotton mills erected in England. Cotton was brought in the early days of the mill by ship, as Cark was a busy port in the 1700s. Ships were built by the river near Crook Wheel and trade was carried out with the Baltic, America and the West Indies. The mill was largely destroyed by fire in 1936.

The Engine inn was previously the Fire Engine inn, and so is not connected, as is often thought, with the railway. The railway was opened in 1857, Cark station being on the line between Ulverston and Carnforth. It was not until later that it was extended beyond Ulverston. The extensive excavations and building of the embankments led to the silting up of the estuary and thus the end of shipping activity.

Cark has its own little church, a Methodist chapel. There has been an active Methodist society in Cark since before 1876; before the church was built and opened in 1904, meetings were held in the Mill Yard.

Cartmel

Everyone loves Cartmel. Beside its traditionally hospitable and welcoming atmosphere, its outstanding features are the magnificent priory church founded about 1190 by William Marshal, the Regent of England, the steeplechase race course – and the food!

The Market Square, with its obelisk lamp stand and antiquated stone fish-slabs – the traditional meeting place of Cartmel youth, and the village pump (where once the milk-man was caught diluting his milk), all testify to Cartmel having been a market town and the centre of commercial life for surrounding villages. Not so long ago the village was self-sufficient, with almost every trade represented to serve the whole neighbourhood. It was said that the villagers made their year's rent on Race Day by catering for visitors and bookies, most of whom had walked the two miles from Cark station.

Through this beautiful monastic township winds the river Aye. Ducks paddle and trout rise under its picturesque bridges and hanging flowered shrubs. Luckily the monks of old were told in a dream to build their priory beside this water, and not, as they intended, on top of Mount Barnard overlooking the fertile valley.

Legend has it that the monks started Cartmel Races as their Whitsun recreation. At first the wooden grandstand and paraphernalia of the races was all taken down and put away each year in the tithe barn in Barn Garth. Now it is a permanent course. Lord Cavendish, patron of the priory, can be seen on the stand, surveying indulgently the ocean of parked cars and coaches and the happy Bank Holiday crowds enjoying their punting and picnicking and fairground fun on his land. A popular Steeplechase Service is held in the priory on the Sunday between the August races.

The old Gothic-style village school is still the most popular primary school for miles around, and the modern comprehensive Priory school is a worthy successor to the original grammar school held in the priory gate house in 1624.

The era of monks was later followed by an era of spinsters! Twos and threes of sisters, taking in guests, dressmaking or teaching under the roofs provided for them by considerate fathers. At one time there were 45 of them. A succession of vicars was thus armed with a supply of lady helpers, and generations of Cartmel children owe much of their gentle culture and religious education, not to mention tea-parties, treats and outings, to these wise and great-hearted ladies, eccentricities and all.

Cartmel attracts the learned and intellectual, and the village is like a magnet to business and professional people who want a special atmosphere for their retirement years. It is the combined spiritual and secular influence of the great priory that makes Cartmel unique.

Cartmel Fell 🌿

Cartmel Fell is a scattered parish covering a wide upland area of great beauty to the west of the river Winster and including the hamlets of Bowland Bridge, Gill Head and Tower Wood. It enjoys expansive views of Whitbarrow Scar on one side and the Coniston range on the other, and has remained unspoilt through the centuries.

The focal point of the parish is St Anthony's church, tucked away in a remote fold of the fells with its adjoining parish hall, which was the village school until 1971. Built about 1504 to serve a small community of hill farmers whose church had previously been seven miles away at Cartmel Priory, and to provide basic education for their children, St Anthony's is a simple Lakeland chapel, with low rough-cast walls, pierced by Perpendicular stone-mullioned windows. There are large enclosed pews on either side of the nave for the families of the three halls: Burblethwaite, Cowmire and Thorphinsty.

It was at Burblethwaite, in the centre of the parish, that Anthony Knipe lived in the 15th century, and it was in accordance with his will that the church was founded. Cowmire (pronounced Comer) Hall is an elegant 17th century house of three stories built on to a pele tower of much earlier date, probably 14th century. But it is Thorphinsty Hall which seems to be the oldest, for the earliest reference to it appeared in 1275 when Henry, son of Henry de Thorphinsty, claimed a messuage and ploughlands against the Prior of Cartmel.

Below the church stands Hodge Hill, a 16th century statesman's house of great charm, which is now an hotel. High up on the fell between Cartmel Fell and High Newton is another building of great historical interest: the Heights Friends' meeting house. Originally a barn, it served the small community of local Friends from the 17th century until the 1920s.

A house of great architectural significance in more modern times is Moor Crag at Gill Head on the eastern shore of Lake Windermere. Designed in 1899 by Voysey, a prominent member of the Arts and Crafts Movement, it exemplifies the trend away from traditional architecture to a more enlightened design to take full advantage of the magnificent setting. The gardens, sloping down towards the lake, were laid out by Thomas Mawson.

Gill Head has seen much change in the past 200 years, for during the 18th century and up until the 1850s it was a hive of industry. Two large mills were situated along the gill, the upper one being first for flax and then for bobbins, and the lower one a saw-mill. By the middle of the 19th century, however, when the Victorian vogue for building villas along the lake shore was in full swing, the mills and land were sold off, and nothing now remains of the old industry except the boat-house, which now forms the foundation of a lakeside residence, and two of the dams. Gill Head was a noisy place when the mills were in operation, but now the grinding of the huge water-wheels and the continuous rasping of the saws have been replaced by the noise of a modern era, for the main Bowness to Newby Bridge road, a mere track in 1850, now carries heavy traffic, and power-boats along the lake have replaced the gentle sail and steam of yesteryear.

Casterton 🦋

The two hamlets of High Casterton and Low Casterton are situated on the left bank of the river Lune, north and east of Devil's Bridge on the A683 Sedbergh to Lancaster road and one and a half miles from Kirkby Lonsdale.

The earliest mention of Casterton was in 1086 in the Domesday Book, yet it would seem that a community had been in existence for centuries before this. The place name Casterton means literally 'the farmstead near the fortification', and suggests a Roman settlement linked with the Roman road lying between the village and the fells.

Coal mining was carried out on the fells, the name Collier's Lane being given to the road leading from the main road to the pits, still well used today as a route to High Casterton and a strong reminder of times past. Lime quarrying in Casterton Woods and the remains of at least two lime kilns in the parish point to further employment at a later time.

The name Carus-Wilson figures frequently in Casterton history. The Carus family acquired the manor of Kirkby Lonsdale in 1558 and a descendant of this family reacquired Casterton Hall by marrying Elizabeth Wilson. He adopted the name Carus-Wilson and his eldest son William founded the Clergy Daughters' School at Cowan Bridge in 1823, moving the school ten years later into new buildings at Casterton, where Casterton School remains today as a boarding school for 360 girls. It is interesting to note that the school register for the latter half of 1824 contains the names of the four Bronte sisters. The junior department of the school is now known as Bronte House, accommodated in a building also founded by Carus-Wilson as a school for servant girls.

It was William Carus-Wilson who in 1833 built Holy Trinity church for the use of the schools and the village. The village has been served in the past, indeed within living memory, by shoe repairers, a blacksmith, an hotel and at least two general shops, a butcher and a post office. This compares with one combined shop and filling station and the hotel which serve the district today. The industry of today has changed too, comprising garage repairs, a publishing firm, a maker of educational toys and a cabinet maker.

With the closure of the village school and greater general mobility by private car, Kirkby Lonsdale has become increasingly the focus for shopping and social activities for Casterton people. The village hall, nevertheless, provides a home for a successful rural nursery. There is a well patronised nine-hole golf course in the village and regular swimming classes for all ages take place in the Casterton school pool.

Castle Carrock

Castle Carrock, a small village with about 80 dwellings within its boundaries, nestles with its back to the foot of the north-western tip of the Pennines, a designated Area of Outstanding Natural Beauty. Outlying farms clinging to the hillside enjoy panoramic views over the Eden valley to the south, the Solway Firth to the west, and the Scottish hills to the north, with, in the foreground, a man-made reservoir, storing much of Carlisle City's water supply and home for many wild fowl.

Evidence of early habitation in the area includes pit dwellings on Castle Carrock fells, the discovery of an ancient stone coffin containing artefacts dated from the Stone Age at Greenwell, a nearby hamlet on the bank of the river Gelt, and a large stone cairn, six metres high, prominent on the skyline to the south of Castle Carrock, known as Cardunneth Pike. This is identified as a meeting place and burial site for 'important people' of the Bronze Age, 1800 BC–500 BC, which served notice to other Bronze Age peoples in the Eden valley of the extent of the builder's influence and territory.

Castle Carrock or Castel Caerog, despite its name, does not boast a castle; rather, it is believed, there existed a fortified manor house east of the church, with a moat filled by the Castle Carrock beck. Nothing remains except a massive stone, possibly a lintel, in a field.

Today, Castle Carrock has settled back into a peaceful and tranquil existence. St Peter's church, the Watson Institute (the village hall), two public houses and the school all cluster near or fronting the Marr (the village green). A combined shop and post office and, a concession to modernity, footpath lighting, complete the facilities. Three working farms remain within the confines of the village, surrounded by houses of all periods with a mixed population; some 'native' some 'new', some retired and some 'working away', most playing a full part in the life of the village.

The present church, St Peter's, was rebuilt on the original site in 1838, possibly using some stone from the ruined manor house, and refurbished in 1888. The rectory, across the Marr from the church, was built in 1727 for a Joseph Pattinson, rector from 1722–1738; a typical Georgian rectory, it is still provided with a ring in the front wall to tie up one's horse, and is next door to one of the newest homes in the village, both quite happy to be neighbours.

The first school was a small building at the gate of the churchyard, as shown in an old painting now hanging in the church vestry. The present building dates from 1874 when it was built by local landowners, including one Ralph Watson, for the village. The original one room has been extended at various times to match the requirements of the day. At the time of the enclosure of common land, the school was endowed with 24 acres of land, the rents of these 'school lands' providing extras for the use of the school, outwith those now provided by the Local Education Committee. A useful legacy from Georgian days.

Causewayhead ✍

Causewayhead, an undoubted part of the Roman road which led from the station at Bowness to the camp at Ellenborough, lies about one and a half miles south-east of Silloth and is dominated by the lovely old church of St Paul, erected in 1845. A piece of land was donated by the Earl of Lonsdale for burial purposes in 1893. The graves of some of the airmen who were killed while flying during the Second World War are to be found here.

The parsonage house was built in 1851, but has since become a private residence, with a caravan park attached. The vicar of Christ Church in Silloth now combines his parish with that of Causewayhead. The parish once boasted two schools – The Nab Corner and Colt Park school, a public elementary school with an average attendance of 80 pupils. Opposite the parsonage was the Sunday school and mission hall. Here the WI held their meetings and the village dances and suppers took place.

During the war the area became a RAF training centre and maintenance unit, covering a large acreage with hangars and runways. Passes were needed by civilians to move about in certain areas.

The village once had its own blacksmith's shop and an inn called the Forresters Arms. Now only the farms, the cottages and the church remain, Runways are overgrown but there are still some of the old hangars remaining, put to good use by the farmers.

Clappersgate & Brathay ✍

The hamlet of Clappersgate is situated a mile from Ambleside on the Coniston road, beneath Loughrigg fell.

In the 16th century Clappersgate was classified as a port, since it had a wharf on the Brathay river where slate from local quarries was loaded and taken down river to Windermere and onwards to the south. There was a horse-operated mill at Clappersgate, an inn, a store and two farmhouses. The port is now the boat house and harbour of the Croft, a large house built about 1850 for a prosperous Liverpool merchant. The inn and store have now disappeared but there is still a cluster of picturesque houses and cottages. The Croft and its stables have been converted into flats and small houses. At the entrance to the stable yard there was once a vagrants whipping post.

Turning left in Clappersgate the Hawkshead road leads down to the Brathay bridge (formerly the boundary between Westmorland and Lancashire). The name Brathay means 'the broad river' and above the bridge is a broad pool where, despite human intervention, trout still lie!

Just over the bridge, on the left, the house now called Old Brathay has some historical and literary associations. Originally 'Low Brathay', it was a farm in the Middle Ages and there was an inn nearby. The present house dates from the 16th century and in 1880 was occupied by Charles Lloyd, a member of the Quaker banking family and a friend of the poet Wordsworth. Lloyd frequently entertained the Wordsworth family as well as Coleridge, Southey and other members of the Lakes literary circle. In 1805, John Harden, diarist and artist, came to live at the adjoining property, Brathay Hall. Here de Quincey, Dr Arnold of Rugby and Constable, the artist, were all visitors. It was probably whilst staying here that Constable produced an over-romanticised drawing of the Langdale Pikes showing a lake at the foot where none exists. Both properties now belong to the Brathay Hall Trust and are centres for leadership and development training.

In 1880 Brathay Hall was sold to a Mr Giles Redmayne and six years later he built the church at Brathay, now known as Holy Trinity. Redmayne had made his fortune in the Italian silk trade and the stuccoed Italianate appearance of the church reflects this interest. Although incongruous in a Lakeland setting the building has a melancholy Victorian charm.

A Sunday school was built near the church in 1859, in memory of Giles Redmayne and later, further up the leafy valley of the Brathay, between Skelwith Fold and Skelwith Bridge, a day school, with a house for the master, was built on land given by the Duke of Buccleugh. The school is now a community centre, serving a wide area.

Cliburn

Cliburn is a small village of about 200 inhabitants situated in the Eden valley halfway between Penrith and Appleby. The name Cliburn means 'stream by the bank', the stream in question being the river Leith which runs through meadows at the foot of the hill on which Cliburn is built. This small river, which flows into the river Eden four miles away, has carved through rock to form a river cliff 30 to 40 ft high and so the village is aptly named.

In common with many small villages Cliburn has lost most of its services and institutions. The primary school closed in 1983 and the sub-post office in 1988. The local railway line was closed years ago and the bus service now consists of one bus a week. There are no shops in the village now although mobile shops call regularly. However, Cliburn is not 'dead'. There are still two working farms in the main street as well as a garage and car showroom and a small curtain-making firm. The little pub, the Golden Pheasant, is a meeting place for locals and the village hall is booked every evening for a variety of activities. Recently a volunteer transport service has been set up to help compensate for the poor public service.

The main street of the village runs downhill from north to south and is lined with attractive sandstone buildings, the stone for which would have been brought from quarries in the nearby Whinfell Forest. The majority of the buildings date from the late 18th and the 19th centuries – although there has probably been a settlement on this site since Saxon times. Notable exceptions, however, are Cliburn Hall, built on the river bank at the foot of the village, and St Cuthbert's church opposite.

Cliburn Hall, now a farmhouse and extensively modernised about 20 years ago, was built in the 14th century as a pele tower by Robert De Cliburn, the lord of the manor. St Cuthbert's church is an attractively sited building perched on the river bank and approached by a short avenue of lime trees. Originally Norman it has been added to and restored over the years but the Norman nave and chancel still survive, as does the Norman font.

Apart from the council houses and a handful of new bungalows it is likely that most of the houses in the village have changed their use over the years. Cliburn has survived as a community by changing with the times and shows every sign of continuing to do so ensuring, we hope, that there will be a thriving village here for many years to come.

Clifton 🌿

South of Penrith and Eamont Bridge and called after the two cliffs above which it stands, lies the village of Clifton, straddling both the railway and the A6 with the M6 running alongside. Here the last battle on English soil was fought when rebel Highlanders, retreating from Derby, clashed with the Duke of Cumberland's dragoons on Clifton Moor. A stone in the churchyard marks the spot where some of the dragoons were buried, and a brass tablet records the burial of Highlanders by the Rebel Tree, an oak, at Townend, the southern end of the village.

The 13th century church is dedicated to St Cuthbert, as it is tradition-ally one of the places where the monks from Lindisfarne rested with his body when they fled from the Danes in the late 9th century. It must have seemed a very attractive place to the weary monks: a raised mound in rich farmland, supplied with wells and streams and spectacular views of the Pennines and Lake District hills.

It was because of Border raids that pele towers, such as that at Clifton Hall, at the northern end of the village, were built. These sturdy towers provided homes for the farmers and their families on the upper floors (usually two) and protection for their livestock below.

Early parish registers indicate that almost every trade and profession was represented in the village. Occupations listed include those of attorney, clockmaker, dressmaker, cordwainer, blacksmith, carpenter, gamekeeper, shoemaker, weaver, tollgate keeper, miller, painter, potter, engineer and farmer. Today's villagers are not quite so self-sufficient, but there are still working farms as well as a thriving village shop-cum-post office, a school, hotel, an inn and a sawmill. The first school in the village was provided when Mary Scott left £40 in 1764 towards payment for a schoolmaster.

Clifton once possessed two railway stations: Clifton Lowther (where Edward VI arrived to stay at Brougham) and Clifton Moor. Lord Lonsdale had a private waiting room, a personal railway siding, a coach house and stables to facilitate the loading of his horses and luggage for holidays at Barleythorpe, now a well known stud farm in Leicestershire.

Outside the village on the road past Clifton Dykes, lies Wetheriggs pottery, which first started making bricks and tiles in 1760 when it was part of Lord Brougham's estate. Some of its pantiles can be seen on an old gamekeeper's cottage, unusual where most of the houses are roofed in local slate. The pottery made all the earthenware needed by farmers and people for miles around, a slipware in brown, green or blue. The pottery still makes slipware in the same distinctive pattern decorated with white clay poured through a cow horn with a goose quill in the end. The pottery is now an industrial museum.

Industrious is perhaps a good word to describe this village, which is not a pretty postcard village, but an interesting and vibrant community.

Colby 🦢

Colby village stands on an eminence one and a quarter miles from Appleby, the county town of Westmorland. Its history can be traced back to at least 1086, when a family named Colby owned all the village.

In the past Colby had twelve farms which milked cows. Today there is one dairy farm and five working farms. It had two water wheels; one was a corn mill and the other wheel was used for threshing cereals. There was a blacksmith's forge, a public house, a farm that sold milk and its own home made icecream, a general store, a greengrocer's shop, a small tin church and a Methodist chapel. None of these survive today. In recent years a joiner's shop and a small knitwear business have been established.

Most of the old houses are built of sandstone which was obtained locally from a quarry. Some of the houses date back to the early 17th century and one still displays blocked up windows reminding us of the time when the number of windows in a dwelling were eligible for tax. The village has twice as many houses today but the population of 124 is less than in 1821 when 141 people lived there.

There are residents in the village who still recall the days when the domestic water supply was gathered from three pumps scattered in different areas around the village. The old wells are now overgrown but evidence of their existence is sometimes visible as water trickles across the village road in several places.

There is a good community spirit in the village with old and new inhabitants integrating well. The Women's Institute flourishes and the village sports day and Christmas social are enthusiastically supported. A neighbourhood watch scheme has been introduced recently. Colby may be a village with roots in the past but it looks forward with enthusiasm to the future.

Colthouse 🌿

Colthouse is more like a hamlet than a village, though it does have its own place of worship in the old Quaker meeting house. Near the north-east end of Esthwaite Water, it lies under the lee of Claife Heights, the long and beautiful fell that separates the Esthwaite valley from Winder-mere's western shore. As with nearby Hawkshead it was not in the Domesday Book, and not until 1127 was its uncharted wilderness granted to the Cistercian abbey of Furness.

By far the most significant occurrence at Colthouse in the 17th century, was the consequence of George Fox's visit to Hawkshead in 1653. Many local people were influenced by his teaching, and Colthouse became an important Quaker centre.

The Colthouse Quaker burial ground of 1658 is one of the earliest in the country, though the meeting house was built later in 1688, just before the Toleration Act. Previously, secret meetings were held in houses or barns, and several, including one in the burial ground, resulted in prosecutions. George Fox also believed education to be important, and local Quakers learnt to read and write when most people signed their names with a cross. Not only had a school been started in the meeting house, but what was far more unusual, a lending library.

In 1779, Wordsworth became a pupil at nearby Hawkshead grammar school, and lodged for many years with other boys at Dame Ann Tyson's Colthouse cottage, Green End. His love of the countryside greatly influenced his famous autobiographical poem on the growth of a poet's mind: *The Prelude*. From 1882 onwards Beatrix Potter came to know and love the Esthwaite valley, and in 1896 she 'went to the Friends' Meeting at Colthouse' and 'liked it very much. It is a pretty place, peaceful and sunny, very old fashioned inside, with a gigantic old key in the door'. She also met 'a roly-poly stout lady in a black silk dress' who was a relative of the Satterthwaites.

Colthouse is still a small rural community, and Town End, owned by a Satterthwaite descendant, continues to be farmed. Surprisingly for a holiday area, the hamlet has no tourist facilities, though knowledgeable Wordsworth scholars, often from America and Japan, sometimes visit it. The meeting house is still used, and attracts Friends from distant places.

Colton & Oxen Park 🌿

Colton is a hamlet, Oxen Park a village, divided by the road from Greenodd to Hawkshead. They cover a large area of mainly unspoilt countryside between Windermere to the east and Coniston Water to the west.

Holy Trinity parish church stands on the top of the hill at Colton hamlet with a parochial church hall, once the village school, alongside. A striking panorama of the fells and range of mountains can be seen from this point. Three miles to the south at Tottlebank, a Baptist church was founded in 1669, under the Act of Uniformity. Charles II decreed that Non-conformists could not worship within five miles of a corporate town, thus Tottlebank is just five miles from the market town of Ulverston.

Colton hamlet comprises three farms, two houses, two cottages, a residential home for the elderly and a vicarage, with a further farm and two houses on the periphery.

Oxen Park village consists of a farm and a few dwellings, a repair garage, post office and a small hotel. The old blacksmith's shop still stands and was used for shoeing horses within living memory. Many properties date from the 18th century and some are of earlier foundation. At the edge of the village is an isolated homestead known as New House, which no doubt would have been so named when it first became a private habitation, for this was originally the poor house for the district, housing vagrants, tramps and homeless souls. A house in the village is dated 1679 and has a wall sign depicting the trade of a blacksmith, whilst a further dwelling was formerly the Black Lion inn and is dated 1730. Currently employment can be found on the farms or in forestry – Grisedale Forest being only a few miles away.

Employment in the 1920s included hazardous jobs in the gunpowder industry at Blackbeck near Bouth and at Low Wood, Haverthwaite. Many tragic accidents through all too frequent explosions were reported from these works, often resulting in wives being left with young families. The railway at Haverthwaite and Ulverston stations also employed people from the village in the 1920–1940s era. Basket makers, or swillers as they were termed, plied their craft into the 1970s. Corn mills were another local industry, often worked along with a smallholding or poultry farm. Charcoal burners worked in the woods, living 'on the job' for weeks at a time. Charcoal was used for iron making. A number of bloomery sites for charcoal smelting can still be seen and the industry was practised in recent times. Bobbin mills were another source of employment within the district, also tanning with tan yards situated at Lowick, Oxen Park and Rusland.

Coniston 🦢

Wordsworth, in his guide to the Lakes in 1810, recommended travellers to approach Coniston by crossing Morecambe Sands and approach peacefully into the Vale of Coniston. This is still an enchanting way and leads naturally into the centre of the village.

Before the copper mines, dating from Jacobean times, were revitalized about 1859, and slate quarries opened, Coniston was a scattered rural community, mainly settled around Coniston Hall, built in 1270 by the Fleming family. Nearby Bowmanstead (by the Ship inn) where the bowmen lived, produced bows and arrows and men to defend the Hall and help the hunt.

The present church was completed in 1891 during a period of great prosperity for the community, when many wealthy patrons, including John Ruskin, settled in the area. The Barrats of Holywath (built in 1786) were already prominent patrons of the village. The original school building was attached to the old chapel and was demolished to extend the graveyard, which dates from Elizabethan times, and a new school was built in 1854. This is now a Diocesan Youth Centre, two schools having been built in the 1960s.

The village, most likely a Saxon settlement, probably had a chapel from earliest times, but the first record of one was in 1500, a chapel of ease from the mother church in Ulverston. The Methodist and Baptist chapels were opened for Cornish miners and quarrymen, and the Catholic church for Irishmen who came in great numbers. The row of cottages in Coppermines Valley was once known as Irish Row.

Modern Coniston is still a working village with a long history of self-help. A branch of the Order of Oddfellows, a Mutual Friendly Society, flourished before the days of the social security system. The Co-op came from Sawrey in the late 1800s, originally in one of the Kirkbeck Cottages, until its transfer to the present premises in Yewdale Road early this century. It must be one of the few remaining independent Co-ops still in existence and still paying a dividend to its members. Up to 1960 it also gave the children a film show at Christmas as well as an orange and half-a-crown.

The Institute, the centre for most village activities and well used, houses the Ruskin Museum, well worth a visit. Brantwood, Ruskin's home on the east of the lake, is open to the public. His grave may be seen in the churchyard.

The village centre grew mainly between 1880 and 1920. The Garth estate was built in 1948–9. There have been four developments since, the last around the garage in 1990. The Monk Coniston estate, owned by

Beatrix Potter, stretched from Coniston to Skelwith Bridge and was bequeathed by her to the National Trust.

Donald Campbell broke the water speed record on the lake in 1955 and was killed attempting to regain it in 1967. His memorial is by the bus shelter.

Corney

Corney is a small community, made up mainly of farming families, spread over an area rich in ancient settlements. The parish lies in West Cumbria, between Waberthwaite and Bootle, and stretches up onto the fells behind those villages.

The Brown Cow inn, the centre of much of village life, was built around 1800. The inn provided bed and board for huntsmen and hounds. Lighting was by oil lamps and candles until electricity came in the late 1950s. Nearby was the smithy, originally thatched, then roofed in tin and, much later, slated. Always a very busy place, the blacksmith repaired farm implements and made ploughs and harrows as well as shoeing horses.

Another focal point for the community is the church, dedicated to St John the Baptist. At a height of about 600 ft above sea level, it looks down on much of the parish. There has been a church on this site since the mid 12th century, although the current building was only erected in 1882. During the building work, great quantities of human remains were found beneath the floor – evidence of the site's long history. Corney folk have a reputation for longevity – one gravestone shows John Noble (1658–1772) died at the age of 114!

Outside, in the churchyard, there is a sundial dated 1882. It was the gift of Edward Troughton, Corney's most famous son. Born in 1753, and brought up on a farm called Welcome Nook, Troughton left Corney as a young man to seek fame and fortune in London. Despite being colour blind and deaf from birth, he became famous for his work on the scientific instruments of the day, especially sextants and naval theodolites. The Royal Society awarded him the coveted Copley Medal and Greenwich Observatory commissioned a statue of him. True to Corney longevity, Edward Troughton died at the age of 82 in 1835. He is buried in Kensal Cemetery in London but never forgot his birthplace and, indeed, another of his sundials stands on the front lawn at Welcome Nook.

Corney has always been a predominantly farming community. Stone walls and hawthorn hedges keep the Herdwick and Swaledale sheep from straying when they are in off the fell. Seven dairy farms are spread over the lower land. There are eight other farms, mostly running hill cattle and sheep. In addition, there are some 24 cottages spread throughout the settlement.

Side by side with the traditional farms, Corney has its share of the small businesses which are so much a part of thriving country communities. In its day, Corney has been the home of a Youth Hostel, a carpet factory and a works to produce tannin from sycamore bark. This tannin was sent to the tanneries at Haverigg, near Millom, some twelve miles south. Sadly, these have all gone now, to be replaced in recent years by businesses which have taken traditional rural crafts and developed them in such a way that they can survive in today's business world. Gillfoot, near the centre of Corney, houses a thriving agricultural engineering business. The farm buildings at Skellerah Farm have been adapted to house Ashdown Smokers, producers of traditionally cured and smoked foods.

Cotehill ✤

High on a hillside six miles south of Carlisle, Cotehill village enjoys outstanding views of the East Cumberland fells and the vales and hills to the north. The name is believed to have derived from Goathill, where once wild goats had their habitat. The area is surrounded by lovely countryside for walking and a large forestry plantation which is part of former Inglewood Forest. The church dedicated to St John has an unusual 'beehive' shaped bell tower and a lovely east window. It serves both Cotehill and Cumwhinton. The incumbent is also chaplain at the local Garlands Hospital.

The village population is about 350. There have been a lot of new houses built during the last ten years. Most people commute to Carlisle for employment although like nearby Cumwhinton, many used to work in the gypsum works. The former vicarage is now a home for the elderly with 26 residents. The school is still used and has an active Board of Governors. There is a village shop, Methodist chapel, post office and local pub. The children enjoy a Rose Queen ceremony and sports day every summer. The older people have a thriving over sixties club known affectionately as the 'Hill Toppers'. Sadly the local garage has closed and the policeman once known to every local resident has gone too.

There is a great community spirit in Cotehill and all events are usually well supported – long may it continue.

Crofton ✤

Crofton, in the parish of Thursby, was once a magnificent estate of 3,703 acres. The main entrance is through a distinctive archway off the A595, upon which once stood a replica of a proud stag.

Called Crofton Place, the house was the principal residence of the Brisco family, whose descendants united the county's wealthiest families; a baronetcy was created in 1782. Described as a noble structure of

Grecian design, the mansion built in 1838 contained 365 windows and an interior designed by the Adam brothers and Italian craftsmen.

A short distance away a mount of conical form, clothed with trees, called Tarquin, now Torkin, was said to be the residence of two gigantic brothers and also used as a tumulus for some ancient chieftain. The remains of neolithic and stilted villages, along with some artefacts, have been found in the area. Roman remains and other finds have included old coins, some of French origin.

In 1935 Crofton estate was sold to the Land Settlement Association (LSA) for £18,400 and life at Crofton changed completely. Primarily developed for unemployed miners from West Cumberland, the estate became a thriving community with greenhouses, pigs, poultry and financial help from the Association. A manager and experienced staff occupied some of the 69 houses the men helped to build. Over the years preference was given to applicants with experience and capital. The beautiful old mansion, declared unsafe, was demolished in 1957, when the ghost of the Lady in Grey vanished too.

In 1970 the LSA, deciding that the estate was no longer viable, withdrew their services. Some tenants taking advantage of the compensation offered, left along with the staff, leaving half the estate houses empty. Some of the tenants chose to stay and eventually bought and still work their holdings. The rest of the houses are now all privately owned. The remainder of the land of 365 acres was bought by the former Cumberland County Council and developed into three starter farms for young farmers.

The latest development, Project Crofton, is not yet completed. After years of neglect the lake has been restored to its former glory and is now a wildlife sanctuary. Restoration work is progressing on the imposing stable block. The walled garden is to be Victorian in style with a commercial garden centre and cafe. A car park for 100 cars is replacing a bank of trees and rhododendrons. The remains of one of the county's first private gasometers have been destroyed along with part of a 200 year old wall. Three bungalows and a farmhouse have been built in the last 15 years but there are no plans for any future private development at Crofton.

Crook 🐚

Crook is a pleasant Lakeland village midway between Kendal and Bowness-on-Windermere. The houses and farms form a scattered rural community. Most are cement-rendered and whitened according to the Westmorland tradition.

Crook Hall is now a farmhouse. It stands on high ground to the south of the church and the present building dates from the 18th century. It is on the site of the manorial hall and demesne farm of Crook of medieval times. Formerly called Thwatterden Hall, the house was built by the

Philipson family who also built the pele tower (still surviving) at Hollin Hall, at the eastern end of the village, in about 1450. Several farmhouses date back to the 17th century and many are still working farms. A prominent landmark on the hill top above Yew Tree Farm to the north of the road is The Monument, which was the look-out point for Scottish raiders in ancient times and more recently for the Home Guard during the Second World War.

In a field to the west of Crook Hall is the site of the old church, of which only the tower now remains. The tower is considered unsafe and unstable but plans are currently afoot to repair and preserve it. This was the manor chapel in use from about 1506 to 1880 at which later date it was finally abandoned in a ruinous state. The present St Catherine's church was built and consecrated in 1887. A bell which is in the present church used to hang in the old church and in an earlier chapel, the site of which is not known. It is believed to date somewhere between 1340 and 1405, and is one of the oldest church bells in the North West.

Village life centres around St Catherine's church, the Sun inn and the Memorial Hall which was built by public subscription in 1926. Prior to this time village functions often took place in the premises now known as Mill Slack, in Mill Yard. At that time it was the warehouse for the Crook Mill and was known as the Victoria Hall. Across Dobby Lane (so called as it is supposed to be haunted) is the site of the quite substantial Crook Mill, long since disappeared but which is shown in old photographs to have been a large four storey building employing many workers. Most of the remaining cottages in Mill Yard were workers' cottages and it is believed that a fulling mill was operating on this site in the 1500s. The later mill building, owned in 1849 by John Harrison, did a thriving trade in worsted cloth.

Every village which had a beck had its own corn mill and other businesses made use of the cheap power provided by the water. It has been calculated that if a circle were drawn with a radius of no more than three miles around Crook church, that circle would take in the sites of at least 39 water-powered mills known to have been working at one period or another of local history. It is believed that at least three were bobbin mills and much of the local woodland was coppiced to provide a crop of timber for local industry.

Tourism plays an increasingly important role and helps boost the village economy. Several families take in visitors and there is a mushroom farm, a market garden, saw mill, caravan park, an hotel and a pub. Crook is a peaceful, pastoral farming village protected, it is hoped, from further wholesale development by virtue of its position safely inside the boundaries of the Lake District National Park.

Crosby Garrett Viaduct on the Settle-Carlisle Railway

Crosby Garrett

Crosby Garrett, a small, attractive but obviously working village on the south-westerly side of the upper Eden valley, is four miles from Kirkby Stephen and seven miles from Appleby-in-Westmorland, perhaps just off the recognised beaten track for most tourists, although both the proposed Northumberland to Derbyshire Bridleway and Wainwright's Coast to Coast Walk pass through parts of the parish.

Archaeological finds within the parish boundaries have proved that man has inhabited the area at least since Stone Age times. There is evidence of ancient dwellings at Severals and of burial grounds at Bents and Raiset Pike. The open common lands and the ancient field patterns defined by stone walls give a distinctive landscape to Crosby Garrett.

The village as it is seen today probably had its origins in Saxon times and the oldest part of the parish church of St Andrew is the remnant of a Saxon arch. The church is built on the highest part of the ridge known as Arklow which is thought to be the site of pre-Christian sacrifices.

Looking westwards from the church over the village, the 54 ft high viaduct on the Settle-Carlisle railway, with the fell as background, dominates the scene, while Crosby Garrett Fell, a regulated common of 2,000 acres, rises to a height of 1,254 ft above sea level at Nettle Hill.

The village comprises some 50 houses and seven farms grouped mostly round undulating common land intersected by Crosby Garrett beck. The population is about 100 adults and 17 children. The community is served by a small post office/shop, a Methodist church, a Baptist church and the Anglican church. There is a bus service to Kirkby Stephen on Monday mornings for the market. The school, built in 1894, is now the village hall while the former pub, the Fleece, is now a farmhouse, Chapel View.

Apart from agriculture, the only industry in the village is a substantial transport undertaking whose red and white vehicles will be familiar to motorists all over the county and beyond. About one-third of the adult population commutes to work in surrounding towns, while about 20 are either self-employed or work on the farms. Although such a small community, Crosby Garrett is very much alive with annual shows by the amateur dramatic society and 'Its a Knockout' attracting considerable interest in the locality.

Crosby Ravensworth & Maulds Meaburn

The sister villages of Crosby Ravensworth and Maulds Meaburn can be approached from Shap, passing the circle of standing stones at Oddendale, or from Appleby down Meaburn Edge. Descending from Crosby Fell one passes the ancient settlement (Romano-British) called Ewe Close.

The river Lyvennet, a tributary of the Eden, flows through both villages. There is much evidence that these two villages formed a remote community hidden away in this lovely valley. The Romans were here in force. Agricola's men thrust an enduring road through the forest and valley known as Wicker Street or the Gateway to the Pass. During this period Christianity came to the village via Ireland.

There are several great houses in the parish. Crosby Hall was acquired from the Lowthers by the Todd family who continue to farm there today. The house was once fortified with a pele tower which has now been demolished. Meaburn Hall is a lovely house dating from the early 17th century. It has a long history connected with the Lowther family and was famous for the pleasure gardens and bowling green. The two attractive stone summerhouses remain today, a reminder of past history.

Crosby Ravensworth parish church was originally built in 1190 and granted to the abbey of Whitby and dedicated to St Lawrence. Today it is a large austere church of great beauty. There is a flourishing junior school in Crosby Ravensworth.

The highlight of the year is the Crosby Ravensworth Show. It started in a small way in 1856 but today is recognised as an important event in the county and hundreds of people are attracted to it from miles around. There are many exhibits in the giant marquee covering gardening prowess, handicrafts and cooking. Outside are equestrian events, a dog show and a great exhibition of livestock competing for prizes.

Lancelot Addison, the father of the celebrated essayist Joseph Addison, was born in Maulds Meaburn in 1632; a stone obelisk in a field by Hill Top farm marks this event. Another monument is at Black Dub which shows the place where Charles II stopped with his forces in August 1651 when being pursued by Oliver Cromwell.

The two villages and surrounding country constitute an area of outstanding beauty with an atmosphere of pleasant serenity.

Cross Canonby 🦢

Crosby, Birkby, Ellengrove, Allerby Hall and part of Bullgill combine as Cross Canonby parish, recorded as a township in the 11th century.

Sandstones from an earlier church were reused in Cross Canonby, St John's 11th century church, the mother church of Maryport. A Roman chancel arch gifted from Maryport Aluna Fort has two statue alcoves. In 1990 excavation in Swath field revealed relics 1,700 years old with a 2nd century fortlet. On the coast below is Salt Pans, where deep-dug basins remain and a gravestone depicts the salt inspector writing in his office. This has been developed as a tourist attraction.

The squire lived near the church, with a village green, vicarage, four farms, four cottages and alehouse comprising Cross Canonby, now expanded to 26 dwellings. Farmers had grazing stints on the shorebanks where camping holidays, now forbidden, were enjoyed. Many buildings are sandstone, possibly made from large slabs hewn from Cross Canonby quarry and manhandled to site. One barn dated 1787 which was used for dances and school tea parties is now converted to five three-storey spacious homes.

Crosby, a farming and mining village, had dwellings situated around village greens where householders tethered their larger animals. Twenty farms kept two blacksmiths and a saddler busy while allotments, shops, post office, four pubs and resident policeman supplied community requirements. The Methodist chapel built in 1863 is closed. Now there are six farms, a post office cum village store and the Stag inn for villagers' use. Crosby has expanded fourfold and the parish council attend to village amenities. North East Housing offices occupy Moor Park residence and a new vicarage awaits an incumbent.

Birkby, midway between Crosby and Maryport, had a village green, farms, smallholdings and gentlemen's houses. The pit and mill, both once thriving, are closed. The first motorcar in the parish caused great excitement when seen on Birkby green. New bungalows, an hotel and converted buildings make Birkby a desirable area.

Nearer Maryport, Ellengrove toll bar house is occupied and a derelict laundry stands near the river Ellen. Ellen Bank residence, the former home of the Ritson family, is an attractive hotel situated on the Maryport to Carlisle road.

The 19th century opening of Rosegill and Bullgill pits provided work for miners, who mainly lived at Crosby Villa in houses built in long terraces. A chapel, post office and shops were provided together with allotments for gardens, poultry runs etc. Children walked two miles to Crosby school, taking their sandwiches and bottle of tea which was kept warm by the school fire. Bullgill passenger and goods station was quarter of a mile away near to the pit, which closed in 1897 and Rosegill Pit closed a few years later. The suffering caused by the closure was intensified by the General Strike when a Police Clog Fund and school food helped to ease distress. Only the pub and allotments remain and Crosby Villa is a pleasant place where many retired miners now live. The mill at Rosegill too is closed and Bullgill station has also been demolished.

This is an area where beautiful Solway views and glorious sunsets westward combine with the panorama of the Cumbrian mountains eastward which, added to its other amenities, make Cross Canonby parish outstanding.

Crosthwaite & Lyth

Turning in from the A590 there is a sign stating this is the start of the National Park. A sprawling village with farms and cottages in small hamlets, the main buildings are the church, parish rooms, Memorial Hall, school, the Punch Bowl inn, a village shop and post office. Planning permission is difficult to obtain but in the last few years more houses have been built and there are eight council houses and recently a Housing Association has erected a block of six flats for young and elderly people. Being only four miles from Morecambe Bay and the Gulf stream (as the crow flies) the weather is mild, and being sheltered, it is ideal for farming. Well known for its damsons (these were brought from Damascus for their dye when the area was involved with the woollen trade), at the end of April the orchards come alive with the white blossom. Later the hedges are a picture with the hawthorn blossom.

The name Crosthwaite means a cross in a clearing and it is thought there has been a chapel or church in the area for centuries, but the one used today was built in 1878–9 and is called St Mary's. Villagers brought stone for the building and much of the expense was defrayed by the Argles family. This family owned most of the farms and though many have been sold they still own several. They were also responsible for the building of the Memorial Hall which stands in the middle of the village and is the envy of many other villages; it is in excellent repair and can hold 100 people.

There is still a corn mill on the river Gilpin, though not in use. The mill dates from 1829 when James Wilson was the miller. The last one was Joe Kegg, who ground oatmeal and poultry meal until it was no longer viable. The mill is now a field study centre but is fully preserved. There is evidence of several other mills and lime kilns, but the only trade left is the blacksmith's shop at the end of the village.

Culgaith 🐏

Situated just off the Penrith – Scotch Corner road, approximately seven miles from Penrith and Appleby, Culgaith is sited on a promontory above the fertile Eden valley, overlooking the Pennines on one side and the Lakeland fells on the other.

The Midland railway built in the 1870s runs near the village. Despite the station being closed in 1970 a daily service between Carlisle and Leeds is offered from Langwathby, three miles away. From a cluster of dwellings, farmsteads and small businesses, the village has, in recent years changed its character, with people travelling outside to find employment. Houses have been built wherever space allowed bringing new family names with them.

Mechanical power has replaced manpower on farms, but small family businesses seem to be thriving again. Projects include a market garden, currently being expanded, a haulage business, two building firms, engineering works, milk retailer and an extensive pig rearing farm. Lads who gave their lives in the wars are remembered on a memorial set in the centre of the village, opposite the Victoria Institute, the venue of village activities. The pub, the Black Swan, offers hospitality and there is a village shop/post office.

The small Wesleyan chapel erected in 1830 and the church of All Saints offer worship each Sunday. These buildings are steeped in history. Many old customs have died, but tying the church gate with string is still practised today at weddings. The children scramble for pennies before the bridal party and guests are freed to go on their way.

Interesting walks can be taken in and around Culgaith. Millrigg bridge marked the boundary between the counties of Cumberland and Westmorland, while in the opposite direction, a short distance away the rivers Eden and Eamont meet and peace and tranquillity reigns. When walking in this area someone is always willing to chat; the older generation can tell you of the changes that have taken place, and how life used to be when they were young.

Cumdivock 🌿

Cumdivock is not a village but a rural community almost three miles south-west of Dalston. In the mid 19th century the township comprised the hamlets of Cardew, Cardewlees, The Gill and Shawkfoot as well as Cumdivock itself. At the centre stands the church of St John the Evangelist, consecrated in 1872.

Continuing east we come to a line of houses and family farms. This is the original hamlet of Cumdivock. Beyond this is 'Sally Gray'. Robert Anderson, a well known poet and ballad writer of the turn of the 19th century, fell in love with a local girl, Sally Gray. He wrote a poem extolling her virtues and the delights of the countryside. The cottage where Sally Gray lived was used as a farm building until 1930 when it was restored to a family home.

Down the hill from the church lies one of the best documented areas – Shawk quarries. Shawk quarries have been worked since Roman times and it is thought that stone from here was used in Hadrian's Wall west of Carlisle and later on for the building of Rose Castle, Carlisle Cathedral and the city walls. The stone was of a very high quality and it was unusual to find beds of red and white sandstone and a seam of limestone. After burning, the limestone was used for cementing in building.

There appears to have been great excitement in the mid 18th century when a Roman inscription was uncovered on a rock above Shawk-beck. Several accounts of the discovery are recorded and the carving is thought to be the work of the second Augustan legion in about AD 208. There is also some carving of a later date. Unfortunately an account in 1937 stated that it had been destroyed and the fact that no one in the locality has seen it recently appears to bear this out. The high rock on which it was discovered was even then known as 'Tom Smith's leap'. This was reputedly named after a man who, 'whilst being pursued for some felonious action resolutely jumped from the cliff to evade capture and was killed on the rocks below'. Various local 'embroideries' of the tale are told today. The quarries were recently reopened for the restoration work on Carlisle Cathedral and Citadel.

The workers' cottages in the quarries and surrounding area have disappeared and only foundations remain. The public house and school room which served the community are no longer there.

Cumdivock is still a very rural community and the population is essentially stable with many families having lived here for generations. The pleasant rolling pastureland, the springtime white blossom of the wild-cherry, sloe and hawthorn and the superb views across to the Caldbeck fells serve to make this a favoured place in which to live.

Cumwhinton 🐾

Known in ancient times as Quintins Combe or Combe Quinton, the village nestles in a valley near the Pow Maughan beck some four miles south-east of Carlisle. Still comparatively undeveloped it retains its rural feel, although nowadays there are only three working farms within the village. Many of the houses are built of local red sandstone quarried nearby during the 19th century. The quarry is now a nature reserve.

The famous Settle railway line passes through the village and attracts many enthusiasts at weekends when special steam trains pass through. The station is no longer used and the waiting room and offices have been converted into a private house.

The school built in 1895 is thriving with over 80 pupils and three full time teachers. The village shop is still a meeting place for a chat as well as purchasing and is owned and run by village born and bred Reg Feddon, aided by his wife and sister.

Until 20 years ago the main employment was at the local gypsum works. A rich vein of alabaster lies beneath the area and was mined until the building of the M6 motorway. Today the population is 300 and most people work in Carlisle, although many are still involved with the local Garlands Hospital which has always drawn some of its workforce from the villages nearby.

There is no church – worshippers go to church at Cotehill (one and a half miles south). However a church service is held once a month in the village hall where all activities take place. There is also a public house. Known as a caring village there is a prayer meeting once a week which meets to pray for the sick. This takes place in different people's homes. Although the population has changed over the years from country people to the modern commuter, great effort is made to retain the closeness of a village community.

Cumwhitton 🐾

Cumwhitton is a small picturesque village situated about nine miles from Carlisle, seven from Brampton and 16 from Penrith. All but the five newest houses in the village were built from red sandstone which was hewn from a quarry about a mile or so from the village.

There is a rather lovely little church, St Mary's, and there are records of a church from the 13th century though probably there was one much earlier. The original 'village' was Celtic and there was certainly a hamlet or hamlets here in Saxon times.

There are two mosses in the parish, Cumwhitton and Moorthwaite, from which residents in years gone by cut peat for fuel – there is also 'a bleak, hilly, trackless waste' where one of the King Henrys (possibly Henry VI after the battle of Hexham) was reputed to have encamped during a campaign, thus giving the area its present day title of 'King Harry'. Near the centre of this moor is the remains of a druidical circle known as Grey Yauds. Some houses in the parish still use water from springs on King Harry, this water having a reputation for being some of the purest in the country.

In 1950 there were nine individual family-run farms within the village, a Methodist chapel, a shop, a post office, a garage, a joiner's shop, a haulage contractor, a pub and a resident vicar. Today, after amalgamation, there are only three farms, a shop and post office combined, a coach operator/garage and a pub. Nowadays the vicar lives at Castle Carrock and is responsible for four parishes, and the chapel closed in the early 1960s.

In common with most villages on the periphery of a large town or city, the population of Cumwhitton has changed over the years, now mainly comprising professional people who commute daily. This has inevitably changed the character of the village. In spite of this, Cumwhitton is a very active village with a Young Farmers Club, a Women's Institute and a 'Treat Committee' which organises a Christmas party for the under fives of the parish, a pantomime or cinema visit for school children and a Christmas dinner for the over sixties, and raises funds throughout the year with several social events in order to pay for these functions. There is also an active Hall Committee which looks after and raises funds for the upkeep of the village hall where most village activities take place.

Dacre 🌿

The village of Dacre is very small – tucked between the hills, four miles south-west of Penrith. It is picturesque and quiet but access in winter's ice and snow can be hazardous, as Dacre Banks or the Vicarage Hill have to be negotiated and both are very steep.

Though small the village has a very long history, being mentioned by the Venerable Bede in AD 698. The name Dacre was probably taken from the sizeable beck which runs through the village.

The castle used to belong to the Dacre family and some of the lords of Dacre led raids against the Scottish Borderers. It is now a private residence. At one time the Kinsman family lived there – Mrs Bunty Kinsman was a famous beauty and leader of London Society. Before that two gentlemen interested in heraldry lived there and flew different flags each day, which looked quite splendid high on the tower.

The church, which is very beautiful, is thought to have been built on the ruins of an Anglo-Saxon monastery. In the churchyard stand four ancient stone effigies known as the Dacre Bears and these are quite famous.

There is no school in the village now but two buildings used as schools still exist, both are now dwellings. The cottage just below the inn bears a signboard – 'Dacre School – builded 1749'.

Years ago all transport was horse-drawn, so there was a flourishing smithy. As well as shoeing horses, the blacksmith mended farm implements and made the iron caulkers everyone wore on their clogs. It was quite an adventure going for these caulkers – sneaking past the huge farm horses to reach the inner sanctum where the big fire glowed and the bellows puffed and the hammers rang on the anvil. But, when the caulkers got worn and shiny, they were marvellous for sliding on the castle pond!

In days gone by, farmers always washed their sheep before shearing time and the deep pool by the High Bridge, known locally as 'The Wash Dub', was used for this. The sheep were driven into stone walled pens then down a little wooden platform over the edge of the 'dub'. Two men stood there and threw the sheep into the deep water, then with their crooks pushed them underwater. The poor creatures then swam to the other side where the water was shallow and climbed out up the bank where they stood dripping and bleating. Many children learned to swim in the 'Wash Dub'.

Dalston ✍

Amidst the undulating countryside that lies to the south-west of Carlisle is the charming village of Dalston, on the banks of the river Caldew.

By 1800 Dalston was a small, nucleated village centred around the village square. The surrounding countryside consisted of scattered hamlets and isolated homes surrounded by large expanses of moors, commons and wastelands. In the late 18th century cotton manufacture was introduced to the village by George Hodgson of Manchester. Harnessing the river Caldew as his power source, Hodgson brought the Industrial Revolution to this small community. The village quickly witnessed the emergence of four cotton mills and a flax mill. A forge and two corn mills also played a vital role in sustaining the local economy. Most of the present day buildings date from this period and reflect the prosperity such industry brought to a previously agricultural environment.

The sandstone building of the church of St Michael, with evidence of its Norman origins, dominates the eastern end of the Square and is approached by entering beneath a memorial lychgate. The Victorian Methodist chapel nestles neatly between several Georgian properties along the green. It is one of the few red brick buildings to be found in the village.

Today farming and textiles are still prevalent but many other small businesses are in evidence, although inconspicuous by comparison with the industries of the 19th century. With the throbbing pulse of the Industrial Revolution long past, Dalston is somewhat dormitory and relaxed in atmosphere. However, beneath this air of tranquillity is a community still very industrious in its outlook. The village boasts a

The Square, Dalston

tennis and bowling association, a male voice and ladies choir and a drama society amongst its numerous organisations. The parish hand-bells, over 100 years old, are once again being rung by local people.

Each August the showground ceases to be used for grazing and becomes the focus for the annual Agricultural Show. Local farmers exhibit their stock and the Industrial tent houses a display of the tremendous talents that local people, young and old, have in horticulture, floristry, arts and crafts and not least regional baking.

These talents are nothing new. From Cardew Hall, John Denton wrote a history of Cumberland in the 16th century. Dalston was also the birthplace of Susanna Blamire, 1747–1794, the Muse of Cumberland who wrote songs in Scottish dialect and delightful poems about Cumbrian country life.

Dean 🦢

The parish of Dean consists of five small villages which lie between the western lakes and the sea. Farming remains basic but most people, including the many professionals, work in the towns or at Sellafield. The total population of the parish is approximately 600.

At Branthwaite steep hills descend into the village, where Brow Bottom enjoys the prestige of being the uncrowned 'centre'. Branthwaite Hall with its 14th century pele tower is on the fringe of the village in a very picturesque setting. Gone are the village hall, reading room, shop and corn mill, while still remaining are two pubs with excellent eating facilities. The village atmosphere is still enjoyed, with the population increased, and children playing in open places. Natural beauty surrounds the village, although opencast mining now and the threat of more in the future will undoubtedly leave its mark on the landscape.

Legend has it, that at Neuk Cottage in the early 17th century, a headless female corpse was found in the old barn; this ghost is reputed to appear in white wandering and wailing – looking for her head. Beware the Branthwaite Boggle!

Dean village is pleasant rather than pretty with the buildings mainly strung along each side of the road, more than half of them built since 1965.

The little church of St Oswald is partly 12th century, the base of the preaching cross possibly even older. The priest lives in a neighbouring parish, and divides his time between both. Gone is the all-pervading influence of the Victorian archdeacon who left the pulpit to do business with the owner of some passing cattle, and then resumed the sermon, or so they say. For some life still centres round the church, which encourages activities throughout the year. Five farms prevent the village from becoming purely residential, the Royal Yew inn provides meals and attracts visitors. The post mistress and school workers also find employment within the village.

Deanscales is a small village situated east of Dean, originally a settlement of cattle herders' dwellings, with few farms. Past trades included a blacksmith, repairing farm machinery and horse shoeing, also a joiner's shop. Approximately 40 homes now exist in the village, with some new properties. The inn formerly called the Beehive has now reverted to its ancient name of the Old Posting House and it still retains the old mounting block for travellers on horse back. Deanscales quarry provided limestone for road repairs, and a kiln burnt limestone for the land.

In the past Pardshaw comprised of farms, an inn, a clogger's shop, and a Wesleyan chapel. In the mid 17th century George Fox, the founder of the Quaker movement, held the first meeting in the area on Pardshaw Craggs; 'Fox's Pulpit', two blocks of limestone, still stands facing north. A large temperance rally was held on the craggs in June 1857. Over 14,000 people were present, and both inns in Pardshaw and Deanscales were sold out of beer! Pardshaw Hall became the Quaker meeting house, now the only service held is the occasional burial, and the Wesleyan chapel is a Youth Hostel.

Ullock is a small village set back from a stream. This is spanned by a pack horse bridge and finally joins the river Marron. At the beginning of the 20th century it was self sufficient, housing a baker, blacksmith, joiner, cornmill, dressmaker, post office, and a shoe and clog maker.

Dent 🦢

Situated in the south-east corner of Cumbria, Dentdale is within the boundaries of the Yorkshire Dales National Park. It provides a beautiful setting for Dent 'Town', which is the village of Dentdale. In addition there are two hamlets, Cowgill and Gawthrop. Travellers on the Settle-Carlisle railway, alighting at Dent station, may be disconcerted to find themselves almost five miles from the village itself! The reprieving of the line from closure has been important for Dent. Not only does it imprint its presence on the face of the dale, with its two magnificent viaducts at Artengill and Dent Head, but the great and heroic effort involved in its construction is an integral part of local history.

Archaeological evidence indicates that there was a Roman presence and there is a long history of religious fervour. In the reign of Henry VIII, the people, then devout Catholics, took an active part in the Pilgrimage of Grace. The medieval church of St Andrew, dominating the village, celebrated its 900th anniversary in 1980 and within the churchyard the fine Jacobean grammar school still stands. Dent also has an interest in Quakerism, lying as it does in the heart of the area where the movement began. A Society of Friends was formed in Cowgill in 1652. Cowgill also has an Anglican church built in 1838. Methodism has been established in the dale for over 200 years and there are still three chapels open.

Dent remained self-contained until the Second World War. In the 1930s the village supported 20 shops, three banks and five public houses meeting all local needs. In the 18th and early 19th centuries it well merited its name of Dent 'Town' for its prosperity rested on a flourishing domestic industry: hand knitting. This was very necessary as a source of income to supplement the mixed farming. Bringing repute to the village, the 'terrible knitters' of Dent produced vast quantities of hose and gloves, mainly for the London market. 'Terrible' was a compliment to their skill and speed. Both men and women knitted, often while walking to and in the fields, using 'sticks' tucked into their belts holding one of the four needles. These intricately carved sticks, often made and presented as betrothal gifts, are now valuable and much prized heirlooms. The lives and times of the hand-knitters have been vividly recorded by Adam Sedgwick in his memories of his childhood and youth in Dent: *A Memorial by the Trustees of Cowgill Chapel* (1868). In Adam's day, the narrow cobbled streets seemed even narrower, because wooden galleries jutted out from the houses. Up there in good weather, knitters sat and talked while their needles flew so fast the eye could not distinguish their movement.

There are numerous caves in this area; best of these is Ibbeth Peril cave. The entrance is behind a small cliff overlooking a plunge-pool a hundred yards downstream from Tommy Bridge. Four hundred feet of crawling leads into a magnificent chamber with stalactites and a waterfall. Casual visitors should beware as it is easy to get lost inside and rainfall can flood the entrance without warning!

Dovenby 🌿

Dovenby village straddles the A594 Maryport to Cockermouth road and is situated about halfway between these towns.

When local people think of Dovenby, they think of the Georgian-fronted manor house, Dovenby Hall. The building is large and commodious and frequent restorations have been made. The pele tower is probably Norman and is built of stone taken from the nearby Roman road. In 1890 the Hall was owned and lived in by the Ballantyne Dykes family. There is a ghost at the Hall known by the name of the Grey Lady. Many years ago a girl living at the manor wanted to marry someone her family did not approve of. The distraught girl committed suicide and was buried in the Hall Park. It is said that two members of the Dykes family, who knew nothing of the story, have seen the spectre in an upstairs room.

In 1928 Colonel Hubert Trecheville Ballantyne Dykes sold the manor and demesne and it became a home for mentally handicapped people. Large houses were built in the grounds to accommodate them. Today some handicapped people remain at the hospital but it also houses a number of elderly people who require nursing and care.

Dovenby school, which was built in 1628 and rebuilt in 1845 continues as a flourishing centre of education. The post office and small shop run by Mr and Mrs Benn closed some years ago. The last recorded blacksmith was Mr Jonty Carr, who is still remembered in the area. The Ship inn continues to provide repast and refreshment.

The village still has its farms and cottages but in the last 30 years about 15 new dwellings have been constructed. The farms and Dovenby Hall estate have always provided work for villagers.

Drybeck 🪶

Drybeck has a population of under 50 souls. It is situated on a loop of road adjoining the B6260 Appleby to Orton road. The hamlet gets its name from the small stream, or beck, along which the farms straggle. In summer the beck frequently dries up altogether.

The evolution of larger farm holdings has resulted in some of the houses becoming homes for people working outside the settlement. Changes to the farmhouses appear to have been minimal since the dates of building – 1732, 1737 and 1753 were inscribed over the doorways. Drybeck Hall is the most imposing dwelling, built in 1679 by, or for, 'WS and GS'. Socially, old village ways are still retained here, with neighbour helping neighbour; especially in the constant farming tussle with the seasons.

Carboniferous limestone underlies the area and evidence of it is all around. There are several small disused quarries, their products still seen in the buildings and in the miles of dry-stone wall dividing the fields. These walls sport patches of yellow lichen and soft green moss on their greyness, as they continue to solidly provide shelter for stock in the storms of winter, and in the chill spring winds of lambing time.

Early in the summer the hedgerows are patched with crabapple blossom, then elderflowers and delicate wild roses. Some of the old unspoilt meadows and pastures are sprinkled with drifts of our traditional wild flowers; primroses, cowslips, ragged robin and a host of others including some of the limestone-loving orchid family. Forestry provides good cover for the many game birds while of the wild birds which can be seen and heard, the curlew, with its clear cry, is perhaps best remembered by visitors. Sometimes one can be fortunate enough to see a hare scudding over a field, or even an occasional deer.

Dufton 🌿

Dufton is a very attractive village nestling among the eastern fells just above the Eden valley, in an area now designated as one of Outstanding Natural Beauty, three miles from Appleby. Curiously, for such a small village, the area covered by the parish is one of the largest in England.

Dufton is at the centre of the Helm Wind area and the arrangement of houses provides some protection against this local wind, the only one in this country to have a particular name. The Helm is an often violent north-easterly most frequent in late winter and spring. It drops from the steep scarp slope of Crossfell, 2,930 ft, known earlier as Fiends Fell and said to be the haunt of evil spirits until St Paulinus erected a cross on its summit.

Houses of individual character and architectural interest border the village green, some with date stones showing origins in the 17th, 18th and 19th centuries. Many of the houses are built of locally quarried red sandstone. Situated also around the green are the Stag inn, the village hall, built in 1911, the post office which is also a well-stocked general store, and the popular Youth Hostel which closes only during November and December. The school and the Wesleyan chapel, 1820, which has a curious white statue on an external wall, are now private houses. Set back from the road, at the east end of the green, is Dufton Hall, part of which dates from the 16th century.

The London Lead Mining Company began mining in Dufton in the 19th century and had considerable influence in the village. After typhoid deaths in Teesdale, the Quaker company installed a new drinking water supply in Dufton, in 1858. Four taps are still in evidence as is the splendid sandstone horse trough which dominates the green. The steep approach to Dufton from Appleby, known as the Smelt, is so-called after the smelting mill which operated near Flakebridge.

The church, dedicated to St Cuthbert, is about half a mile out of the village, built, according to tradition, at one of the places where the Lindisfarne monks rested when they carried St Cuthbert's body as they escaped from the Vikings in AD 875. The church was rebuilt in 1784 and repaired at later dates but records go back to 1292. In the outside south wall of the chancel there is a small figure of possibly Roman origin and in the west wall of the nave there is a grave slab which is thought to depict a Norman forester.

Dufton is a beauty spot and has an interesting history but it is very much a living village. By holding monthly events, the village hall committee maintains the large hall. The 'Fellside Royal', an agricultural show held on the last Saturday in August, is a highlight of the village's year. Previously held on the village green, it moved to the show field near the church in 1957; this beautiful setting helps to attract competitors and spectators from all over the country.

Farming features prominently in the village but there is also a furniture maker, a family-run catering business, a one-woman milk round and a family now in its fourth generation of making hay rakes. Two of the village farms have campsites and caravans and some housewives offer bed and breakfast.

Dundraw ✍

Dundraw is situated about three miles from Wigton, three quarters of a mile from the main B5302 to Silloth. It is a small civil parish of ancient origin. The original houses and buildings were clay daubins. At the present time there are four farms and seven houses.

A wealthy bachelor named Joseph Nelson lived at Moor Row House, near Dundraw. He died in 1893 and £500 from his estate was used to build a mission room at Dundraw which was completed in 1901. A new ecclesiastical parish of Waverton cum Dundraw was formed in 1902, prior to this Dundraw was in the ecclesiastical parish of Bromfield.

A non denominational Mission Hall was built in 1898 by Jack Todd and Tom Todd, and for a number of years Dundraw had two places of worship. They were both well attended by people from the surrounding hamlets, Moor Row, Wheyrigg, Kelsick, Lesson Hall, Waverbridge and Aikhead. They are both now closed for worship but one is still used as a hall for any parish activities.

Waverbridge gets its name from the river Waver. There are 19 houses, and one farm, mostly occupied by retired and professional people. Once there was a public house, the Spread Eagle, a blacksmith's forge, an agricultural implement manufacturer and cycle agent, a joiner's shop and a working water mill. Now there are no commercial properties, only desirable residences and very good views. The school was built in 1844 by Charles Ray of Lesson Hall for 50 pupils, and was closed in 1970.

Kelsick is derived from an Anglo-Saxon word meaning a spring or well. Some years ago while boring for coal on the moss, a spring of hot water was struck, which continued flowing for some time.

During the Second World War two aeroplanes crashed, one near Lesson Hall and a second one on Kelsick Moss on 7th July 1942. It was a two seater Miles Master trainer. The instructor baled out and broke his leg on landing, and the pilot, a New Zealander, went down with the plane. It fell on soft ground and the pilot and engine were never recovered until the very dry summer of 1976, by the Dumfries Aviation group organised by Peter Connon. Just a few years ago the pilot's parents came over to Kelsick to visit the place where their son crashed. Tragically their plane crashed near Rome on their return and they were both killed.

Once there were ponds at Dundraw, Moor Row and Kelsick, the latter being opened out in 1990 by conservationists.

Dian House at Moor Row was a 'call house'; people called with horses and traps for food and ale on the way home from Wigton after taking their butter and eggs to market on Tuesdays.

The only place where you can eat and drink now in the area is at Wheyrigg Hall, formerly a farm which was worked by the Asbridge family for generations until it was turned into an hotel.

Eamont Bridge

Situated at the confluence of the rivers Eamont and Lowther the area around Eamont Bridge has been inhabited since very early times, and the remains of two ancient fortifications can still be seen: the large Mayburgh henge, dating back to around 2500 BC and King Arthur's Round Table, about 1800 BC.

The village itself is typical of many northern villages, the houses being built along both sides of the road, many of them joined together regardless of style or size. This practice dates back to the time of the Border raids when the animals could be driven in to the main street at the first signs of the marauding Scots. The street would then be blocked off and defended at each end. Many of the houses date from the 16th and early 17th centuries when the inhabitants of the old village of Brougham moved here, their homes having been demolished to make way for the building of Brougham Hall.

In the middle of the village is a large fine looking rose-pink washed building which was once the local mansion house, then the workhouse, often the last resting place for those who had struggled over Shap Fell looking for work. It is now business premises. The whitewashed cottage whose front room serves as the post office once provided accommodation for the workers at Lord Brougham's estate laundry on the banks of the river. The laundry itself has been converted into a home.

In the past the traveller on horseback would have welcomed the existence of two old coaching inns at the southern end of the village, the Crown, and the Beehive, where real hives of bees were kept outside near the front door! Motorists remember it as an irritating bottleneck where, before the building of the M6, a long wait could be guaranteed before they could cross the 16th century hump-backed bridge over the river Eamont, which marked the old county boundary between Cumberland and Westmorland. This sturdy structure built for the packhorse and stagecoach era still copes with the weight of today's traffic.

Edenhall 🌿

Nestling in the tranquil fertile valley of the river Eden, some four and a half miles south-west of Penrith, lies the small village of Edenhall. The finding of hatchets made of metal and polished stone indicate that there was a settlement in this area before Roman times.

It is thought that the village church of St Cuthbert was built on the site of one of the saint's many resting places during the 9th century. It lies approximately half a mile outside the centre of Edenhall where the earlier settlement of thatched houses surrounded the church. These cottages were either burnt or fell into disrepair at the time of the Black Death. Returning from the church one would pass an old stone cross, sited on the top of a plague stone on which money was left for goods during the epidemic.

The Musgrave family, who once owned the estate, lived in Edenhall from 1500 to 1900 and in 1821 a magnificent new mansion was built; sadly this was auctioned off in 1934 and removed piece by piece. The present owner of the estate now lives in the coach house. Older inhabitants of the village can recall happy times spent at balls and concerts held in the Long Room of the Hall and Christmas parties held in the servants quarters where all the children received a small gift from the tree.

One of the legends handed down in Edenhall is the story of the medieval glass chalice probably brought back to the Musgrave family by a Crusader. It is said that one night the butler went to draw water from St Cuthbert's Well, when he saw a glorious company of fairies with their queen dancing and holding court. Disturbed by his approach they left the goblet, chanting 'If the cup should break or fall, farewell to luck of Edenhall'. This priceless goblet and its leather case of a later date was purchased by the Victoria and Albert Museum in 1957 and remains safe in a glass case for all to see.

The village school which was built by Sir Phillip Musgrave in 1815, closed in 1934 and is now used as two private houses. None of the thatched cottages or village shops remain and the once small fishing inn is now a large hotel.

Cricket is still played on the cricket field although they no longer wear the red and black blazers and caps. The Flower Show which originated in 1906 is once again an annual event in conjunction with Langwathby, now organised by the Women's Institute who have their own hall in the village.

Some people who live in Edenhall still work on the estate and further local employment is provided by the brickworks on the village outskirts. Many of the charming red sandstone houses and the vicarage, dating back to 1723, were made from sandstone from the local quarry.

For many people a stroll down Ladies Walk along the river bank, gazing at the primroses and violets at springtime and watching the fishermen spin for salmon or trout, is where the luck of Edenhall still remains in this unspoilt village.

Egton-cum-Newland 🌿

This parish, consisting of several villages and hamlets, lies on the northern shores of Morecambe Bay and is part of South Lakeland District Council's area.

The shoreline here became a port, for loading and taking away limestone, slates from Coniston and charcoal and iron from the many bloomeries in the area. Shipbuilding became the major trade and flourished all along this water frontage and set the pattern for the villages, much as they are today. All this was swept away with the coming of the railway and viaducts built across the bay. Over the years the railways altered transport and travelling and so village life continued its rural way with farming, woodcutting, basket making and quarrying and bobbin turning. As most of these trades died out others took over and now we are mainly a dormitory for workers at Glaxo Chem's huge works in nearby Ulverston.

Egton-cum-Newland parish starts here, about one mile from the town's boundary, at Newland, a small quiet hamlet just off the busy A590. It was once famed for its iron furnace, one of the largest of the old bloomeries, and its buildings still remain. A few farms are found amongst its narrow lanes which all run downhill to the sea. Northwards is Arrad Foot, now bypassed, with an old pub and a few houses, with the local big house now a thriving hostelry for the traveller.

Onwards now to Greenodd and Penny Bridge, the main heart of the parish, passing the new car park and picnic area and fishing access at Barr End, which is very popular. Greenodd has two pubs, a post office, grocer's, bakery and butcher so is well served for basic needs. Penny Bridge is a place name that came into use after a local family named Penny built a stone bridge over the Crake, thus making obsolete the old ford. It is purely residential and has an old cosy inn on the village's main street, all uphill to the near summit where stands the Penny Bridge church of St Mary the Virgin – a splendid edifice built on the site of a former chapel.

Elterwater & Chapel Stile 🌿

Elterwater and Chapel Stile are the two villages of Great Langdale with half a mile between them and sharing their church and school. The whole of the two Langdale valleys, Great and Little, comprise the community.

Chapel Stile grew round a simple stone chapel perched on a rocky ledge under the steep fell; before 1821 Langdale folk were carried to be buried at Grasmere over the fell via Hunting Stile. In 1857 the two squires of High Close and Elterwater Hall had the present church built; the 20th century St Francis window was made by a stained glass artist who lived and worked for much of his long life in Chapel Stile. The churchyard has the grave of 'G. M. Trevelyan Historian of England', but most of the valley folk rest in a quiet green patch beyond the village.

The oldest 17th century houses are by the church; later quarrymen's cottages were built down the hill, and on the main valley road are the school (1824), the post office and the Langdale Co-op – a unique independent store important to the valley and carrying a remarkable stock. Both villages grew in the heyday of 19th century quarrying and the gunpowder works.

Elterwater was named by the Norsemen 'Swan Lake' and swans still frequent the tarn. The village has its tiny green nearly filled by a maple tree which blazes golden every autumn. Of several 17th century houses by the high stone bridge over the Langdale beck, one was the home of the linen industry, and another's barn has been a youth hostel since 1935. On either side of the maple tree is the Britannia inn, a busy pub for locals and tourists, and the village shop and the bowling green. Up the brow stride the quarryworkers' cottages which became council houses or holiday homes; and beyond the old joiner's and wheelwright's premises (now self-catering cottages) the blacksmith had his forge and cooled his iron in the Smiddy Dub, now a silted-up soggy bed of rushes.

Elterwater Quarry has eaten a huge hole in the hill above the river. Now the green slate is luxury material and shipped all over the world to grace the most prestigious architecture. The slate is taken to Kirkby Ireleth for processing and few Langdale men work in the industry which used to be the major employment. Far fewer men work in farming than formerly but the land tended has not diminished and farming is what preserves the valley's beauty. Far more people work in tourism, from bed and breakfast to hoteliers.

The gunpowder works site eventually became the beautifully designed and equipped Timeshare complex with handsome timber lodges set among the trees. It is appreciated by Langdale folk who nevertheless keep a wary eye on the Timeshare's urge to expand outside its boundaries and thereby imbalance the community life.

Embleton 🌿

The name is derived from Eanbald's Tun, Old English meaning farmstead or land belonging to Eanbald. It was a Norman manor but a community existed in Brigantian times. This community was centred round what is now Brook House Farm. The present village is in the broad valley running east to west which opens up to the sky at the northern end of Lake Bassenthwaite. It has approximately 300 inhabitants, most of whom live alongside the old A66 road. It has no centre and is a very scattered parish. The church of St Cuthbert is on the south side of the valley on a very ancient site which is reputed to be one of the places where his body rested during the long journey made by the monks of Lindisfarne. It was in Embleton that the iron sword, thought to have belonged to a Brigantian in the first century AD, was discovered in the mid 19th century.

Farming is the main occupation. It still has a post office, also an inn, an hotel and a well used village hall. Not so long ago it had a school and a vicarage.

Embleton is closely linked with Wythop, a small hamlet situated on the south side of the valley in the shadow of Sale Fell. It also has a church, St Margaret's, beautifully situated on the fell side with extensive views. Branching off the Embleton valley southwards is the lovely Wythop valley, the secret valley, mentioned in one of Wainwright's guide books. Here one can wander in peace and solitude although the busy A66 is only a short distance away. In this valley lie the ruins of an early church dating back to the 16th century. Pause and think back to those early days when people had to walk miles to church along the green tracks which wind round the shoulders of the fells. At the end of the valley is the ancient Wythop Hall and beyond it are the remains of the old silica works which came into existence about 1933/34. This was during the depression when the employment of around 70 men must have been a godsend. Unfortunately, the works closed down in less than three years.

Embleton also had its own quarry, which was started in 1907 by Joe Bounday, just above the Wheatsheaf inn. The Keswick Granite Company took this over in 1910 and employed about 80 people at one time. This closed in 1950.

Wythop mill was originally owned by the Wythop estate. It was used solely to provide timber for the repair of estate property, fences etc. It has now been renovated and is again in working order and a popular place for tourists to visit.

Ennerdale Bridge 🌿

You can never forget the mountains in Ennerdale. The village stands at the mouth of the loneliest of.the great valleys of Lakeland. In winter the mid-day sun bearly clears the steep fellside of Grike, while Red Pike, High Stile, Steeple and Pillar stand out against the eastern sky.

Today the one road into the valley leads only to a handful of farms and to sweeping forestry plantations but in the past the valley was full of activity. In prehistoric times iron was smelted beside Smithy beck at the head of the lake, while a hundred years ago haematite ore was mined on both sides of the valley, the workings at Kelton Fell actually supporting a railway system. Spinning, weaving and bleaching took place, and one ancient mill is still lived in, though no longer working.

Ennerdale Bridge grew up to support all these activities at the point where the valley road crosses the river Ehen and meets roads from the south over Cold Fell and from the north past Kirkland. Once it provided most of the requirements of an isolated community, with its own smithy, garage, reading room, Co-operative store and village policeman but now most of these needs are met by neighbouring towns and the village is lucky still to have church, school, village shop and post office.

The village is divided by the river Ehen, from which it derives its name, into two distinct parts; one clustered around the church and the Fox and Hounds public house, the other around the school, shop and Shepherd's Arms hotel. Over the past 30 years the village has altered dramatically and recently built houses and bungalows greatly outnumber those which formed the core of the old village. Each new building development has been fiercely resented but the newcomers have, in time, become a welcome and vital part of the community.

Although few people now depend on farming, everyone in Ennerdale is constantly aware that they live in an agricultural community. The surrounding fells with their dry-stone walls, in-bye fields and pastures are maintained and protected by local farmers. The high point of the year is the Ennerdale Show, traditionally held on the last Wednesday in August.

St Mary's church was founded in 1534 as a chapel of the abbey of St Bees. Wordsworth wrote in his poem *The Brothers* of the homely priest of Ennerdale, as he and his wife sat spinning 'upon the long seat beneath the eaves of the old cottage'. The church which he saw was replaced in 1857 by the present Romanesque building, which stands with simple dignity in the old churchyard.

This then is Ennerdale, so recently a farming community where changes came slowly and were resisted, yet now adapting to a new role, one dependent for employment on neighbouring towns yet independent in defence of its own identity. Many people pass through the village on their way to other beauty spots but we consider ourselves fortunate to be able to stay here.

Eskdale

'There must be something very attractive about the 'King of Prussia', for every neighbouring parish has a road leading directly from it to that well-known inn.' So wrote C. A. Parker in his description of Eskdale in 1904. Nowadays sporting a fine signboard portrait of King George IV, 'The King' is still a point of reference for anywhere in the valley, as it commands the main road junction.

The valley has a network of old routes, some of which have grown into tarmac roads; but many more have survived as unspoilt footpaths and pony tracks. One such path leads over the bridge at Boot up over Burnmoor and down to Wasdale, whose churchyard was not consecrated for burials until 1901. Over this Corpse Road the coffins from Wasdale were carried to St Catherine's, and the sad tale is still told of the pack horse which took fright, reared and disappeared into the mist with the body of Thomas Porter of Wasdale strapped to its back.

Beyond the village of Boot, with its crossroad up the village street or down to St Catherine's on the riverbank, is the winding road up to Hard Knott Pass, four miles ahead on the skyline. This is the entry into the valley from central Lakeland, zig-zagging down past the Roman fort to the valley bottom and the old farm of Brotherilkeld – owned by the National Trust since 1961, but still farmed by the Harrison family.

The isolated Woolpack Inn and the nearby Youth Hostel are well frequented by hill-lovers for most of the year, but on the last Saturday in September the narrow road is thronged for the Eskdale Show. A mile down the river is Penny Hill, one of the Lakeland farms which Beatrix Potter bought for the National Trust, whilst two miles further on is Stanley Ghyll with Dalegarth Force. The Stanleys of Austhwaite farmed this valley for 500 years.

The village of Eskdale Green changed considerably a century ago, when the Rea family bought Gate House farm and developed the Gate House estate. The school was moved down the road to a new building with St Bega's church above, and several houses went. Nowadays, the centre of the village is the post office cum outdoor shop, facing the Eskdale Stores. This is a real 'Ginger and Pickles', with everything from tea towels and tobacco to Woodalls' Cumberland Sausage – not surprisingly, as the owner is a cousin of the maker of this delicacy.

Behind Eskdale Green is a narrow track into Miterdale, always a sparsely populated and lonely valley, and famed locally as the site of the 'Beckside Boggle'. This gruesome story is of the wife, left with her young child whilst her farmer husband attended to business in Whitehaven. At dusk, a strange woman, with her head wrapped in a shawl, approached and asked for lodging, and much against her will the wife made her welcome to the fireside, where she had been preparing to make tallow candles. The stranger fell asleep, and her shawl slipped to reveal the coarse skin and features of a man, and a hand clutching a knife. Desperate with fear, the wife raised the heavy pan over the fire and tipped it over the stranger's head. Before he could struggle, he was choked and entombed in boiling mutton fat. And the farmer returned early next day to find his wife distraught, with this ghastly corpse concealed on a ledge. They buried the body, and kept their counsel, but somehow the story came out, and ever since there have been tales of strange hauntings up that valley.

Early in September, the Puppy Show of the Eskdale & Ennerdale Foxhounds is held in the field by 'The King'. This pack was founded by Tommy Dobson, who died at the age of 83 whilst hunting in Langdale, and his portrait is carved on his gravestone in the churchyard. Three generations of the Porter family have been Master of Hounds since, and, when lambing starts, Edmund Porter answers calls from farmers as readily as his predecessors.

Farleton 🌿

Farleton gives its name to junction 36 of the M6 motorway. The limestone hill, Farleton Knot, is a landmark to the east of the motorway and was a beacon hill. There are several springs, old disused quarries, and lime kilns. There was once a chapel, and a field alongside the northbound carriageway is still known as Chapel Hill. Unfortunately there is no trace now of the tithe barn shown on early maps. Several of the houses and barns have date stones and some of the houses have carved wooden panels or spice cupboards.

It is a good area for stock and crops and once was renowned for northern dairy shorthorn cattle. The Lunesdale Agricultural Show, formed in 1839, used to have classes for the crag sheep of Farleton. Nowadays there are a variety of breeds of cattle and sheep, some of the farmers showing their stock at local shows and sales, and further afield.

The canal is culverted under the M6 and has several bridges through Farleton. The Duke Bridge also has a smaller arch for stock to pass through. The house opposite is named 'The Duke' after one of the Dukes of Cumberland and was once a coaching inn. There is a derelict packet house, and stable, and a winding hole for turning the barges. Stone used to be loaded at this basin.

One thing sadly gone is the Farleton and District Ploughing and Hedging Association. Competitions were organised by them for many years but these ceased in 1969. In an old minute book there is mention of a special prize in 1914 for the hedger with the largest family – a man with 13 children won! Some of the trophies are now on loan to, and competed for, by the Southern District of Cumbria Young Farmers' Clubs.

Field Broughton 🌿

The village of Field Broughton lies to the north of Cartmel and about four miles from the south of Lake Windermere.

Today most of the village is taken up with farming, this being mainly livestock farming. For the most part the fields are small and surrounded by stone walls; the craft of 'stone walling' requires considerable skill. For this reason also, the majority of the local fox-hunting is carried out by the local farmers on foot with their hounds, the rocky outcrops being unsuitable for horses.

There is a lime kiln by Field Broughton church which was used until 1920, producing quick lime, and then when slaked producing lime for the fields, for building and for whitewashing. There is also an old lime kiln at Beckside, adjoining Wood Broughton.

Much charcoal burning was done over the years – coppices being grown specially for this purpose. The charcoal was then used to melt iron to be made and beaten into the many tools required for use on the land, for tilling, timber work for wagons and buildings, and presumably for iron pots and pans.

All the land was common land until it was divided and sold to a few wealthy people in 1796, making some people very prosperous and others very poor. There still remains one piece of common land in the village on which stands the village pound – used for holding straying animals for many hundreds of years. Behind this common land stands the old smithy – the last village blacksmith being Edward Swainson, but for the last 60 years blacksmith work has been done in Cartmel, or, as now, by the travelling blacksmith.

The sum of £50 was left by Miles Burns around 1731 towards building a chapel at Field Broughton. The chapel was also used as a schoolroom. Later another schoolroom was built at the back of the chapel by the lime kiln, the money being raised by public subscription. Then, on the death of her husband in about 1888, Harriet Margaret Hibbert wished to build a new church in his memory, and so the old church and schoolroom were removed in 1892 and on the 10th May in that year Mrs Hibbert laid the foundation stone of the new church. She died a few weeks later in France, and never saw the completion of the church.

The parish room is still used today for social functions, adult education classes and WI meetings. The ground floor is now incorporated in this use but was originally Mr John Whinnerah's joiner's shop, he being the estate joiner for the Hibbert family.

Today there are the farmers, the butcher with his home-killed meat who visits the hamlets twice a week, the coal merchant and the nursery-man. The doctor now lives in Cartmel – no longer at Stonydale or Broughton House, but still with his own dispensary. The children all go to school in Cartmel.

Finsthwaite & Staveley 🦖

The river Leven drains Windermere at its southern end and Staveley-in-Cartmel lies to the east of the lake. It includes part of the area known as Newby Bridge and was once a place of industry and agriculture, having many farms, a mill, a limestone quarry and a bloomery. This latter was started by the monks of Cartmel Priory about 1230 for the smelting and forging of iron ore, the woods around the area affording plenty of timber for this purpose.

From the A592 winds a lane to the beautiful little church of St Mary, formerly a chapel of ease, which dates from 1600. It was restored in 1678 and 1793 when the south aisle and tower were added. The last restoration was in 1896.

Although now bisected by the A590 the two halves of the village remain relatively peaceful with quite a few of the old properties remaining, as do some of the descendants of the families who lived here long ago.

The village of Finsthwaite, a settlement dating back to Viking times, lies in the hills above Lakeside to the west of Windermere. It can be reached by a narrow winding lane past the Swan Hotel, which stands at the end of the quaint Newby Bridge with its five arches of unequal size and sharply pointed buttresses.

Obvious all around are the extensive woodlands, originally of oak, birch and hazel with a small amount of pine forest. This gave rise to the industry of woodcutting for use in the furniture and building trades, but with the opening of a bobbin mill in 1835 the forests were converted to the smaller coppice trees. Smaller pieces of wood were used in the production of charcoal – a viable commodity of those days when iron smelting and manufacture of gunpowder were also local industries. The gunpowder factory buildings can still be seen at Low Wood near Haverthwaite.

An outstanding feature of the village is the church of St Peter, consecrated in 1874, which replaced an earlier church built in 1724. The design had won first place in a competition organised by the Diocesan Church Extensions Society as being specially suitable for a mountain chapel. The church clock, still hand wound, was installed in 1919, subscribed for by the parish in memory of its dead of the First World War.

Along the lane further towards Hawkshead lies Graythwaite, another peaceably settled area of the Vikings. Surrounded on all sides by woods where red deer still roam, it has become an estate owned and run by the Sandys family, who settled here as tenants of Furness Abbey in the 16th century.

Flimby

The suffix 'by' in Flimby suggests Danish/Norse origin for the village. Nearby Risehow has the remains of a Roman signalling station – part of the Roman coastal defences along the Solway.

In 1279 land here was given to monks of Holm Cultram Abbey (present day Abbeytown). After the Reformation, Henry VIII granted Flimby to Thomas Dalston of Carlisle, who in 1546 sold the land to John Blennerhasset. The family resided at Flimby Hall until 1772 when William Blennerhasset sold the property to Sir James Lowther. Flimby Hall is now a farm.

Flimby as a parish was separated from Camerton in 1546. The present parish church of St Nicholas was rebuilt in 1794 on the site of a previous church. 'Old' Flimby is around the green of Flimby Cross.

Many farms have gone. There were large sand and gravel quarries around the village – one opposite the school, occupied now by a large housing estate; another on the southern edge of the village is the rugby pitch for Flimby ARLFC. The collieries, brickworks, coke ovens and chemical works have gone. Modern factories are on the site of Risehow colliery and on the southern edge of the village.

There is a good male voice choir and Flimby Saxhorn Silver Band has done well in competitions. Each year the village carnival takes place on the first Saturday in July; it is thought to be one of the best in the area. The lorries are beautifully decorated and people come from miles around to see it.

Flookburgh 🪺

Flookburgh was, at one time, a market town of some importance, largely because it was situated on the major cross-bay route which connected Lancaster with Furness. Having been granted a charter by Edward I, later confirmed by Henry IV, and again by Charles II in 1665, Flookburgh was able to hold a market and two annual fairs.

Up to the First World War, fleet ships came up to Sandgate to fish the mussel beds off the Furness Peninsula. This came to an end due to silting in the estuary as a result of the building of the railway. Flukes, or plaice, were caught in the autumn and cockles in the winter. Later shrimping became more popular. Youngs came to Cark in 1950 and developed the business of potted and frozen shrimps. In the 1950s men would go by rail to Kendal, Ulverston and Barrow to sell their fish from barrows.

At one time the land south of the village would have been sand and, at exceptionally high tides, the sea washed over the streets. Today the sea is one mile away along a straight road over reclaimed land which leads to the campus of the Lakeland Caravan Park.

Flookburgh has what looks like a large market square but it is, in fact, the site of the old chapel and graveyard. A chapel stood on this site from the 13th century, served by the canons of Cartmel. The market cross stands in a second smaller square opposite the Hope and Anchor inn. Further down the street is the Manor House, built in 1686, and almost opposite is the Crown inn. A few hundred yards up the Cark road from the square, is Flookburgh's parish church, dedicated to St John.

Flookburgh has suffered two major disasters. In 1669 the plague raged through the village. Because of the severity of the outbreak, bodies could not be carried to Cartmel and were buried in two excavations in Ecclestan meadow on the west side of the village (now the site of new housing). This was followed in 1686 by a fire, which destroyed 22 houses, many other buildings and even burned fruit trees in the orchards.

Barely a mile south-west of the village is a crescent of houses known as Ravenstown, taking its name from the farmstead Raven Winder. The original houses were built for staff of a naval aerodrome towards the end of the First World War. The streets are named after First World War battles. The original plan was abandoned and the houses were bought by Messrs Vickers to house staff from their Barrow shipyard. Now Ravenstown is occupied by private owners and more building has taken place.

The area below Ravenstown is known as Winder and from medieval times was divided into two estates – Raven Winder, named after a Scandinavian, and Canon Winder, so called because it came to belong to the canons of Cartmel Priory. Both retain halls of great antiquity, now farms and part of the Holker estates.

Frostrow

Along the river Rawthey lie Derry Cottages. The original Derry Hall was built in the 17th century by Christopher Thornburrow, extensions were added in the 1830s and, shortly afterwards, it was converted into four cottages. Derry is believed to be a corruption of 'Dairy'.

'John Fawcett of Gateside in Frostrow, left by will in 1703 ten shillings yearly for ever to the poor of these two places (Frostrow and Soolbank) to be distributed by the churchwardens and overseer in penny wheaten loaves on St John's Day in Christmas'. Gateside once belonged to Green Farm and was a dame school before being pulled down. Now there are just turf covered bumps in the ground. A footpath leads across the fields above Bird's Nest to Wardses and Bank Cottage. Walk up the road past Low Hollins and High Hollins and across to High Side, commonly referred to as 'Africa'. From here there is a superb view of the Howgills and Sedbergh.

Farfield Mills was built in 1836–37 by the Dover family when Hebblethwaite mill was proving too small to cope with the volume of business. Over 100 hands were employed, including outworkers, many working there all their lives. A cutting 350 yards long was constructed by the side of the river Clough to provide the water flow necessary to power the millwheel. The mill was eventually closed in 1937. During the Second World War it was taken over by Armstrong-Siddeley for making aero-engines, later it became a wool store and then a cheese factory. Now it has become a weaving mill again.

The Row are five three-storeyed cottages built in 1851 for workers at the mill. Previously there was a small cottage there which was pulled down and the land sold to the Dovers for £9. It must have been a cheerful, noisy place – according to the 1871 and 1881 censuses over 40 people lived there and practically every house contained a large family; grandparents, sons and daughters and grandchildren.

Garsdale Bridge crosses the river Clough just by the Row. Once called Garstall Garths it was only half the width of the present bridge. It was widened in the early 19th century.

Gaitsgill 🌿

The hamlet of Gaitsgill lies in a valley seven miles south of Carlisle and 18 miles north of Penrith. A small stream, Penbeck, flows through the village, and joins the river Roe near the second of two arched stone bridges.

At the present time it has a population of 54, which is six less than that shown on a survey done by one of the residents in 1942. In those days most of the village and the surrounding farmland was the property of the Holme Hill estate, which provided employment for many of the people. Today the three farms belong to the Church Commissioners, and the remainder of the houses are privately owned.

A new property is named 'St Jude's' after the little chapel on whose site it stands. The chapel was built in 1868 by the Salkeld family of Holme Hill for the use of all estate residents, but was demolished just 100 years later as the parish could not afford two churches. The stone from St Jude's was used to build a vestry at the parish church at Raughtonhead, a mile and a half away.

The only remaining public building in Gaitsgill is the Primrose Hall, which belongs to the Church Commissioners and is run by a committee of volunteers from the parish of Raughtonhead. It was built in 1885 at the expense of Lt Col Joseph Carleton Salkeld of Holme Hill mansion for the use of the estate workers, and named after the Primrose League. This was an association for supporters of the Conservative cause, who were, according to their song 'ready to do or die for their Country, their Queen, and their God'. Originally a large primrose carved in stone was set above the porch of the hall, but this is no longer in evidence.

In past years the Primrose Hall has also been used as a reading room, for Sunday school, knitting circles, the Girl's Friendly Society and, in the war years, by the Home Guard. Now it is used by the Women's Institute, the Young Farmers, the Youth Club and the Mothers and Toddlers Group, as well as for dances, sales and other functions which help to pay for its upkeep. Gone are the days of Gaitsgill's tailor's shop, cooper and churnmaker and small village store. The only businesses here now are the three dairy farms, each milking 80–100 Friesian cows, one of which also rears pedigree sheep.

Although Gaitsgill is becoming a village mainly of commuters, it still retains its old-fashioned rural style, and there is still much evidence of community spirit among the residents.

Gamblesby & Unthank 🌿

The village of Gamblesby and the hamlet of Unthank are situated about ten miles east of Penrith, in the Eden valley and hard up against the Pennine Fells, an area generally described as East Fellside.

Today's Unthank is not located where the first squatters settled, as in 1597/98 the inhabitants of the original village succumbed to the plague or Black Death. A new hamlet grew some way from the old settlement, initially a tiny group of thatched dwellings surrounded by a wall to keep out the Scottish raiders.

This whole area frequently fell victim to the raiders and Gamblesby also developed to protect its inhabitants by keeping its farm buildings within the perimeter of the village, stock being gathered onto the village green. There is talk of gates along the Glassonby road but these were not to keep the raiders out, but were a set of whale jaws erected just outside the village, joining at the top to form an arch and beneath which traffic passed, until one day a hay cart knocked them over!

Until the 18th century the residents of Gamblesby and Unthank had no place of worship of their own and had to travel to the parish church at Addingham for spiritual enlightenment. Weddings were much enjoyed and there grew a tradition that as soon as a wedding at Addingham was over, the wedding party, which had mostly arrived there on horseback, would race back to the village, a prize being awarded to the winner.

In 1772 a visitor arrived in Gamblesby who was to fundamentally change the spiritual habits of the local population – John Wesley. Legend has it that he arrived on horseback from Newcastle across the Pennines and preached on the village green. He returned many times and in 1784

Gamblesby, showing the Smithy and Methodist Chapel

he planned and erected a chapel on the green. A century later in 1888 a larger, grander chapel was built in its place, but the spot is still revered by all Methodists.

Farming has always been and still remains by far the major occupation of the inhabitants of Gamblesby and Unthank but old practices have died, such as 'threshing day' when every farmer in the area sent a person to help with the threshing on the village green, the hard work being mitigated by the threshing dinner and tea provided. On Saturdays, outside the mill, could be seen rows of horses and carts brought over from Alston, the Pennine market town. The horses were used down the mine all through the week and then were brought over the Hartside pass on Saturday to collect flour for the people and oats for themselves.

The smith was also an indispensable member of the village, shoeing the horses and fettling the plough. The stocks, made by William Toppin in the late 18th century are still in place on the village green as a reminder to would-be miscreants. They were last used to punish the theft of a turnip!

Mention must be made of the famous cricket green, which had a hump so large that a fielder in one corner could not see the wickets. The hump was removed after a huge fund-raising campaign in the 1960s.

Gilsland 🦢

Gilsland village is unique in that it is in two counties, three parishes and two parliamentary divisions. Running through the centre of the village is Poltross Burn which marks the boundary between Cumbria and Northumberland. Denton Upper and Waterhead parishes in Cumbria are in Penrith and the Borders parliamentary division whilst Thirlwall in Northumberland is in the Hexham parliamentary division.

Hadrian's Wall, of which there are fine examples including Poltross Mile Castle, remains of the bridge abutment over the river Irthing at Willowford, and Amboglana camp, tells of the rule of the Romans.

To the north lies Spadeadam Waste – a large tract of unproductive land, part of which has been planted by the Forestry Commission and part developed in the 1950s to test the Blue Streak rocket. It is now used by an RAF Signals Unit and the peace of the countryside is frequently shattered by the screaming noise of low flying jet planes on exercise. Rare species of flora and fauna abound on Spadeadam, Butterburn Flow and Gowk Bank which are conservation areas.

The Spa Hotel is one of the first objects which attracts the attention approaching Gilsland from any direction. From its site there are magnificent views of the Alston fells and Lake District mountains. Owned by the North East Co-operative Society, it was formerly a convalescent home where miners and people from that area came for the sulphur and iron waters and bracing air.

Over 60 years ago, Gilsland was a self sufficient community with two dressmakers, a blacksmith, a baker's shop where fresh supplies were baked daily on the premises, a clogger, a shoemaker, a joiner, three butcher's shops, three grocery shops, two of which supplied livestock feed, a fancy goods shop, cycle shop, post office, garage, Station Hotel and two public houses, the Samson and the Bridge inn. The licensee of the Bridge inn was responsible for collecting a shire toll for livestock crossing the border either direction for Cumberland County Council. Today there is a grocer's shop, post office, a garage, the two licensed premises, the hotel and a building firm.

Agriculture, quarry work and coal mining used to be the main sources of employment but the last two have been worked out, leaving only agriculture. Once a labour intensive industry but now highly mechanised, most farms are family worked as well as family owned. Stock rearing of beef and sheep is the main enterprise with only one farm in the village producing milk. Over the years the number of farms in the area has decreased as small holdings have been amalgamated into bigger units. After 63 years trading the Cumberland and Dumfriesshire Auction Co have closed their sale ring in the village.

Glassonby

The small rural village of Glassonby is situated in the Eden valley some nine miles from the nearest town of Penrith. It comprises nine farms, a village hall, Methodist chapel, smithy, a small horse-riding establishment, a forest tree nursery, and the parish church of Addingham. At the end of 1990 there were 75 adults, 33 children.

A local community bus was started ten years ago giving a twice weekly service. The local small shop closed and when the postmistress moved away the post office closed too. The brewery who owned the local pub, the Pack Horse, took away the licence and sold the house to the tenant to live in. The smithy is used very occasionally for ornamental metal work and welding, the village hall built by public subscription in the 1930s is used for bingo in the winter months.

There are two stone circles, 'Long Meg and her daughters' and 'Little Meg'. An open air service on a June evening conducted alternately by the Methodists and Church of England was held each year around the stones, a great local attraction, people travelling on foot and bicycle and some partaking of a little refreshment at the nearby Druids Head inn before their homeward journey.

The land around Glassonby is rich in minerals, anhydrite and gypsum, and a mine close to the river Eden provided employment. Since the mine's closure subsidence has been noted in fields, and a few years ago a large part of a road leading out of the village collapsed.

Severe winters used to occur with drifting snow on the narrow roads running parallel to the fell, and the cold north-east wind known as the 'Helm' wind peculiar to these parts has to be experienced to be believed.

Gosforth

Situated where the roads from Eskdale and Wasdale meet, Gosforth has long had an important function as the place where the folk from the remoter valleys came to shop for goods and services. Add to that its role as first changing-place for horses on the road south from Whitehaven (this supposedly accounts for the large number of pubs in the Square), and it is obvious why it became the bustling village it still is today.

Surrounded by open country and the fells, many of its inhabitants have traditionally relied on agriculture for their living, mainly in sheep-farming, but Gosforth at one time had mills, blacksmiths, grocers, bakers, tailors, masons, slaters, bootmakers, cloggers, milliners and even a chemist as well as several doctors. Nowadays there are still over 20 shops and businesses in the village, but more of its inhabitants rely on British Nuclear Fuels for employment, and there is a large complement of professional people who live here but work in nearby towns and villages. This has changed the character of Gosforth to a certain extent, as have the concomitant housing estates, but the village has done a very success-ful job of absorbing these modern 'invaders', much as must have happe-ned 1,000 years ago when the Vikings arrived. It has expanded where necessary, but retained the feel of a country village, together with its community spirit.

The Vikings were responsible for the best-known landmarks – the Gosforth Cross (the tallest sandstone monolith in Britain, carved with both Norse and Christian symbols), the 'fishing stone' and the hogback warrior tombs in the church, and the carved stones built into the toolshed which is now a listed building! The Viking influence is also seen in the name of the river, the Bleng, and many surrounding fells and farms.

As one might expect in a village of some 1,200 inhabitants, there is a thriving social life. During the summer the big event is the Gosforth Agricultural Show, now over a century old and attracting entries from all over the county.

As is usual in a country parish, many events centre round the church and school. Gosforth is the largest church in a united benefice with Nether Wasdale and Wasdale Head. Nether Wasdale still boasts its own Mayday celebrations, with the schoolchildren dancing round the maypole. In Gosforth, church and school are separated only by a road and the ties are close.

Part of the village hall incorporates one of the oldest buildings in Gosforth. This was built in 1628 by John and Margaret Shearwen (there are still Sherwens in the village), and now houses the library and the Supper Room. About 30 years later the Gosforth Hall was erected, using the same local sandstone and in the same vernacular style. Another old building (now a private house) is the old high school at the northern entrance to the village. The story goes that 'Wonderful Walker' taught here as a young man in the early 18th century.

Grasmere 🍃

Grasmere probably originated from the name Grisemere (Lake of the Swine), so called because one of the early uses of the forest was for herding pigs. Gradually, as the forests reduced, sheep became the main stay of the valley.

Early roads, of necessity, had to keep above the swamps of the low lying ground, and it is still possible to follow long stretches of the old packhorse tracks. Coaches were the main mode of transport between Grasmere and Kendal, but coaching did not long survive the close of the century. In 1905 steam motor buses were introduced, known the 'Yellow Perils'. Nowadays cars and luxury coaches bring hundreds of thousands of people to the village every year. No longer does Grasmere depend for its prosperity on sheep. It has become one of the most famous of the Lake District villages and a centre of tourism.

Perhaps the most famous of all Grasmere's inhabitants was the poet William Wordsworth, who arrived with his sister Dorothy on the 20th December 1799, and took up residence at Town End, the house now known to all as Dove Cottage. In 1802, Wordsworth married Mary Hutchinson.

Grasmere church, dedicated to St Oswald, the Northumbrian king who was killed at the battle of Masserfield in AD 642, stands upon the bank of the winding river Rothay. The date of its foundation is uncertain, but a church may have stood on the site in Saxon times. St Oswald's well is now covered over, but it is remembered that water used for christenings used to be fetched from it. The tower walls, three or four ft thick, are of unhewn boulders, probably taken from the beck and bound together with strong mortar. The roughcast was removed and the walls pointed in 1891, but when this proved inadequate to keep out the rain, the walls were again cemented and roughcast in 1910. Beneath the tower is an ancient font, believed to have come from Furness Abbey.

Some of the yew trees in the churchyard were planted by Wordsworth. Near one of them, close to the river, is his grave with the simple inscription, 'William Wordsworth 1850. Mary Wordsworth 1859'. The next grave to the north is that of their daughter, Dora, while to the south lies the poet's sister Dorothy. Nearby are the resting places of other members of the family.

Rushbearing is a festival surviving only at Grasmere and two or three other places in the north of England, and has been observed annually at Grasmere for many centuries. It is a relic of the days when the earthern floors of churches were strewn with rushes for warmth and cleanliness. When the need for rush-strewing ceased, the ancient custom was never dropped and has been preserved as a pastoral festival. It now takes place on the Saturday nearest to St Oswald's Day, 5th August.

Grayrigg 🌿

Grayrigg is a small village on the A685 road halfway between Kendal and Tebay, with some fine views of the Howgill Fells to the east and Whinfell Beacon standing guard to the north. There are about 30 houses in the village and although ten of these have been built in the last few years, the village remains largely untroubled by property developers.

The community is swelled by the parishes of Docker, Lambrigg, Dillicar, Whinfell and Patton which all contain scattered farms and cottages. Until about 40 years ago most of the people living here were employed in agriculture but now many small farms have been amalgamated and, in some cases, the farmhouses, cottages and barns have been converted to suit modern housing needs. Grayrigg with its school, church and post office is the centre for all these dwellings and village life survives well.

The present church was built in 1837 although there had been a place of worship on the site for centuries. The Quakers were once an important part of Grayrigg's community. They started meeting at Sunny Bank but in 1696 built their own meeting house at Beckhouses where they also established a school. The Quakers met there for the next 200 years but the numbers dwindled and the building was eventually sold and made into a house.

The shop and post office, across the road from the school, was built by the present postmistress in 1980. (Yes, she did actually help with the building!) This is a real village shop where the proprietor is always willing to assist locals or strangers. Next to the post office stands the Coronation Hall, built to commemorate the 1911 Coronation. There are still men around who can remember helping to cart stone from Grayrigg Hall land to build it.

The picturesque almshouses opposite the vicarage were built in 1869 with money provided by Miss Mary Rowlandson of Kiln Head.

Grayrigg Hall, down the lane by the church, was built to replace the original Hall further out of the village where the Duckett family lived for generations. The old Hall fell into disrepair and was finally demolished in the early 1700s. The Agricultural Show held at Grayrigg Hall on the first Thursday in September, is one of the oldest in the country.

Mount Pleasant House standing across the lane from the church has played various roles. It is said to have been the vicarage before the present vicarage was built in 1843 and was a public house (the Brown Cow) during the building of the railway. The navvies were paid there and probably some of them would spend a considerable part of their earnings there. The respectable residents of Grayrigg no doubt locked their doors on pay nights! The other pub in the village was the Punch Bowl on the corner of the Lambrigg road. The licence lapsed in 1922 and it is now an attractive guest house.

This end of the village was at one time the 'industrial estate' with a joiner and wheelwright, a shoemaker, the post office and shop and the smithy. The joiner's shop is still in use but the others are gone now. The smithy closed and was converted into a bungalow (Anvil Cottage) in 1953. The pump house which provided water until a piped supply arrived in 1937 was demolished in the 1961 road widening scheme.

Great & Little Broughton 🌿

The twin villages of Great and Little Broughton lie on the north bank of the river Derwent, the 'sunny side' as old villagers call it. They are quiet spots, despite their name, for Broughton derives from the Scandinavian 'broch – ton' meaning 'fortified place'.

Defences were necessary for centuries until the Scots ceased to be the enemies, but there's a relic of the Border wars in the name of Scot Hill, Great Broughton's village square, where it is likely that captured Border raiders were executed. It is certain, however, that Scot Hill was the execution place of two Broughton men condemned for their part in the Pilgrimage of Grace, also known as the Great Northern Rebellion, which followed the suppression of the monasteries by King Henry VIII.

The Broughtons have a long industrial history. There is a tradition (but no remaining traces) of copper smelting at Broughton Hall, and for many years Little Broughton was the home of an extensive industry making tobacco pipes of clay. They became colliery villages in the Industrial Revolution, and for more than a century coal mining was the principal occupation. Opencast coal mining today continues the tradition, but most villagers work in new industries on the coastal belt, especially the large number of 'off-comers' who live in new housing estates which have sprung up in and around the villages.

Religion has always been a strong influence in the Broughtons. Originally a part of the parish of Bridekirk, they broke away and built their Christ Church more than a century ago. The Baptist chapel at Little Broughton was established in 1648 by a Colonel in Cromwell's army when Roundhead troops were stationed at Broughton during the siege of Cockermouth Castle. There is a long-standing Quaker influence and the Friends meeting at Little Broughton goes all the way back to visits by George Fox himself.

Most famous of all sons of the Broughtons was Abraham Fletcher, of Little Broughton, whose formal education lasted a week and cost his parents threepence at a local dame school. A clay-pipe maker by profession, he studied in a loft over the porch of his Little Broughton home, and eventually wrote a definitive work on mathematics, *The Universal Measurer and Mechanic*. Apart from that he spent a useful life in his native village as doctor (his herbal medicines were always in demand), scribe and lawyer.

Great and Little Broughton are separate villages, but they are as one today. This was not always so, but the differences seldom went beyond healthy rivalry usually expressed in the past on the field known in olden times as 'Challen Jackers' (which may be interpreted as 'Challenge Acres'). By coincidence, most of Challen Jackers between Great and Little Broughton remains an open space as The Welfare Field.

Great Corby ✿

Great Corby is located six miles east of Carlisle, one mile south of the A69 Carlisle/Newcastle road. The population of the village is approximately 500.

The village was originally an agricultural settlement closely related to the activities at Corby Castle, the home of the Howard family. This large house, situated on a cliff above the river Eden, commands fine views. The castle started as a pele tower in the 13th century; this was enclosed within later additions over the years until it took its present form between 1812 and 1817.

In the village itself adjoining the green is a square exedra built in 1833 as a blacksmith's shop, with a covered open space in front supported by thick sandstone piers. This was used for shoeing, and is now a motor repair workshop.

The other feature of architectural interest is the 600 ft long, 100 ft high railway bridge by Francis Giles completed in 1834. This connects Great Corby to the station at Wetheral, the village on the west side of the river. The sandstone bridge also supports a cast iron footbridge with a wooden path which until 1956 was subject to a toll of originally a halfpenny and later a penny. This provided an alternative route to a ferry service by rowing boat based at the still-present Ferry Cottage on the Great Corby side of the river. Fine views of the river are obtained from the footpath.

The character of the village has changed because of its increasing attraction as a commuter village and the decline of its farming role. Its attractiveness lies in its accessibility to Carlisle, the relatively small size of the village, its largely unspoilt basic form and its pleasant rural surroundings.

All the shops, the chapel and several former farms and barns have been converted into houses, and groups of cottages made into larger dwellings. The coal merchant and joiner have gone. The reading room now serves as a village hall and is adjoined by a playing field.

Because of the impact of the surrounding woods and the nature of agricultural land holdings, the village has retained a tree-filled backcloth and many open areas within which provide pleasant airy spaces.

Great Salkeld 🌿

Nestling on the western bank of the Eden valley is the small village of Great Salkeld, five and a half miles from Penrith. The village is an old one built mainly of local sandstone with traditional Cumbrian windows. Many houses have fine views of the river Eden and of the Pennines towards Cross Fell and Hartside. There are traces of Roman occupation at North Dykes.

The oldest building in the village today is the church of St Cuthbert. It is thought to stand on the site of an older wooden church. The carvings reflect the Norse influence in the area. In 1380 a tower was added, with six ft thick walls and a narrow oak door which is reinforced by an iron grating and massive bolts. It was used as a look-out and a safe refuge from raiding Scots.

The other foundation of interest is the village school. The first school was held in the church tower as early as 1515. A school house was built in 1686, but when a new school was built in 1856 there had been no school for a number of years. This new school could accommodate 96 pupils. It remains open today but with fewer pupils on the roll.

The village has changed over the years. In 1905, it was more self supporting than it is today. People grew much of their food and the village had local shops and craftsmen to supply their other needs. Most people were employed in or near the village. They worked on farms, smallholdings or on large estates such as Nunwick Hall. By 1965, the population had fallen to 380. There were few smallholdings and most of the younger or qualified people could now travel to work in Penrith on public transport. There were only two shops and a post office left.

Today the population is about 350 men, women and children. The church, school, chapel and village hall are still well supported. The one public house which remains is also still a social centre.

The village of Great Salkeld is not isolated and so has contact with a new industry – tourism. The buildings which once formed the laundry for Nunwick Hall are now part of a holiday cottage complex. There are several holiday homes in the area and the local public house welcomes visitors but Great Salkeld remains a quiet rural spot.

Greysouthen 🌿

Greysouthen is a village of about 350 people, lying roughly halfway between Cockermouth and Workington. There are no signposts to the village on the major roads in the area, so that visitors to Greysouthen are usually lost, or have come upon it by accident on the way to somewhere else, or are armed with detailed instructions and a map and endeavouring to visit an inhabitant!

The visitor who does find his way to Greysouthen will notice the high stone walls which are a striking feature of the village, and which are one of the reasons why it was made a conservation area by Allerdale District Council in 1984. The walls, which are up to twelve ft high, surround the grounds of the Mansion in the centre of the village, and the gardens of smaller houses along the main street.

The Mansion began as a small 17th century farmhouse, to which more rooms and more grandeur were added over the years. It was later given an imposing facade which looks out over the once landscaped grounds. It is the back door which opens on to the Main Street, opposite to a row of houses which in the 17th century would have been farm buildings, a barn, perhaps a cart shed and the blacksmith's forge. Behind them was the orchard, and all were once part of the Mansion estate.

In the 19th century, Greysouthen was part of a thriving coalmining area and small rows of miners' cottages were built in the village. The population then was almost twice its present level and Greysouthen prospered, as did the old village inn, the Punch Bowl. The miners of Greysouthen had quite a reputation in the area for the amount of ale they consumed and the Cockermouth magistrates of the time are reported to have declared that if it were not for Greysouthen their services as magistrates would no longer be required.

The Punch Bowl has been converted into flats, but externally has changed very little. The Mansion, too, while outwardly the same, has recently been converted into flats, and houses have been built within the high walls of the former kitchen garden. Indeed, while the external appearance of Greysouthen has been largely maintained, new houses have been tucked into many nooks and crannies in the village and redundant farm buildings have been converted into homes.

There are still seven working farms in Greysouthen, but most working inhabitants now go out of the village to their jobs. The local mines closed long ago, but there are still men who worked in the mine at the nearby village of Clifton.

In spite of having no school, church or pub, Greysouthen remains a thriving community, with the village hall the meeting place for its inhabitants.

Greystoke ✣

Lying just outside the Lake District National Park, this pleasant village still retains its central small green and ancient market cross, and a large number of stone – built houses and cottages which have slate roofs. Many of these are listed buildings. The cross is mentioned in a Parish Register dated 1623. At that time there were also footstocks for the punishment of wrongdoers. It was an obvious site for a busy market. Today it is a meeting place for the youth of the village.

One of the six central roads leads through a grand archway, and is the main drive to Greystoke Castle. The Howard family have always lived there, and claim an unbroken line of descent going back to the Norman Conquest.

On Church Road can be seen the Sanctuary Stone. Formerly lying on the Church Causeway near the bridge, it was moved in 1908, for its own protection, into a recess in the wall by the swimming pool, and enclosed by iron railings. The stone is blue whinstone or cobble, and has a hatchet mark pointing towards the church. The right of sanctuary is said to have been granted in early times to all churches. Once beyond the stone, fugitives from the law could claim sanctuary within the precincts of the church. In a field next to the church, is another stone known locally as 'Spillers'. This is hollowed out on the top, and is believed to have been a plague stone, where coins could be left to avoid possible contagion.

The beautiful and ancient church is dedicated to St Andrew, and was first mentioned in records in 1255. It is much larger than most lakeland churches because it was a collegiate, or mother church in the Middle Ages. The college of Greystoke was closed at the Reformation when the chantries were abolished. From 1958 to 1979 a bold experiment re-established a college in Greystoke with a somewhat different purpose. This was a pre-theological college to help men gain the necessary qualifications prior to entering full residential training.

An art and craft exhibition is held in the church in May and August, and this attracts visitors from a very wide area, as does Greystoke itself throughout the summer months. Tourists often photograph the ancient village school which we are indeed fortunate to retain. It was erected by the Howard family in 1838, and has nearly 50 infant and junior children on roll.

Many years ago the village boasted four public houses, only one of which remains overlooking the green. The Boot and Shoe is run by the third generation of the Tweddle family. Also in Greystoke is a very successful racing stable, owned by Gordon W. Richards. This large stable has trained around 700 winners since it began, including two Grand National winners, *Lucius* and *Hello Dandy*.

A group of ladies, nicknamed the Magnificent Seven, sally forth on most weekends in summer with one or two husbands in tow. They attend various popular country gatherings, especially grass track race meetings, feeding the crowds on soup and snacks from their caravan. The money raised, and this is usually well over £2,000 each year, is shared between local organisations and charities, and national charities. Traditionally village committees have always raised huge amounts of money which benefit the inhabitants of all ages. Each Christmas parcels are distributed to householders over 60 by the parish council. This money derives from a bequest of many years ago.

Grinsdale

Grinsdale is situated on the river Eden and the Roman wall and vallum runs through the village. The river has always been a threat to the village, and in the 1940s it was necessary to change the course of the river away from the houses. The village hall has long been a focal point of village life. The original building was burnt down in 1934 and was rebuilt on a smaller scale the following year. During the Second World War there was a knitting circle established by the women of the village. They provided knitted comforts for the troops and wove camouflage netting from hessian strips, a hard and dirty job. These days the hall is used for dances, whist drives, keep fit classes and other social events for the villagers.

The main occupation of the village has always been agriculture, three farms in the village producing milk and other mixed crops from the land. There are now 18 families living in the village compared to 22 according to records kept in 1747. In those days there used to be a tannery at Grinsdale Bridge and a blacksmith's shop in the village. The original bellows and blacksmith's tools are still intact inside the building, which is still standing. In the 18th and early 19th century there was a linen industry and many people became weavers. There was also a manure industry, but all these folded with the advent of modern production methods.

The church is dedicated to St Kentigern and villagers have to walk over two fields to worship there. It was restored in 1740 and again in 1895, but the original church probably dates back to the 12th century. There was once a rock between the church and the river where a human footprint could be seen. The person responsible had probably walked from the river northwards when the rock was just soft slate and left his print in it. Unfortunately the whereabouts of this rock today is unknown.

Even though this is a small community there is always something happening in the village. There are quite a few young families in the village, and as we are situated on a no-through road, children can play in safety. The members of one family occupy five of the 18 houses in the village, so this is very much a close community.

Hallbankgate

The fellside village of Hallbankgate is midway between Carlisle and Alston at the northern end of the Pennines, approximately 700 ft above sea level. Hallbankgate is the centre of several small hamlets, scattered houses and farmsteads.

It was once a thriving community with coal mines, quarries, a brick-yard, railways and farms, but today only the farms and one quarry survive, and their workforce is greatly reduced. Today, lack of buses is why many of the older inhabitants move into the local market town of Brampton. The Kirkhouse, just outside the village, was once a considerable industrial centre with coke ovens, gas works, foundries, blacksmiths, waggon shops, even to the building of an occasional locomotive. Equipment for the collieries was made here. It supplied the church with gas for lighting purposes and had its own fire engine, propelled by levers, which took six men to work. Here was the 'Tommy' shop where everyone who worked for the Thompsons had to buy their groceries.

In the 1950s the mines closed and the miners and their families moved away. Many of the cottages were pulled down or left to become derelict. In the late 1960s and early 1970s things changed and new people moved into the area and renovated these cottages, not only for holiday houses, but to live in themselves. Farlam Hall, for so many years the home of the Thompson family, is now a well known hotel.

The pub, the Belted Will, was closed many years ago by Rosalind, the radical Countess of Carlisle, and became the Temperance Hotel until in the 1970s it once again became a public house. The church, situated just outside the village was built in 1860 and replaced a much smaller one, whose registers date from the year 1663 but mention was made of it as early as 1169.

The village shop, originally named 'Naworth Collieries Co-operative Society Ltd', established in 1873 by the lord of the manor and leased to the Co-operative movement, is now owned by members and shareholders. At one time this large three-storey building supplied the needs of the parish and surrounding area. It had a manager's house adjoining, committee rooms and storage space. It consisted of grocery, drapery and butchering departments, tailor's shop, cornmill and even a hearse to be hired out at funerals. The hearse ended its days as a hen-house! It also had travelling shops. Today only a well stocked grocery department remains with a post office sharing part of it and the rest of the building, except for the manager's house, has been made into flats.

For 30 years the village had a recreation ground, laid out by the 'Miners Welfare' which had tennis courts, putting green, football and cricket pitches, swings and a pavilion. Sadly this too has gone and sheep and cattle graze where village activities were once held. However the school has a playing field where games are played and the school fete is held.

A railway once ran through the village and George Stephenson's famous *Rocket* ended its working life here and was later presented to Kensington Museum, London by the Thompson family.

One of the worst disasters was in 1908 when Roachburn Pit was flooded and three miners died. The loss of this pit caused a great exodus from the parish.

The great industrial past is over but the village is still very much alive.

Hawkshead Green End; Colt House on the left is where Wordsworth lodged as a schoolboy

Hawkshead 🦔

Hawkshead still appears to be the same tiny village of higgledy-piggledy stone cottages, archways, squares and cobbled nooks, beloved of Wordsworth and Beatrix Potter. In reality of course, its way of life has changed more in the last 50 years than in the previous 500 years.

Situated near the head of Esthwaite Water, it nestles under the old church of St Michael, and lies roughly half-way between the lakes of Coniston Water and Windermere.

Like its neighbours in High Furness, Hawkshead did not feature in the Domesday Book. In Norman times it was in a kind of no-man's land of swampy valleys and tangled woodland, until in the early 12th century it came under the monastic rule of Furness Abbey.

After the Dissolution of the abbey in 1537, there was a period of unrest, and even by the late 16th century the customary tenants and dalesfolk were often living at subsistence level, and suffering outbreaks of plague and famine. Hawkshead was fortunate, however, when Elizabeth I ratified its Code of Customs in 1586, and when Archbishop Sandys remembered his native area. It was he who in 1578 made Hawkshead a parish which before had been merely a chapelry of Dalton, and who in 1585 founded Hawkshead Grammar School. Today this school, closed in 1909, is only remembered as the village school attended by Wordsworth. In fact it was much more. Now a museum, it still contains an important antiquarian library, and once nurtured many pupils often of humble birth who, via St John's College, Cambridge, became outstanding in many fields. The 18th century astronomer William Pearson, FRS, is just one example.

Even for a rural area, Hawkshead's prolonged remoteness was unusual. This was because the village was never on an important route or river crossing, and until as late as the beginning of the 19th century, there were no roads suitable for wheeled traffic; access being only by foot or horseback along rough and stony packhorse tracks.

Now the village has gone from one extreme to another. Tourism has become an important Hawkshead industry, catered for by pleasant inns and guest houses, teashops, gift-shops, a post office and other shops, and facilities for other leisure pursuits like fishing. Even the quiet outlying farms are now also part of a more cosmopolitan life.

In spite of all, Hawkshead still retains something of its old community spirit. It is fortunate in having its own new junior school, an active church community and chapel, and a successful play group run by volunteers.

Today, the High Furness area is still one of the most densely wooded places in the country. Though its old woodland industries like charcoal-burning and bobbin-making have slowly disappeared, the latter recently, a few areas of semi-natural and old coppice woodland remain, while thousands of acres of deer forest are maintained by modern forestry methods.

Hayton 🌿

Hayton in May has a wonderful dawn chorus; it also has a night chorus of owls of which there were many, but since a number of farm buildings and barns have been made into houses and flats the owl population has diminished, and there are fewer bats.

Hayton's population has increased from 1,112 in 1931 to 2,257 in 1981. As it is only seven miles east of Carlisle and accessible by car it is a very popular place for commuters. Even so, it is still a village and seen at its best when the damson blossom is out, and when there are carpets of crocuses on the side of Castle Hill, a man-made hill rising well above the village. Snowdrops spread across the churchyard and overflow onto the 'Trods', a public footpath, which was a corpse road across the fields from the hamlet known as the How.

St Mary Magdalene church has an altar in memory of Betty Hodgson, which was built by a village craftsman, William Ivison from a locally grown oak. The church had a private chapel belonging to the Graham family of Edmond Castle. Next to the church stands Norman House, which was the Sunday house of the Grahams, where all the family and servants came to spend Sunday and attend services in the church. It is now a private dwelling.

Hayton beck runs down the middle of the village. It is now channelled through a culvert, although it surfaces in the fields by Briar Lonning and through the fields known as the 'Saughs'. Within living memory, the village got all its water from three pumps – one at Townhead, one in the middle of the village known as Martha's Well and one at Townfoot. Townhead, at the eastern end of the village was once a self-reliant hamlet of twelve houses with its own saw-mill and sandstone quarry, supplying stone for many of the cottages in the village.

However, it is not only buildings that make a village; it is the people too. Hayton was a self-supporting village with a blacksmith's shop, now a garage; Mrs Palmer's bakery sold delicious home-baked bread and cakes, now a private house. A shop run by Miss Louisa Hodgson sold everything from tea to paraffin and she kept all her dry goods in shoe boxes and knew where everything was. The post office is now combined with the village shop in a building that was once the Red Lion inn. The White Lion, now called the Stone inn, is a few yards down the road. Albert Scott the cobbler had his workshop in a hut at the top of the garden, behind Cobbler's Cottage in the beck bottom. There clogs were taken to have their caulkers renewed.

Hayton (Aspatria) ✺

The small village of Hayton is set in idyllic rural surroundings about two miles west of Aspatria. The oldest and most historical building in Hayton must be the splendid castle which dates back to the 11th century. Standing majestically on a elevated site and approached by a long winding pathway, the castle commands a superb view and is surrounded by its rolling acres of farm and woodland. It is the family home of Mr and Mrs David Mitchell and their two sons, having previously been the home of David's parents and grandparents.

The only natural fortification of so illustrious a building appears to be the small stream called Patten beck on the south and west and running northwards. Any earlier defences – and there would certainly be some – have been obliterated by modern farm buildings. Along the roadway passing the entrance gates and continuing eastwards is a small group of modern cottages aptly named Patten Garth.

Almost in the centre of the village and across the green is the parish church of St James. The building was completed and consecrated on 5th November, 1867. It contains a lovely hand-carved pulpit – the work of the late Miss Ruth Atkinson in memory of her father. The font standing within the doorway at the west side of the church is said to be over 800 years old and previously stood in the chapel at Hayton castle where the villagers worshipped before the present church was built – the chapel at the castle is long since demolished. On a warm summer evening there is a feeling of peace and tranquillity surrounding this little church. One can hear the distant whirr of farm machinery, the birds coming and going in the old gnarled trees, dogs barking and perhaps the two elegant peacocks which live at the big house across the green.

Towards the west end of Hayton is the public room which serves the village people well. Sadly the village school was closed many years ago – the building has been converted into dwellings. The vicarage standing nearby is also a dwelling, as the church is linked with the parish of Aspatria and shares the same incumbent. The village consists of many farmsteads, all very productive, and generally handed down by previous generations. The land is rich and fertile and hundreds of cattle and sheep are bred here. Many of the farms carry large dairy herds – the milk being collected daily by the tankers from the local creamery at Aspatria.

Hethersgill 🌿

Hethersgill is situated between Longtown and Brampton, ten miles from Carlisle.

A famous inhabitant was George Graham the clock and watch maker. He also invented several valuable instruments for astronomical observations. It is uncertain as to where he was born; his indenture describes his father as George Graham 'late of Fordlands', although it is possible he was born at Horsegills. He was made a Fellow of the Royal Society and is one of the few Cumbrians to be buried in Westminster Abbey.

St Mary's church is situated in the village, erected in 1876 as a chapel of ease to Kirklinton, built of stone from the local quarry in Gothic style. In 1984 a licence was granted for weddings, previously all weddings were at Kirklinton church.

A Wesleyan Methodist chapel was built at Ullermire in 1833, but was replaced by another in the village in 1901. The former is now used as a store room. The land for a second chapel was given by William Moffat, a gentleman's outfitter who delighted in calling himself 'Sark MP'. Sark was an old name for a shirt and MP stood for Methodist Preacher. The chapel was closed in 1979 and purchased two years later and converted into an art studio/gallery. The Home Office granted permission to disinter the remains of the Sark MP and have them buried in the churchyard. There was an added stipulation that this work must be carried out after midnight. The Methodist minister, the local vicar, the undertaker and the local policeman carried the remains through the village and buried them in the churchyard – quite sensational.

Most dwellings had their own peat rights; the Long Pole was the central focal point for aligning these rights. Today Scottish Agricultural Industries work the peat moss. It is quite big business giving employment locally, varying from 60/80 employees and up-to-date equipment churns out tons of peat for horticultural purposes all over the country. Adders thrive on the Moss in the summer. The notorious tinkling holes were a great danger, so named because of an overgrown hole with a ditch running underground. When the local sports held their hound trails, on one occasion three hounds disappeared into a tinkling hole – the holes have now gone with the new drainage system.

A clay quarry was worked at Prior Rigg; the clay was dug out, transported to Sandysike and made into bricks. This has now finished. The smithy at Boltonfell has also finished. The local tradesmen are mostly allied to agriculture, consisting of stick makers, trough makers, joiners, electricians and builders. A new centre is being tried by one farmer, llama farming, the only such enterprise in Cumbria.

In December 1979 the locality was shaken by an earthquake and as we were near to the epicentre it was five on the Richter scale. This was followed by another a week later, not quite as severe. Structural damage was caused to chimney stacks and walls.

Heversham & Leasgill

Much has been written about Heversham's ancient parish church ('the oldest recorded church in Westmorland') and its famous grammar school founded in 1613. But it is people who give life to a community, and indeed the very name of the village, which, with its associated hamlet, Leasgill, nestles at the foot of the hill called the Head six miles south of Kendal, is generally accepted to derive from a 7th century Anglian chief, Haefar, bearing testimony down some 13 centuries to the antiquity of the settlement.

Haefar may have vanished into the mists of time, but the descendants of Edward Wilson, founder of the grammar school, live on to this day, playing a prominent role in the life of the district. The school itself, for much of its history a private day and boarding school for boys, has produced many notable scholars, its most famous son being Ephraim Chambers, whose *Chambers' Dictionary*, the forerunner of modern encyclopaedias, was published in 1728.

The Wilsons also made their mark by buying in 1614 what must surely be the oldest residence in the village, Heversham Hall. The fabric of the Hall dates back to the 14th century remains of a pele tower, though its history goes back nearly a thousand years, having been until 1539 the headquarters of the steward appointed by St Mary's Abbey in York to farm lands which the abbey owned in Heversham.

Today the land is still farmed, and the Hall still belongs to the Wilson family, who, since 1723, have lived in Dallam Tower, the splendid mansion they built for themselves near the neighbouring village of Milnthorpe.

Heversham Hall, with its massive six ft thick stone walls, its mullioned trefoil-headed windows and its superb oak-timbered banqueting hall, is today occupied by another notable village family, the Handleys, whose tenancy of the farm goes back four generations to 1876.

The social centre of the village, the hall known as the Athenaeum in Leasgill, owes its existence to the philanthropy and vision of Frank A.

Argles, who founded it as a room for 'Penny Readings' in 1872 with the aim of providing intellectual stimulus for the village. The Argles family, who lived in Eversley House in Leasgill from 1859, contributed to the village in many ways, assisting in the restoration of the parish church of St Peter , supplementing the village water supply, and providing, in 1891, for a nominal sum, a new site for the village school.

An educational enterprise set up in 1891 was Heversham Metal Industry, by Percy Hibbert of Plumtree Hall, at the instigation mainly of the village blacksmith, Henry Varley. Intended to train men and boys in the craft of making brass and copper ware, the industry continued into the 1920s. Malcolm Sisson, formerly clerk to the parish council, remembers as a lad attending their classes in the old school. Many families still treasure the artefacts made by their fathers and grandfathers, and at least one item, a copper coal-scuttle, was bought by Queen Mary.

Hincaster

Hincaster is a small hamlet of some 70 houses about three miles north of Milnthorpe, on the road to Kendal. The main Kendal road is now the A6 to the west of the river Kent, but a back road goes through the villages of Ackenthwaite, Hincaster, Sedgwick and Natland.

No explanation or remains have been found to support the apparent Roman origins indicated by the suffix 'caster', though many theories of possible sites of settlement – even a bridge – have been put forward, but only a few coin finds have been substantiated.

The underlying rock is limestone, protruding like bones in many fields, which, being porous, prevents much surface drainage except for streams with sources beyond the limestone area. Water is everywhere near the surface as the frequent 'Liable to flood' County Council notices indicate.

In the mid 19th century the demand for gunpowder led to the Stricklands from Sizergh and the Wakefields from Sedgwick supporting the development of a gunpowder mill using the water power which was readily available – 'but don't scare my salmon', said one. By 1880 Mr Swinglehurst, who lived at Hincaster House, had control of the gunpowder works, and became a local squire figure. His house had been gentrified earlier in the century by 'cladding' the rough walls with dressed limestone. Mr Swinglehurst built a small mission room onto one of the cottages on the green where Sunday school was held until the 1940s. Even in the 1920s these gunpowder works drew labour from the village. Later the works were moved to a bigger site at Gatebeck, and later still ICI took them all over. Only worn down mill race walls remain.

The canal, now dry from Stainton to Kendal, was planned in the 18th century and reached from Preston to Tewitfield in 1797 and Kendal in 1819, with an extension to Glasson Dock near Lancaster. The quarter-mile tunnel at Hincaster is of interest. The horses which drew the barges were led over the hill, and the bargees 'clogged' the barges through the tunnel by pushing with their boots on the tunnel roof. Doubts have been expressed recently as to whether this practice actually occurred, but an octogenarian who was born and bred in Hincaster affirms that it was so.

Today Hincaster comprises two distinct and separate groups of houses. The bigger group, near the green, are also the older, having been mostly built, in limestone, before the 20th century. The big house, Hincaster House, is now divided into three; there are several old cottages; and in about 1950 a row of eight council houses was built.

The smaller group of houses lies at the southern end of the village, near the only other big 19th century house, which is also now divided. Behind it is the oldest farm in the village, specialising in poultry and providing some useful employment. In the 1960s half a dozen bungalows and houses were built. The farm has built an attractive group of holiday flats, bringing a little tourism to this village on the edge of Lakeland.

Hoff 🦢

Hoff cannot be classed as a village, nor yet a hamlet, but rather a 'gathering' of cottages and scattered farms straggling the B6260 road which connects Appleby to Kendal and the M6 motorway. The name Hoff is thought to be of Viking origin.

Just west of Hoff is Orton moor through which runs a huge scar of limestone. Amongst the boulders are many visible signs of settlements and barrows of early man. Later, in the 19th century, quarrying provided work for many miners, the limestone obtained going towards building and industrial uses. No doubt the men frequented both pubs, one now converted to a working farm, the other still known as the New Inn although its existence is known as far back as the 17th century. The inn also provided travellers with a necessary staging post, before crossing the lonely, dangerous moorland.

Beside the inn is a row of houses in which four families now live. The date of 1698 is engraved upon the wall, but little is known of its history until its emergence in the last century as a workhouse. One point of interest is the extra height of the upper floor suggesting that, at one time, advantage was taken of the additional light which it provides for weaving or spiining.

There is no church but there was an old Methodist chapel, dated 1895, now converted into a private dwelling house.

The old school has lost the last of its pupils but not its heart. Once a month it is used for an afternoon service conducted by the vicar of Appleby. During the seasons, social functions are held, especially at Christmastime. The Harvest Festival is well attended and followed by an auction of all the offerings, and it is good to see the whole community come together and enjoy some enthusiastic bidding.

The beck, which flows near the boundary of Hoff, was the scene of a violent skirmish between the Scots and the English during the reign of

Richard II. Nowadays it is a haven for red squirrels, the occasional deer, herons and kingfishers. In the spring, the fields are a riot of wild flowers and orchids can readily be seen. One can only hope this timeless existence will be able to continue in a changing world.

Holker 🦡

Holker village is a neat collection of cottages with diamond-paned windows, housing some of the staff and workers on the Holker estate.

At first the only building of any size was the grange that came to be known as Frith Hall. It stands on the shore of the estuary near an old route which led across the sands into Furness. It would have had a barn or barns, a jetty and some domestic accommodation, fragmentary remains of which can still be seen.

The one major development in the history of Holker was the establishment of Holker Hall, which is open daily from Easter to October (except Saturdays). The Hall was once the Elizabethan home of the Prestons, now the property of the Cavendish family. Its situation is amongst the most beautiful of the English countryside, with gardens merging into parkland, and hills on one side and the expanse of the bay on the other. The gardens are worth a visit with their semi-tropical trees and shrubs and unusual collections of plants. There has been a herd of fallow deer in the park at Holker for over 200 years, and more recently introduced is a herd of red deer.

Holme 🦡

Holme, with a population of around 1,200, is in the south of the county midway between Kendal and Lancaster, and very close to the boundary of Lancashire itself. The village is bordered on the east by Clawthorpe Fell, Farleton Knott rising to a height of 801 ft, and the M6 motorway.

The Preston to Kendal Canal which passes through the village is no longer used as it once was by barges bringing coal from the Lancaster pits. One of the wharfs was at Holme and it was quite common for the bargees to walk into the village to buy food and other necessities and board the boat again at some point further-along the canal. The M6 motorway runs parallel to the canal and construction of this particular stretch of motorway was commenced in 1968 and completed in 1970.

The limestone quarry at Holme Park has been in operation many years. Limestone was transported by horse and cart to local railway stations. Today it is producing much material for present day motorways.

Holme Mill is about half a mile from the village and down through the years has been the chief source of employment, starting as a corn mill, then a flax mill, and later making coconut matting and carpets. One of their biggest consignments was the floor covering for the Blackpool Tower Circus ring. The mill closed in 1975 and the site and buildings were sold and are now industrial units, again providing work for local people. The cottages, which were built dating from 1816 for mill employees, have since been sold and are now privately owned.

On the outskirts of the village a camp was built in 1941 for Italian prisoners of war, who were allowed to move freely and mix with local people and were allotted tasks which benefited the village, including redecorating and refurnishing the Catholic chapel for the use of evacuees billeted in the area. At the end of the war the camp became an open prison but is now transformed into a residential school.

In the centre of the village is Holy Trinity church which has celebrated its 150th anniversary, having been built in 1839.

Holme has always been a sporting village. A cricket club formed in 1888 today has two teams playing in the South Lakeland League. A rugby club was formed the same year but disbanded after the Second World War, their ground being sold for a residential development. There have been several such developments over recent years and this has proved beneficial in so many ways.

Holme St Cuthbert

The area in which Holme St Cuthbert lies once came under the auspices of the great Cistercian monastery of Holme Cultram. To serve the needs of the isolated hamlets and farms, some worked by the monks themselves, the monastery built and maintained several small chapels of ease of which two were in what is now known as the parish of Holme St Cuthbert.

In 1840 the vicar of Holme Cultram raised funds to enable the present Holme St Cuthbert church to be built, again as a chapel of ease and this, along with a school and school house, was completed in 1845. The only other buildings in the vicinity are the church hall, used mainly for fund raising and WI meetings, and the Hearse House, which formerly accommodated a four wheel glass-sided hearse and appropriate special harness. This was acquired by public subscription in 1877 for the use of parishioners, non-parishioners being required to pay fifteen shillings. This vehicle has long since disappeared and the only visible clue to its existence is a portion of one of the engraved glass sides now used as a window in an outhouse at Newtown.

Newtown, comprising several farmhouses, some now used as holiday homes, lies about a mile inland from the Solway Firth. In the middle of the 16th century it replaced the village of New Mawbray on the coast when sand began to encroach on the latter and the inhabitants were forced to move inland.

Beckfoot lies on the coast slightly to the north of Newtown and on account of the number of foundations discovered there it would appear at one time to have been larger than at present. Here the Romans built a fort as part of their coastal defences. Indeed the sites of a chain of fortlets and defensive towers all along this stretch of the Solway shore bear testimony to a considerable Roman presence in the past.

Out in the firth to the south of Beckfoot can be seen, at very low water, the remains of a submerged forest, although the stumps of the trees are hard to distinguish from the adjacent rocks on the edge of a scaur. The time scale here could indicate the beginning of the New Stone Age.

Further south on the coast is Mawbray, originally known as Old Mawbray. This village is a collection of 17th century cottages and farmhouses along with a number of modern bungalows and houses. There is also an interesting row of sturdy, low-roofed cottages originally built for salt pan workers. In the 1881 census Mawbray boasted eight farmers, plus the supportive trades of blacksmith, ham and bacon curers, bakers, butcher, grocers, shoemaker, joiners and also an inn. Today the inn, the Lowther Arms, still survives, as does the forge, which has been most successfully transformed into a restaurant.

The demise in Mawbray of the many trades originally supportive of farming has been echoed all around this parish of Holme St Cuthbert. However the old way of life is never forgotten and the atmosphere is such that earlier times can be recalled and talked about as if they were yesterday, since many of the families have farmed here generation after generation.

How Mill 🌿

How Mill is a small hamlet seven miles east of Carlisle and four miles west of Brampton in the parish of Hayton. How derives its name from a circular earthwork or 'how' of sand. Legend has it that there is buried treasure over which the dragon (the dreaded cairn dweller) keeps endless watch.

The hamlet now has just a pub and a post office, but it used to have a busy railway station on the Carlisle to Newcastle line which closed in the 1950s. Attached to the station were the coal vaults, coal being delivered to the village by horse and cart.

How Mill also had a busy auction mart where sheep and cattle were sold every Wednesday. Locals walked their stock to the mart but the animals were often sent by rail. Mrs Gilliland had a hut on the auction yard and was renowned for her hot soup, tatie pot and roast beef.

Across the railway and up a steep hill is Watch Hill house, built by Dr Maclaren of Carlisle as a convalescent home for his patients. After his death it became a private house. Watch Hill was so named because it was a look-out for Scottish raiders driving their plunder of sheep and cattle along Thief Street and back over the border.

The Faugh is renowned for its pub, the String of Horses. The school there was closed many years ago.

To the east of How Mill is Cowran Bridge. The poor house there was given to the parish by Mr Graham of Edmond Castle and is now converted into two cottages. Adjoining this is the penfold where stray animals could be kept in safe custody. This land was leased to the wardens and overseers of Hayton parish for 2,000 years from 1827.

The rural area encircled by Cowran Bridge, Faugh and How Mill is rich in sand deposits. The contour of the whole area has been drastically changed by extensive quarrying. The attendant heavy lorries now thunder through the country lanes.

Howgill

Howgill is a hamlet about three miles north-west of Sedbergh. The range of hills now known as the Howgills were named after the hamlet by the Ordnance Survey cartographers, who discovered that although all the hills had their individual names, there was no collective name for the range.

The road from Sedbergh to Howgill is the old Roman road which continues to Tebay, past the site of a Roman camp. The hedgerows along the lane produce an amazing variety of wild plants.

Howgill is a farming community, mainly given to the raising of sheep but dairy herds are also kept. The only mill, which was engaged in woollen manufacture and employed about a hundred hands, closed about 1870, though the derelict building still stands and the flume which provided water power is still in evidence.

The two cottages at Bantyghyll were the original old church and school. In 1838 the present church was built in its new position on the green and is still the hub of the community.

The hills and dales around are a magnet to fellwalkers and hikers. In all seasons, in all weathers, these hardy souls are encountered, braving the elements to admire the beauty of the area. There is an abundance of quiet lanes and public footpaths passing by the most picturesque farms and cottages which can only be seen when on foot, and the views from the fells can only be described as magnificent.

There are some houses in the area of great age which still contain features of their original construction. One or two still have the original beef-hawks which were used for drying beef in pre-freezer days. There are also some 'backstones' which were used for the baking of a type of oatcake, whilst some still have the original spice cupboards. One farm which was owned by a family engaged in slave-trading still has the slave chains, originally in the cellars, now used as fencing.

Many Howgill families have lived in the area for generations, one family has a record of their family tree which reaches back to the 12th century. It is not just the beauty of the area which makes it so attractive, one would have far to go to meet more friendly, welcoming people.

Hunsonby 🐚

Hunsonby is a small village lying in the Eden valley approximately two miles from the foothills of the Pennines. The oldest part of the village has changed very little; the houses are all built from the local red sandstone and date back from 200 to 400 years old. One cottage is still thatched, the thatch now being covered in tin, and on other houses it is possible to see where they have been heightened and new roofs put on.

It is in an ideal position for a fortified village to defend itself from the Scottish raiders. The road from the north comes through a narrow cutting which could easily be blocked and the road out to the south has to cross the local beck known as Robbery Water. The villagers could therefore easily bring their cattle into the village green and block off the two routes in.

The only business in the village, a joiner's shop, went out of business some 20 years ago having been in the same family for over a hundred years. This property has now been turned into two cottages. A barn in the village has also been turned into two homes and in the 1950s a row of council houses were built and called Moorside, being the name of the field they were built in. Although there has been this increase in houses, because of smaller families and holiday homes the population is not much larger than in 1829 when a directory quotes the population at 151 persons.

The village school was built with money left by the will of Joseph Hutchinson in 1726; unfortunately it closed in 1974. Joseph Hutchinson also left his land at 'Gawtree' (another word for Hawthorn) to the poor and needy of the village and the rent from this land is still distributed. He also left money for a bridge to be built over the beck; this is called the white bridge because of the white railings along it and was built in 1740. A larger bridge which carries the road was built in 1850.

On the main road at the edge of Gawtree Lane the village chapel was built in 1862. It is a large building of red sandstone and can seat over 200. The stone was given free from the local quarry and villagers helped to build it, the cost coming to only £3,320. There had been a small chapel previously but that building is now used as a cattle shed.

Just past the chapel is a barn which has been converted into a house. You can still see the ventilation slits in the walls; this was the local tithe barn.

Near to the larger bridge was a place used to wash sheep; in 1935 this was turned into a swimming pool, being the earliest built in the area.

Hutton Roof 🦢

The village of Hutton Roof, which includes the hamlet of Newbiggin within its parish boundary, lies three miles to the west of Kirkby Lonsdale.

Hutton Roof is probably best known for its crags which lie to the west of the village and for the outstanding example of limestone pavements which are to be found there. The crag is a designated area of Special Scientific Interest – a tribute to both the limestone pavements and the flora which thrives on the limestone soil.

Unlike many similar villages, almost all the farms are owner-occupied and do not belong to one of the large estates in the area. There is a village hall (built and financed in the main by the villagers) and a sub-post office. There is no public house any more, but at one time there were two; the Sportsmans inn and in the late 19th century a jerry house where the navvies who were constructing the Thirlmere aqueduct which runs through the village, used to congregate.

St John's is a relatively small but beautiful church at the northern end of the village right next to the old school building. It is some years now since St John's lost its resident vicar and it is now part of the team ministry of Kirkby Lonsdale. St John's itself had a well known and respected former vicar in the person of Theodore Bayley Hardy, who served as Chaplain to the Forces in the First World War. He was awarded the VC for his gallantry in 1917 and died in hospital in 1918 after being wounded on the battlefield just three weeks before the Armistice was signed.

Despite the fact that this is a limestone area, there were in the 18th and 19th centuries several sandstone quarries within the village, which have been long since abandoned. From one of these quarries came the stone to build St John's church and another was known for producing some of the finest sandstone grindstones in the country. There are stories of the men who lost their lives in the quarries and horses and carts which fell into the pit. There is no doubt that quarrying was a hazardous business and since water – which had been a persistent and expensive problem all along – eventually got the better of them, first one and then another of them were abandoned.

With the march of time, the village is beginning to alter noticeably; not least with the number of farms which have been sold, split up and the buildings converted to private dwellings. There are also a good number of holiday homes within the village, Hutton Roof being easily accessible to the motorway and the Yorkshire and Lancashire towns. The population had been steadily declining until very recently, but with the conversion of the redundant farm buildings there has been an influx of new people to the village.

With newcomers also come new ideas and a relatively new activity within the village is the Country Fair and Fell Race held on the Bank

Holiday Saturday at the end of May. The race covers some seven miles across Hutton Roof Crag, Newbiggin Fell and Farleton Knot to finish in the village field where the Country Fair provides crafts, stalls and teas.

Ireby 🐾

A picturesque village about 550 ft above sea level, Ireby is situated just outside the Lake District National Park, with Carlisle 18 miles away to the north. It is a beautiful setting with wonderful views of Skiddaw and the surrounding fells.

It was once a thriving market town with four public houses, a saddler, blacksmith, cobbler, two funeral director/joiners, a tailor, butcher, full-time post office and other shops. The two remaining pubs are the Black Lion and the Sun (once frequented by John Peel, who lived in the neighbouring hamlet of Ruthwaite). The post office now opens only four mornings a week. The two largest employers in the village are a tarmac business and a road haulier. Apart from farming, the other businesses are builders, a coal merchant, a motor repairer, a private hotel, a horse trainer, a piano teacher and a restorer of antique clocks and barometers.

Some of the old customs have died out. It was customary when a death occurred in the village for everyone to be 'bidden' to the funeral. It was last done by Mrs Dina Lightfoot, who would call on all her neighbours (always wearing plimsolls and curlers) and bid them to the funeral. The deceased's family paid half-a-crown for this service about 30 years ago. The tradition was carried on from her mother.

The last annual Agricultural Show was held in 1956. Since the mid 1970s, a Country Fair has been held every five years to raise money for charity. People generally dress as for a Hiring Fair, which used to happen twice a year.

The most ancient building in the village is the Old Church in a field about one and a half miles from the centre of the village. It is a little 12th century edifice, only the chancel surviving; being still consecrated, a service is held there annually. It was superseded by St James's church built in 1845–6, standing at the Boltongate end of the main street, with the new rectory to the rear and a former vicarage (now Woodlands private hotel) beside it. An earlier vicarage forms part of a private house close by.

The Wesleyan chapel is now closed due to a falling congregation. Other useful buildings include the Globe Hall, bought by villagers in 1953 and managed by a residents' committee. It is the venue for weekly bingo and bowling sessions, school gymnastics, a snooker club, dances, parties and charity sales, plus the Ireby Players' productions (usually a pantomime and a summer show) and regular domino drives.

Ireleth & Askam-in-Furness

Geographically there is no division between the village of Ireleth and small township of Askam-in-Furness. However, the history of the two villages is completely different, with Ireleth dating back to the 17th century and Askam-in-Furness a comparative newcomer.

Ireleth is situated on the southern banks of the river Duddon, seven miles north of the well known shipbuilding town of Barrow-in-Furness, famous for its nuclear submarines. Eight miles to the west lies the ancient township of Ulverston. In a commanding position above the village stands St Peter's church overlooking a breathtaking view of the Duddon estuary, with the distant mountains of the Lake District as a backdrop.

In early days a packhorse turnpike road ran through Ireleth. This was used for transporting iron ore and other goods down to the shores of the river Duddon for shipment to various parts of the country. The village was also a thriving farming community with many farms practically alongside each other. Most of these are now private dwellings.

In the 17th century a free school was founded when Giles Brownrigg, who had been born in the village and made a fortune in London, gave land and established a trust to endow a school for the children of Ireleth. Later on the school also served as a chapel. With the growth of the population this school was replaced in 1862 by the present St Peter's school, and shortly afterwards a new church was built.

Adjoining Ireleth, lower down on the coast is the small township of Askam-in-Furness which owes its origins to the establishment of a large ironworks built to exploit the finding of iron ore. Smelting began in 1867 by the Furness Iron and Steel Company, and this served to give the people of Askam-in-Furness employment and the benefits of industry. Like most industrial towns of that age, long rows of terraced houses were built to accommodate the expanding workforce.

With the eventual working out of the ore, closure of the ironworks in 1919 was inevitable, and what promised to be a town of some size finished up more the size of a large village.

Askam-in-Furness is fortunate in having a beach which is noted for its profusion of flora and fauna. Many of the most striking plants have been introduced by man, including the purple flowered Duke of Argyll's tea plant and the horseradish plant cultivated since the Middle Ages. The foreshore is one of the prime breeding sites in the country of the rare protected natterjack toad. There are many local fishermen using the beach and their craft make a colourful sight moored on the leeward side of a long pier composed of slag from the old ironworks.

The villagers support an Inshore Rescue Service which has been responsible for saving many lives from the treacherous fast flowing tides of the Duddon.

There is a fine modern primary school and the town boasts its own brass band which plays at the annual carnival and fetes. The railway station built by the Furness Railway Company and opened in 1877, is a notable example of the Swiss chalet design, and still serves the community.

Irthington

About seven miles east of Carlisle and three miles north-west of Brampton is the red sandstone village of Irthington, close by the river Irthing from which it takes its name. Included in Irthington parish are the small villages of Laversdale, Newby, Newtown and the hamlets of Ruleholme and Old Wall.

Irthington lies astride the Stanegate Roman road which ran from Corbridge to Carlisle and Roman remains and coins have been discovered here. Newtown village is on Hadrian's Wall and many wall stones have been used in local buildings. Very recently a Roman well was unearthed at White Flatt.

The Norman baron of Gilsland, Robert de Vaux, had his stronghold on the mound behind Nook Farm and in 1169 gave Irthington church as part of the endowment for the new Lanercost Priory. In 1201 King John stayed here. Now a mound, covered with daffodils in spring, is the only sign of the old castle.

Cavalier Randal Mulcaster of Stonewalls, Laversdale's 'Randie with the long sword', is buried in the churchyard. Lachlan Murray, who stayed here when Bonnie Prince Charlie's army returned to Scotland, was appointed schoolmaster and parish clerk. His wife kept a shop and it is said that when short of paper she tore out pages from his church registers to use as wrappers for tea, cheese and tobacco. Several pages are missing! Growing in the hedges is a tiny white double rose and the legend is that where it grew, Prince Charlie's men were welcome 'be it a castle or a clachan'.

Many farms and cottages date back to the 17th and 18th centuries, and have peat cutting rights. One WI member cut, dried, turned and gathered peat on Breaks Moss 30 years ago. Some families have lived here for centuries. In 1854 Robert Irving was the builder in Newtown, today his descendant Robert Irving is also a builder here. Newtown was once known as 'little Ireland' because of an influx of Irish, perhaps escaping from potato famines. Some lived in weavers' cottages where they wove cloth on hand looms, and sent letters home saying 'what a fine place it was, three pubs with drinking after hours and the nearest policeman a mile away.'

The church is dedicated to St Kentigern, who perhaps preached at the 'Ha Well' (Holy Well) in the 6th century. The church has been restored though much of the chancel and chancel arch are Norman. One memorial window is for Robert Bowman who died in 1823 in his 119th year. He supposedly 'lived very abstemiously, was never drunk but once, and in his 109th year walked the 14 miles to and from Carlisle.'

Irthington has a well stocked shop and post office and there are pubs in Irthington, Laversdale and Ruleholme. The village hall built in Newtown in 1906 is in constant use. There is a good quality of life in this flourishing rural parish with its pleasant walks along paths and lonnings, an abundance of wild life and many reminders of bygone days.

Irton with Santon 🐚

Irton with Santon is a scattered parish with the hamlets of Santon, Hall Santon and Santon Bridge nestled between the hills and the sea. Approximately two miles long and one and a half miles wide, it is bounded by the rivers Irt and Mite. The Irt was once famous for its pearl-producing mussels.

There has been a church on the site of St Paul's Irton since the 13th century. It is built on an elevated position with spectacular views of the Wasdale valley. The present church, with a peal of eight bells and eleven beautiful stained glass windows, was rebuilt and dedicated in 1857. Standing in the churchyard there is an ancient Celtic 9th century sandstone cross.

About a mile from the church stands the manor house of Irton Hall (now converted to private homes). In the grounds stands the huge oak tree where Henry VI was reputed to have hidden in 1464 when seeking refuge during the Wars of the Roses.

At Santon Bridge, on the banks of the river Irt, is the Bridge inn, an old hostelry now modernised and venue for many functions, one of which is the annual Biggest Liar Competition. The village post office stands on the river bank opposite.

The parish is rich in agriculture with 25 farms in all. Many are fell farms where flocks of the famous Herdwick sheep are reared. Legend has it that this breed of sheep swam ashore from a sinking Viking ship just off the coast at Ravenglass and made their way to the hills where still today the pure Herdwick sheep is found.

The Greengarth Hostel which accommodates workers from the nearby nuclear power station at Sellafield provides employment for a number of parishioners, whilst others are employed in agriculture or commute to nearby towns.

Part of the picturesque village of Holmrook lies in the parish of Irton. The Lutwidge Arms Hotel proudly stands on the hill overlooking the river Irt. In times past an open air auction of farm animals took place here. Anglers countrywide have and still do come here for the excellent salmon fishing. Two garages serve the community, each with their own store 'open all hours'. A small reading room stands on the river bank. There is little parking here and this lovely village often goes unnoticed by the passing motorist.

Ivegill

The district of which Ivegill is the centre lies some eight miles from Carlisle and radiates from a crossroads on one of the many roads linking Carlisle with Penrith. The crossroads are overlooked by the small mid-Victorian Church of England school, which was modernised in the 1960s.

A half mile on past the lovely little Victorian church on the right and the herb farm on the left, you reach the aptly named village of Ivegill, standing in the ghyll through which flows the river Ive. Here surrounded by a cluster of houses and farms stands the old packhorse bridge, evidence of the existence of a small community dating from at least the 15th century.

At Ivegill the two main dwellings were the homes of Quaker families – Bernard Barton at Ive Bank and the Newley family at the Grange, which was reputed to be a Quaker burial ground and is still today a well preserved 16th century farm steading. Bernard Barton was apparently a man of influence having a farm and several fields bearing his name.

Follow the river to Linton Ghyll, where the old properties stand as evidence of hundreds of years of habitation, to the manor of High Head where the castle now lies in ruins after a disastrous fire in 1956. Standing amidst fields looking to the Caldbeck Fells and the Lake District hills is the old chapel of ease, built in 1358 and in the mid 19th century used as the parish church.

To the east of High Head on rising land is a further settlement of farms which is known as The Beacon, so named because it was used as a link in the chain of bonfires lit to warn the citizens of Carlisle of the coming of the Armada in the reign of Queen Elizabeth I.

The other major settlement is the Broadfield estate which lies to the east of the crossroads and nearby Itonfield. The road to Broadfield passes Macey Bank and Monkcastle and has more evidence of forest and common land of the Middle Ages at Sceugh. This estate was, in the 19th century, owned by the Oliphant family, who also owned property in Ivegill, and the compact Broadfield estate is still owned by their descendants, the Oliphant-Sheffield family.

Renovations and new housing bring to the community business and professional people from Carlisle and Penrith and retired people to appreciate the peace of the countryside, to replace the blacksmith, joiner, steam threshers, clog maker, miller, shopkeeper and butcher. It is only by welcoming the new residents can we hope to stay as an independent community with a viable church, school and village hall.

Keekle & Padstow 🕮

Our village of Keekle and Padstow is made up of four different hamlets, Keekle, Padstow, Galemire and Goosebutts.

It lies in the heart of Cumbria with a view of the beautiful fells at Ennerdale. Keekle is a row of 51 terraced houses built over 150 years ago and at one time it had three public houses and two shops.

It has a very impressive viaduct with seven arches, which used to carry a railway line from Cleator Moor to Workington, mainly used for coal from Walkmill Pit, Moresby. It was also used for passenger service, enabling people to go on day trips to the seaside. It was built in 1877 and opened for use in October 1879. The structure still stands today, now unused, but very beautiful. Quite near is the remains of an old road bridge which is seen on old photographs and can be used today to cross the river. There is a great variety of wild flowers and wildlife to be seen in this area, making very interesting nature walks.

Padstow reputedly derives its name from Padstow in Cornwall because its first inhabitants, they say, were Cornish miners who travelled to this part of the county to work in the local iron ore mines. The Ewe and Lamb at High Padstow is the only inn in the village now.

Galemire and Goosebutts, almost adjoining each other, have lovely cottages and new bungalows. The main road leads to Summergrove Hostel which belongs to British Nuclear Fuels PLC and is used for Sellafield workers. The hostel was once the lovely Summergrove Mansion, a beautiful old building in the centre of woodland. Before the turn of the century it was well kept and it contained an armoury with suits of armour standing in the hall. It also had its own private Roman Catholic chapel, modelled after the upper room, and mass was said every morning by a visiting priest. The owners, during that time, used to hold garden fetes in the grounds and music was played for dancing on the lawns. Peacocks were a great attraction strolling around, and the private gardens were a profusion of flowers and fruit.

The road from Goosebutts to Hensingham was private with a toll-gate, hence the name Sneckyeat.

One old character who was seen in the village in the 18th century was Robert Bland. He was an amateur poet and he wrote several poems about his family and the Keekle area. These poems still remain at Keekle with his great grandson, Herbert Bland, now almost 90 years old, who still plays the organ for Sunday service at Keekle Mission. The occupation of the old poet was to drive the Heslop engine at the Wreah Pit near Keekle, which was built in 1795, and it stands today in the Science Museum, Kensington, London, for preservation.

The countryside is being taken over by open cast coal mining and it is rather sad to see the beauty of the land being changed when we value the lovely scenery surrounding our village but, one day, it will be returned to its natural beauty.

Keld & Thornship

Keld, on the banks of the Lowther, has 17 homes, three of which are occupied by members of original families.

At the entrance to the hamlet is the chapel, thought to have been built by the monks of the abbey. The date of its origin, as the east window suggests, is early 16th century. The chimney was erected in the 18th century when it was used as a home by a family. It now belongs to, and is maintained by, the National Trust.

The Butter Market, now the craft shop, is visited by all who come to, or pass through Keld. Agriculture is still indigenous to the area, and others find employment in Shap, Penrith and Kendal.

At the larger hamlet of Rosgill with Hegdale is the bridge above which the Swindale beck joins the river Lowther. There are 28 houses here. Rosgill Hall was once the manor house owned by the de Rosghyll and Salkeld families. Now occupied by a farming family, this is one of the six hill farms of the area.

Opposite Rosgill Hall is what, until 1958, was the school. The swings and seesaws further up the hamlet once belonged to the school. The smithy, opposite the swings, was until the 1960s derelict. It has been rebuilt and is now occupied.

Mary's Pillar is a memorial erected by Thomas Castley to his daughter Mary, who died at the age of 24. Mary used to visit this spot, from where she had a splendid view towards the entrance to the Mardale valley, Haweswater and the surrounding hills. This view, it is said, amply compensates any visitor for the effort needed to reach the pillar.

Looking across from Mary's Pillar, due south-west, is Mardale, a once thriving village until 1935, when it was submerged to provide a reservoir for Manchester's water supply. The stones of the then grammar school were removed to build a house a mile or more from the valley, opposite Thornthwaite Hall. Remains of the people buried in the valley were interred at Clifton, and the Mardale plot in the Shap churchyard.

During very dry summers, the water has shrunk until the 'lost village' was again visible. Visitors have come in thousands from far and near to see the phenomena. A Commemoration Service to mark the 50th anniversary of the last service in Mardale church was held on 18th August 1985.

Leaving Mardale, travel east along the concrete road for two miles. Turn to the south-east, and about half a mile on, the very small hamlet of Swindale comes into view. At one time there was a church and a school, catering for the needs of the families. Today there are three farmhouses, two used by farmers, and the third occupied by a potter and his family.

Kentmere ✤

Kentmere is a peaceful valley community which lies nine miles north-west by north of Kendal. The valley has remained largely unspoilt because it lies off the main tourist route with only one access road by car.

The river Kent which rises beneath High Street, is one of the fastest flowing rivers in England. From Kentmere reservoir it flows down the valley through Kentmere Tarn and on to Staveley, Burneside, Kendal and then into Morecambe Bay. The Kent provided water power for a corn mill at Low Bridge, Kentmere, as well as a saw mill at Saw Mill Cottage where Gordon Fox now creates his much prized pottery. Along the river are traces of other mill sites and of the old smelting sites for the lead mines at Millriggs; from which Staveley now derives its water supply. At Ulthwaite, there was a fulling mill (later a corn mill) and further evidence of potash pits can be found in the area which were connected with the Kendal woollen trade.

The Kentmere Reservoir was built in 1845/46 to regulate the supply of water in the river for the mills along its banks, including the paper mill at Burneside and Cowan Head. During the 19th century the Kent powered the bobbin mills and wood turning mills at Staveley when these were in full swing, supplying the wool and cotton industries.

The oldest house in Kentmere is Kentmere Hall (14th century) which was the home of the Gilpin family – famous for killing the last wild boar in England in about 1325.

Kentmere Hall pele tower is similar to other fortified farmsteads which were built for protection against the Border raids. Further reminders of Border service in Kentmere are the Quarters: Green Quarter, Hallow-bank Quarter, Crag Quarter and Wray Quarter. These Quarters were divided into holdings, each of which provided a fighting man to defend the Border with Scotland. This was known as Border tenure and after the Union of the Crowns, James I tried to dispossess the Border tenants. A meeting was held at Staveley in 1620 to petition the King to allow their ancient custom of Tenant Right. After some years struggle the tenants were successful.

The Low Bridge inn at Kentmere, which closed in 1887, made legal history when the case Sharpe v Wakefield went to the House of Lords. Evidence then revealed that there had been an inn on the site for 300 years but it lost its licence because 'it was too far from police supervision'. The case established the absolute discretion of magistrates to grant or refuse a full licence. Reports in the *Westmorland Gazette* of the time are both amusing and illuminating. Half the population were against drink and the other half seemed to be exploiting the facilities to the full!

Kentmere church, dedicated to St Cuthbert, stands plain and simple upon a knoll in the middle of the valley; loved by folk far and near for its simple charm and the fact that it relates so well to its surroundings.

Killington 🦢

Killington is a small and delightful hamlet, with extensive farms and lands between the river Lune and Killington reservoir and Lilymere estate on the west. The hamlet itself lies in a sheltered fold of the hills in the Vale of Lune.

Killington Hall is believed to have been built by Sir James de Pickering in the 1400s – only the south wing, now in ruins, remains. The chapel of St James – renamed in 1586 All Saints – and belonging to the de Pickerings, is in regular use to this day, as is the solid silver chalice given by John Briggs of Kirkby Lonsdale in 1722.

After George Fox preached on Firbank Fell in 1652, a high proportion of the leading families of Killington, which included the Hodgsons of Hallbeck, the Alexanders, the Storeys of Bendrigg, the Parrotts of Grassrigg, and indeed the most influential of all – the Baines of Stangerthwaite, joined the Quakers. The Baines' sons – William and Joseph – helped to build Brigg Flatts Friends meeting house in 1675.

The Killington Need Fire took place in November 1840, the last which was ever lit in Westmorland, indeed even England. About 1839 a dreadful cattle sickness set in causing great suffering and ruination to the farmers. It was decided, as no cure could be found, to resort to the ceremony of the Need Fire. It was imperative to follow the rules. The fire must be lit by friction. The wood used must never have been in a house as this would nullify its magic power. The fire was covered with damp grass, straw or anything which would produce a really thick and heavy smoke, through which the cattle were driven repeatedly and exhaustively. Finally the fastest runner would seize a brand from the fire and rush to the next farm. The brand must not go out, nor could it be relit. In that year of 1840 the fire first lit in Killington was passed from hand to hand, farm to farm throughout the county of Westmorland.

King's Meaburn 🦢

The hamlet of King's Meaburn lies on high ground above the river Lyvennet and it is part of the parish of Morland.

The river normally flows gently and many children play in it in the summer. But after a storm higher up the valley it can suddenly become a raging torrent, capable of sweeping away a child or a sheep.

This is a conservation area and most of the houses are built of local stone, quarried from the village quarry. Many of them date from the 17th century, some still have their mullioned windows and at least three have court cupboards built in as partitions between two rooms. One has a cupboard bed built into its kitchen, where in the past the grandmother of the family would have been housed in the centre of all that was going on.

In the early days of Methodism the local community met in each other's houses. Then a member of the Church of England, a Mr Dent, had a vision that he should provide a meeting place for these followers of Wesley, so he built the first small chapel onto the end of a row of houses that he owned, which was greatly appreciated and used for 66 years.

The village is a haven for wildlife due to the rich variety of habitat within so small an area. The river Lyvennet runs through open farmland, then into a narrow valley with unusual cliffs of red sandstone and limestone. Trees grow precariously from cracks in the rock face, which also provide homes for numerous small animals. Part of the cliffs called Jackdaw Scar are host to a noisy colony of jackdaws, who endear themselves to the village at nesting time by filling available chimneys with sticks.

Agriculture is the chief occupation of the village but it has changed over recent years. A number of small farms have become amalgamated into larger units and some family farms have been lost. There were 16 farms and now there are only nine. The school is closed also. One farm has become a timber yard, producing fencing materials for the surrounding area. Another is the base for an agricultural contracting business. Also there is an electrical contractor and a painter and decorator, several motor mechanics, and the old school houses a falconry school.

In the centre of the village stands the village hall, built after the First World War as a thanksgiving that no-one from the village had been killed. Just beyond the hall is the White Horse pub, the village shop and post office, where local people gather to discuss the latest gossip.

Kirkandrews upon Eden 🦜

Kirkandrews upon Eden is a small village some three and a half miles west of Carlisle in the parish of Beaumont.

Hadrian's Wall passed through on a ridge of high ground overlooking the river; nothing is visible above ground now, but the occasional stone is uncovered along the river bank.

In 1823 a canal between Carlisle and Port Carlisle came through the village. This enterprise was sponsored by the manufacturers of Carlisle to facilitate the export of their goods overseas. At that time Carlisle was noted for the manufacture of checks and ginghams for the slave plantations of the USA and these would travel this way. The canal however did not prosper and 30 years later, with the development of the port of Silloth, the canal was drained and a railway built in its bed. Kirkandrews became the first station from Carlisle on this line. The station and its garden were beautifully maintained by the Hope family, and were always admired by the day trippers to Silloth who packed the trains on Thursdays and Saturdays. Sadly this railway came under the Beeching axe in 1964 and it is greatly missed.

Despite the name, there is now no 'kirk' and when exactly the church, dedicated to St Andrew, disappeared is lost in history, but the churchyard still exists.

There is no public house and no shop, but there is a post office which has been kept by the same family for several generations. There are three working farms in the village and a blacksmith. No horses are shod there now, but they do a thriving business mending agricultural machinery, making gates, etc. Osborne's Seeds also have a warehouse in the village.

Although the former station and school have been adapted as private dwellings and other houses have been divided, the last entirely new house was built some 60 years ago.

The Eden is a salmon river and it is tidal hereabouts. The fishing rights are held by local families. As well as rod fishing there was a net fishery here until recent times, the riparian owners having now come to an agreement to cease netting for the benefit of anglers higher up the river. In former times the night catches, often considerable, were despatched to the London markets from the station.

Kirkbampton 🪶

The village of Kirkbampton is pleasantly situated six miles west of Carlisle and seven miles north-north-east of Wigton. Looking north, attractive views can be seen across to the Scottish Hills and the Solway. Looking south can be seen the Cumberland Fells.

Kirkbampton is a linear village comprising today five farms, village shop and post office, public house, garage, construction company, church, primary/junior school and a bus service to Carlisle.

The village is designated a conservation area and contains a Grade I and four Grade II listed buildings – Croft House Farmhouse, Laurel House, the post office and adjoining house and Solway View House. The Rose and Crown public house was built in 1799 and stands near the church.

The parish church dedicated to St Peter is an ancient Norman structure and a Grade I listed building. Over the north entrance door is a sculptured tympanum. Only three examples of these tympana exist in Cumberland, and the one at Kirkbampton, in situ, with its surrounding arch, is probably the most perfect. A Roman stone found in the walls during restoration work in 1870–1871 is now built in the south wall of the chancel.

There seem to have been numerous defensive works in the parish against the predatory incursions of the 'mosstroopers'. The most notorious one, called Boothill, was killed in a singular manner. He was found asleep on the ground by a person called Hody who, being determined not to let the opportunity slip of freeing himself and his neighbours of a formidable enemy, coolly drew the freebooter's sword out of its scabbard and with it severed his foe's head from his body. The body of the Scot lies interred in Kirkbampton churchyard and his grave is covered with a stone on which is engraved a sword.

The old school with school master's house attached is situated at Longrigg Beck, a short distance west of the village and was built in 1876. When the new Church of England school was built in the early 1960s at the east end of the village, the old school was converted into a dwelling house.

The community spirit is strong and lively with every age catered for. Kirkbampton, despite its mushroom growth of new houses and bungalows, still retains its friendly village atmosphere.

Kirkbride 🦩

The pleasant village of Kirkbride lies to the north-west corner of the Solway Plain which fringes the head of the Solway Firth.

The church is dedicated to St Bride and was first mentioned in the Pipe Roll of 1189. It is thought the stone used in the building came from either the Roman wall or forts in the area. Many stones have traces of Roman handiwork. An archaeological dig was carried out in the glebe field to the rear of the church, when traces of a Roman street and forge were found.

A lonning leading from the church to the Marsh Road is called Wine Lonning and it is believed that it was used for smuggling wine into England and salt from the saltpans to Scotland. The wine was taken to the rectory cellar before being taken to the Wheatsheaf inn a short distance from the church. It is also believed that the Roman soldiers and monks used this lonning to take their horses to water at St Bride's Well and Monks Dyke. To the north of Wine Lonning there is a field known locally as Bloody Field where a battle is said to have taken place. Because of the blood shed, the grass remains green even in times of drought. Past businesses included four cloggers, three builders one of whom is still in existence, six grocery shops, three tailors, three butchers whose bacon and ham was renowned over a wide area, three inns, two nursery gardens from which seeds and alpines were delivered worldwide, two joiners, a toy shop, pot shop, bakery, dressmaker, corn and saw mill, saddler, post office, blacksmith, police station and two doctors. Today the post office is also a busy general store, and two of the three inns are private houses.

Turf cutting was carried out on Kirkbride and Newton Marshes and is still carried on today. One village resident well remembers turf being carted through the village to the railway station for delivery all over the country.

The construction of Kirkbride Airfield began in 1938. Aircraft were ferried across from Canada and the USA before taking part in active service. The hangers today are used for warehousing and local businesses; the officers mess is the White Heather Hotel.

Today the village abounds with leisure activities, including bowling and tennis clubs with beautifully kept greens and courts. County events are held quite frequently. Hound trailing, with successful kennels in the village, has a great following. Records show that in the 1800s horse racing was held on the marsh, as was cockfighting and Cumberland wrestling. Sports days for children go back a long way and are still continued in July with the addition now of a carnival.

The older houses of the village had peat cutting rights on the peat moss; this has now been taken over by the Nature Conservancy Council as an area of outstanding natural beauty.

Kirkby-in-Furness

The passing motorist might be forgiven for thinking that the few old houses and a cluster of new ones lying between the shop, garage and Commercial inn at one end and the school at the other, was the village of Kirkby-in-Furness: but they would be wrong. Situated on the east side of the estuary of the river Duddon, Kirkby-in-Furness is a string of tiny villages or hamlets following the line of the A595, the coastal route into West Cumbria, but mainly bypassed by it – Soutergate, Sandside, Beckside, Wallend, Marshside and Chapels – each separate yet each dependant on the others.

More correctly, and still officially, Kirkby-Ireleth, it was renamed by the railway company and the post office for their convenience. Many of the place names are of Norse origin showing a pattern of settlement for over 1,000 years. The parish church, dedicated to St Cuthbert, stands in the village of Beckside. It dates from the 12th century and has a fine Norman doorway, some early stained glass and two interesting old chests. At the top of the village is the old school, redundant in 1877 when the 'new' school was built, now used as the village hall, and the remains of a water-wheel at the side of Beckside Mill which was working until the 1940s.

Soutergate, the most southerly of the 'villages', is totally unspoiled by modern building. On a quiet afternoon, when no cars fill the narrow street, one could be in another century. Until the 1960s, there was a blacksmith's shop in Soutergate. It was here that not only horses but cartwheels were brought for shoeing. This latter was an exciting event as a large fire had to be lit beside the stream, so that when the rim was red hot and dropped into place, the wheel could be quickly plunged into the water to cool the metal and stop the wood burning. A filmed record of this, made by the late Sam Hannah, is held in the archives of Barrow-in-Furness library.

Sandside is linear, squeezed between the railway and the rock-face of higher ground. Here much infilling of new housing has taken place, not all of it homogeneous, and, extending uphill from the station, has now met that built along the main road. As well as the station, the post office, the doctor's surgery, and the Ship inn can be found in Sandside. Before the coming of the railway in 1847 small ships could tie up at both Sandside and Marshside.

Farming has always been important, and though a few farms have gone, there are many small family farms in the parish where sons are following fathers. Slate quarrying has also been important for centuries. The slate, blue-grey in colour, lies in a vein three-quarters of a mile long and estimated to be workable for at least another hundred years. Burlington Slate Limited who own Kirkby Quarries also own quarries producing light green, dark green and black slate which is all brought to Kirkby for cutting and dressing.

The manor of Kirkby-Ireleth belonged to the de Kirkby family from the Conquest until the mid 18th century. The family lived at Kirkby Hall for ten generations. The Hall, dark and sombre, with its large round chimneys and mullioned windows, dates from Tudor times, is the oldest house in the parish, and is now a working farm.

Situated on the southern boundary of the Lake District National Park, Kirkby-in-Furness has so far largely escaped the second home syndrome but there is a large, well run static-caravan park on the hillside above Chapels and reached either from there or from Wallend.

Kirkby Lonsdale

The name Kirkby Lonsdale is believed to be of Danish origin, and marauding seafarers are thought to have formed a settlement there, although nothing is now left of the original habitation.

The market dates from 1227, when a king's licence was obtained for it, and has continued to be held on a Thursday since that time. The old market place, which contains the market cross, was thought to be too small, and so the present market place was built in 1822.

It is thought that the Devil's Bridge may have been of Roman origin, but there is also an opinion that it may be Norman. A church was founded on a site on the edge of a steep bank rising from the river Lune, but the erection of the present church of St Mary on this site seems to have commenced soon after the Conquest.

Lunefield Hall, a Victorian mansion with a beautiful garden, belonged to the Bective family, and Bective Road consists of houses built for the estate workers. The site has now been turned into the first new residential area in the town.

From 1953–77 there was a flourishing fat stock market on Tuesdays, and store sales on Thursdays, but these ceased in 1977. There are, however, still regular furniture and antiques sales.

Queen Elizabeth School was founded as a free grammar school in 1591. A sum of £100 had been left towards the endowment of a school with a similar sum being raised by the inhabitants, and the school was founded under the control of 24 governors. It was formerly free to all boys in the town and neighbourhood for languages, but a payment had to be made by those taught writing and arithmetic.

There is an excellent choral society, and a very good brass band which has won several awards and has a thriving junior section. Branches of every kind of society flourish in Kirkby and the Institute sees meetings of all kinds. Concerts are held in the church, and the school is also used for functions.

The Old Market Hall still has its original wrought iron gates and the high domed windows on the first floor. Above was the Magistrates' Court, which later became a cinema, where children paid 2d to sit on benches at the front. Behind the Market Hall the hunt balls were held, and any other large function which was too big for the Institute. A local builder converted the first floor into flats, with two more flats at the back, and shops have been built on the ground floor.

Fairly recently a limestone path walk was established between Kirkby Lonsdale and Arnside – another asset to add to the many beautiful and historic features of this delightful town, which draws many tourists.

Kirkby Thore 🌿

Kirkby Thore is not the most picturesque village in Cumbria but it does have magnificent views across the Eden Valley – eastwards towards the Pennines and westwards to the Lakeland Hills. The village lies at approx 300 ft, rising to 500 ft at the north easterly end and so enjoys a very favourable climate, having a very low rainfall average of 30 inches annually.

The British Gypsum plant and mine have had a considerable influence on the area, employing some 600 men. The plant produces plasterboard and relies heavily on the prosperity of the building industry. Gypsum used to produce the plaster and plasterboard arrives by wagon, passing through the village from the mine and recent open-cast site. All this combines to make Kirkby Thore a very busy village, carrying a lot of traffic.

Recent housing development has been frustrated by the extensive Roman sites of camp and settlement of Braboniacum, and so have been built in large blocks unsympathetic to the appearance of a rural village.

The Roman settlement was at the junction where the military road from York to Carlisle joined the Maiden Way, which ran through Kirkland and Alston across the Tyne at Whitley Castle, through Gilsland to the Roman Wall and Bewcastle. There are plans to excavate the site of this camp in the near future.

The church of St Michael in Kirkby Thore is built of red sandstone and the west tower and nave date back to the 12th century. The bell, reputed to be the largest in the county, is said to have come from Shap Abbey when Henry VIII dissolved the monasteries. There is also a Wesleyan

Methodist Chapel which was built about 1800 and enjoys enthusiastic support.

The village is fortunate in having a recreation field, bequeathed to the village some years ago. There are swings and slides for the children and a changing pavilion and football pitch. An annual fancy dress parade and sports are held there. There is also an excellent village hall, built as a war memorial to the men who fell in the First and Second World Wars. The large hall is used for badminton and many other social functions and there is also a supper room and excellent kitchen.

Kirkland ❦

Kirkland is 'church land' and the oldest part of Kendal. It had its own manor court and was not absorbed into the Borough of Kendal till 1908. Kirkland village runs from Romney House, where George Romney the famous artist lived for a while before his death, to Blindbeck which once was a ford and now crosses the street in a culvert. This was the boundary which separated Kirkland from Kendal.

Kirkland's main street follows the curve of the river Kent from Nether Bridge. There is a pleasant riverside walk which goes by the Glebe, church land, to Colonel's Walk. This was so named after Colonel George Wilson, who lived at Abbot Hall in the 18th century and took his daily constitutional by the river. Abbot Hall was acquired by the Civic Trust in 1962 and is now a fine art gallery and museum open to the public. The stables belonging to Abbot Hall have been converted into the Museum of Lakeland Life and Industry.

The parish church, which dates back to the 13th century, is the second widest church in the country, having five aisles. It is a beautiful church and has much to interest visitors. By the fine church gates is the Ring O' Bells, the only public house to be built on consecrated ground, in 1741. Between the inn and the church gates there used to be the stocks and opposite the Wheatsheaf inn across the road the maypole was raised every May Day.

Kirkland used to have lots of yards filled with cottages; most of these had heavy gates across the entrances – local tradition said it was to keep out the marauding Scots. One of the prettiest of the yards is near Pembroke House – the last of the timber-framed buildings of the 17th century. Running through the yard is Cock beck, which has never been known to run dry. This flows through a culvert under the road into the river Kent.

Opposite the church gates is a 'ginnel', an old Westmorland word for a narrow entrance, which goes up to Anchorite Well. Here there used to be a religious order of anchorites living in cells of stone with small openings through which they communicated with the outside world. One of the most noted of the anchorites was Julian de Clifford, who came from an aristocratic family. He had been guilty of killing a man and in order to atone for his sins went off to fight in the Holy Land, eventually returning to become a member of the anchorite order.

Overlooking Kirkland on top of Castle Hill are the ruins of Kendal Castle. Queen Katherine Parr, the sixth wife of Henry VIII, lived here as a child.

Kirklinton 🦡

Only the name, apart from the church, remains. Kirklinton is a parish, telephone exchange and postal area; the post office is in Smithfield, the WI and Young Farmers are named after it, but those following road signs never find a place – it is a 'ghost town'.

The church was dedicated to St Cuthbert in 1374 and tradition holds that there could have been a Christian place of worship on the site in earlier times, which was one of the resting places of St Cuthbert's body during the wanderings of the monks of Lindisfarne.

A Quaker meeting house was built at Sikeside in 1688 when Kirklinton became a centre for dissenting Quakers after the Civil War. It closed in 1931 and has been converted into a house. There was a burial ground at Meg's Hill with a building, which is now an implement shed. When the roof fell in it was discovered that no nails were used, only sheep bones to hold the stones in place.

Because of its location near the head of the Solway, pack horses, cattle, pedlars, farm produce and homespun cloth would all pass on the drove roads through Kirklinton. Smithfield lies on a Roman road which ran between the Roman stations of Castlesteads (Uxeloudunum) near Brampton and Netherby near Longtown. It is now the centre of population. The hamlet which grew around the crossroads was called Redhouse (there are four houses of that name today). There was an important market at Longtown where traders from Scotland crossed the river Esk and in Georgian times dealers came from there to meet drovers and farmers at Redhouse to strike good bargains. In former years the village was commercially important, as many as fifty carriers laden with butter, bacon and grain regularly passed through from Newcastle to Longtown and much of the produce was sold here. The place was given the name 'Little Smithfield' after the famous London market, and is now officially called Smithfield.

The original school 'Cobble Rose' was situated in the field opposite the Robin Hood. Fir Ends school was built at the end of the 19th century at the sole expense of Joseph Dacre of Kirklinton Hall, who also gave the site. It is a good mile from the village and in 1968 the present school was opened.

Today, as in the past, those working in the area are mostly farmers or self employed. The school, pub, garage and post office employ a few villagers and others commute to work. In the 1980s the population of Smithfield doubled when Ryehill Park was built and there will be a further increase when the 'link' houses are completed.

Kirkoswald 🌿

Kirkoswald is situated in the fertile Eden valley, where the Raven beck from the Pennine slopes tumbles down to the flat valley floor. The Raven was a source of water power for the mills and craftsmen; woollen, paper and corn mills and a smithy are recorded. The mill race remains and from the grassy bank of the Raven it is possible to view the renovated overshoot wheel and pick out the wheel rim marks of earlier water-wheels, rubbed into the sandstone of the old corn mill.

The houses of varied shape, size and style straggle up the slope alongside the formerly cobbled street. Many of them were built using stone from the nearby Kirkoswald Castle, a powerful medieval stronghold built in the 11th century soon after the Norman conquest, devastated by Scottish border raiders, rebuilt and fortified many times. Little remains but the staircase (garderobe), tower and the overgrown moat.

The College was the home for 400 years of the Fetherstonhaugh family. The house, which contains fine oak panelling in hall and staircase, was instituted as a college of priests in 1523, and incorporates a pele tower. On the other side of the road, a walkway through lime trees leads to the beautiful ancient church of St Oswald, and behind the church on a small hill the unusual detached belfry, a Victorian replacement copying the original structure dating back to the time of Henry VIII. It is believed that the bell tower was placed here so that the sound of the bells could more easily summon the parishioners to worship.

Everywhere around Kirkoswald there is history. The oldest relics, including a Bronze Age burial urn associated with nearby Long Meg and now in Tullie House, were excavated in the same field at Old Parks as can now be found the 20th century bird bath of local red sandstone, a memorial to the naturalist 'Romany', the Reverend G. Bramwell Evens of BBC Children's Hour in the 1940s, who was a regular visitor and whose ashes are scattered here. Near Nunnery House Hotel, an attractive Queen Anne-style mansion on the site of a Benedictine nunnery until the Dissolution, is a sanctuary stone and nuns are reputed to haunt the place to this day. There are other ghosts, and there are legends. Were there really vampires at Croglin Low Hall?

When in the 1870s the LMS railway came to the Eden valley, the Settle to Carlisle line (often called the Dales line) crossed the river at Little Salkeld and so Kirkoswald was bypassed. The market town of Kirkoswald declined, while Lazonby grew. The cobbled market square is still, however, the heart of the modern village, with the post office and, on the site of the former village pump, the war memorial with the old stocks preserved alongside. Here too are the inns, one of them with the old bull baiting ring in the cobbles of its forecourt. Nearby is the manor house built for the corn mill manager. At the far end of the square, and most important of all, is the Village Hall, well maintained and well used, the meeting place for so many groups. The village school remains, as do the doctor, the village shop and the butcher. Kirkoswald is proud of its record in the Best Kept Village Contest.

Lamplugh 🐿️

Lamplugh parish extends for about six miles from north to south, and three miles from east to west. It is bounded by the parishes of Dean, Arlecdon, Ennerdale and Loweswater. At one time the countryside was covered in trees, giving rise to the couplet:

'A squirrel could hop from tree to tree,
from Lamplugh Fells to Moresby.'

The church, dedicated to St Michael, stands on the site of an old chapel. The vestry was previously part of the Lamplugh family mortuary chapel. Improvements were made in 1768, not least being the substitution of slate to replace the thatched roof. In 1870 James Lamplugh Raper, lord of the manor, provided funds to restore, enlarge and modernise the church.

The iron ore mines of Kelton and Knockmurton were situated in the parish. Opened in 1869 by William Baird and Company, Kelton at that time was the third deepest mine in England. Another mine, the 'Coronation', was opened in 1911. It was behind the Royal Oak inn, now renamed the Pack of Hounds. An aerial flight was erected to transport the coal to Asby/Lamplugh railway sidings. These closed in 1930. Other mines were at Whinnah and Murton Gate – the latter being known as 'Crutches Pit', after the engine driver, William 'Crutchy' Watson. Another local character, a woman called 'Maggie Midge', looked after the pit ponies used to transport coal from Dean Moor Colliery. Two disused limestone quarries are now used for go kart racing and clay pigeon shooting.

The row of houses at Cross Gates originally housed the navvies who constructed the reservoir at Cogramoss. Enterprises in this hamlet at the turn of the century, included John Brown's tailoring business at High House and John Edmundson's smithy at the beck, which was later demolished to make way for a new road. A building near Brook House housed Lamplugh's first school. Later used to house the local hearse, it naturally became known as 'Hearse House'. It is now used to store hay.

The Lamplugh Friendly Society was established in 1788. It is the second oldest in the country. Meetings were held in the Lamplugh Arms, another local hostelry, sadly now closed. On the second Friday in June, annually, a gala was held – starting at the school, led by the Lamplugh

Temperance Band. Following a church service, everyone returned to the Lamplugh Arms for a roast beef dinner, followed by Herb Pudding (a local delicacy).

Richard Brisco of Lamplugh Hall, in 1747 bequeathed a yearly rental of £12, payable out of Skelsmoor lands, to be distributed amongst poor widows and the school. Lamplugh Hall, now a farmstead, has an ancient feature at its entrance; an archway bearing the family crest and the date 1595. Sheep shearing was another event held at the Hall, the day ending with songs and drinks.

Lanercost & Banks 🍃

This is a community rather than a village, a few clusters of houses in the valley and a hamlet up the hill called Banks.

The focal point of the parish is Lanercost Priory, situated in the fertile Irthing valley and built in the 12th century. In the Middle Ages it saw turbulent times, being sacked by the Scots, and some of it is now a splendid ruin. This part is cared for by English Heritage and contains several tombs and memorials. Today services are held in the nave of the priory, which was restored in the 18th century to become the local parish church.

Adjoining the church is the Dacre Hall, once part of the priory, but it has also been restored and now serves as a well used, attractive village centre. It is a popular venue for many social occasions, providing modern facilities in ancient surroundings.

There have been many social changes since the Second World War but very little rural development, only 14 houses having been built in the post war period. Fortunately the small school is still open but numbers are low, reflecting today's smaller families and rural depopulation. Gone are the days when groups of children walked safely a mile or two to school enjoying what they saw – and did – on the way. Looking at the roll of honour in the Priory it is interesting to note that in the First World War 88 young men served in the forces and 20 of them were killed. Today it would be impossible to find 20 men of military age in the parish. The local post office is well supported by pensioners, but there is no village shop, lighting, or public transport and the nearest shopping centre is three miles away.

The manner of collecting rates and taxes in the parish is now very different from pre-war days. A local farmer, John Oliver, collected the rates for 50 years for an annual salary of £15, eventually rising to £60 when two other parishes were added to his workload. Twice a year he would set out on foot or horseback visiting all the houses in the neighbourhood. He was usually treated as a friend and the recipient of much hospitality, never needing to take food on his journeys. It was a very simple and efficient system far removed from the complications of today.

Hadrian's Wall, another part of local heritage, runs through the parish. Over the centuries it has been pillaged to provide building materials but there is a well preserved turret at Banks. As well as being an impressive monument it looks across a wonderful view to the Pennines. The Wall attracts tourists from all over the world which also helps the local economy, as quite a few farmhouses and cottages provide bed and breakfast accommodation during the summer.

Langwathby

Langwathby village, situated between the river Eden and the Carlisle-Settle scenic railway line, has a station used regularly for workers and students to Carlisle.

In the old days the village was purely agricultural, consisting of about 20 small 30 acre farms, situated around the village greens. One of the greens then was a pond which provided the water for the livestock, whereby each farmer produced milk for the people around, kept a few hens for eggs, a pig or two and ducks and geese, and lived very frugally, a humble type of existence. Today there are only six working farms, none of them producing milk, only beef, lamb, pork, cereals and potatoes, with one producing 25,000 eggs per day. During the last 50 years an animal feed manufacturing mill has developed and is now employing about 60 people, whilst the water mill has become defunct. There is also a poultry processing plant.

The oldest custom of the village, celebrated every third Saturday in May, is the crowning of the May Queen to give thanks for the coming of spring.

Before the erection of the stone bridge over the Eden in 1685 there as a wath (ford) which was the longest across the Eden, hence the name Langwathby. This was the main crossing for horse transport from the East Fellside to Penrith town. The bridge was unfortunately washed away in March 1968 and replaced by a steel single span structure.

The church dedicated to St Peter was modernised in 1718, with a porch added in 1836 and choir stalls in 1897. The Methodist church was erected in 1860 with a schoolroom added in 1900.

The social side of the village was started in the Assembly rooms where they used to hold 'twopenny hops', music provided by a villager playing a melodian. In 1904 a reading room was built by the local squire where concerts and plays were performed to provide entertainment, then in 1930 a new village hall was built. In the sporting world the village has provided the only professional cricketers to come from Cumberland.

Lazonby 🍂

Lazonby is a busy working village seven miles north-east of Penrith, in the beautiful Eden valley.

Ancient British artefacts, burial mounds and a Bronze Age fort have been found in the parish and the Roman fort of Voreda was nearby at Plumpton. In the North-west corner of the parish lies Tarn Wadling, now drained, which is linked to the Arthurian story of *Gawain and the Green Knight*.

The Anglican church of St Nicholas was consecrated in 1863, but records show a church here in 1272, when Sir Hugh Morvill gave it to Lanercost Priory. The present church was built by the McLeans, who built Lazonby Hall in 1848. The McLeans also built and endowed the school, complete with schoolmaster's house and caretaker's cottage. An earlier, very small, schoolhouse with an outside staircase stands on a grassy site beside the Methodist church. This is parish land and the pinfold and a blacksmith's were nearby.

The many buildings of hard red sandstone, from the quarries on Lazonby Fell, give a co-ordinated look to the village, though the architecture is very varied. A few houses date from the 17th and 18th centuries, but most buildings are from Victorian to present day. Liverpool's Anglican cathedral has steps made of Lazonby stone and some was even exported to America.

The Settle-Carlisle railway line bridges the main street and its opening in 1876 brought extra business, work and travel opportunities. The railway did not please everyone. The rector at that time objected to the proposed cutting at the bottom of his garden, and the tunnel, to the south of the village, was constructed to protect his privacy. The present rectory is beside the church.

The village grew as a farming community and is still surrounded by farmland, though residents now have all kinds of employment. At one time there were 17 farms in the village with fields in several different places in the area, and watering places were provided in the village for the animals. One of these, Will Pool at the top of the village, was landscaped as a village pond for George V's Coronation and the children love to go there to feed the ducks. The farming year still dictates much of village life.

An auction market for livestock was built near the station about 1910. Weekly sales of prime sheep are held throughout the year but the autumn sales are the biggest in northern England.

Occupying the converted engine sheds is Bell's Bakery which supplies bread and confectionery all over the county.

As well as Bell's store, which houses the post office, there is a Co-operative Society which sells everything from cornflakes to washing machines. The Society began in the kitchen at Scale Hill Farm and celebrated its centenary in 1987, as one of the last independent societies in the county.

Levens 🌿

The village of Levens, formerly called Beathwaite Green, straggles along the southern tip of Scout Scar, overlooking the Lyth valley on the west and the lower reaches of the river Kent on the east and south. The church, with its light coloured spire, stands out as a landmark when approaching from the Barrow road.

The village was originally in the parish of Heversham but the Levens church was built in 1828 by Mary Howard of Levens Hall after a disagreement with the vicar of Heversham. Methodism came to the village of Beathwaite Green in about 1790 when Stephen Brunskill of Helsington organised services. The first chapel was built in 1795. This building still exists (though now as two flats) and is the oldest Methodist building in South Lakeland. The present chapel was built in 1891.

One of the oldest buildings is Nether Levens farm built on the bank of the river Kent in the 16th century. It has an open hall with a huge fireplace surmounted by a great, round chimney. Parts of the original building are now in ruins. Further upstream, Levens Hall is a magnificent Elizabethan house built on to an earlier pele tower.

In the centre of the village an old bank barn, once a shippon and haybarn, was turned into a men's reading room in 1903. In 1970 this became the village institute and is now an attractive, well kept building, fully used by the many organisations which flourish in the village. There is an early record of a dame school in Levens but in 1810 Mary Howard of Levens Hall established a school for girls and a little later her husband started a boys school. These were amalgamated in the present school building.

Levens residents are lucky to be so well provided with services. A bus route comes through the village, the library van from Kendal comes every third week, Age Concern bring a van which provides various services for the elderly, the Health Authority provides a child welfare clinic and there is a voluntary car service. Although some shops have closed in recent years there is still a busy post office run by a very helpful husband and wife team, also a general store and a hairdresser.

At one time Levens had three inns but only one, the Hare and Hounds now remains. This is at Causeway End and in its early days would offer welcome refreshment to travellers who had crossed the mosses.

Lindal-in-Furness

Lindal is an ancient settlement, recorded in 1220 as a grange of Furness Abbey six miles away.

Church Farm is dated 1635 over the doorway, and across the road is St Peter's church, dated 1875. The lime trees stand in a straight line opposite the church. Lindal Moor Farm, overlooking the green, also originated in the 1600s but was modified in the 1880s, when along with other farms, a large number of houses and the village hall (the Buccleuch Hall) were built as part of the Buccleuch estates.

From the turn of the century until after the Second World War there were at least six shops in the village selling grocery, confectionery, general stores and fish and chips. Today there are only two shops in the village – the post office/general store and a hairdresser's.

Iron ore was mined all round the district from the middle of the 19th century to the beginning of the 20th. The area was once a maze of

The Green, Lindal

154

railway tracks and open-cast pits and shafts, but over the last 50 years it has once again reverted to natural vegetation, giving the rural agricultural appearance it has today.

On entering the village off the busy A590 one is faced by the village green – a large grassy area where sheep graze, surrounded by sycamore and horse chestnut trees and encircled by iron railings. This has only been so for about a hundred years, prior to this the greater part of the green was a tarn. On the last Saturday in June the village green is transformed from its idyllic scene to a country fair.

The village also extends to the other side of the A590 with a long row of three storey cottages – these were built for railway workers and miners. The Railway Inn is in this row. Although the railway still runs from Ulverston to Barrow, Lindal station is now closed. Due to the extensive mining subsidence takes place, and at the end of the 19th century, on the railway sidings, an engine disappeared into a 200 ft deep hole and was never seen again.

Lindal Candle Factory has recently opened in this area, a small industry which helps with local employment and provides a beautiful shop which encourages tourists to this part of Furness. There was great excitement in the village in October 1990 when it was officially opened by HRH The Princess of Wales.

Lindale-in-Cartmel

Lindale is situated on the southern boundary of the National Park, just off the A590. The construction of a bypass in the 1970s has made the village a much more peaceful place.

People living in small communities depended greatly on carriers, particularly for the supply of food. One such carrier was called Peggy Keith (c1870), who was something of a character; she smoked a short black pipe and wore a man's overcoat. She used to take her canvas-covered cart to Kendal twice a week to buy supplies to sell in Lindale and the surrounding villages. It was said Peggy never forgot a commission and carried them 'all in her head'. Unfortunately, she came to a sad end. One dark night she fell off her cart and was run over and killed. The business of carrying goods is still prominent in Lindale and both small and large haulage businesses still feature as a major industry.

At the lower end of the village, near the crossroads, is the famous Wilkinson Monument. Local ironmaster, John Wilkinson, (c1728–1808) asked that the 40 ft 20 ton cast iron obelisk be erected over his grave when he died. He had already had a cast iron coffin made for the occasion and specified that he should be buried in his garden at Castle Head, south-east of the village. Although his instructions were carried out, later owners of the house had the obelisk removed and the coffin was re-buried in the local graveyard. Among John Wilkinson's achievements was the construction of the first iron boat, which was launched on the river Winster.

The church of St Paul lies in a hollow amid a very peaceful churchyard where snowdrops abound in season. The church bell at one time belonged to the priory church in Cartmel and was used for bidding worshippers to mass. It was in disuse for some time, but on becoming the property of John Wilkinson, the ironmaster, was used for calling his workmen together. Later it was transferred to Lindale church.

There is a window in Lindale church worthy of note, situated on the north side of the church. It is a fine example of Victorian stained glass work and is dedicated to the memory of the infant James Henry Edward Kenneth Deakin. However, it is the motto beneath the family coat of arms which makes the window unique. The inscription goes back to the 15th century when Squire Giles Daykin (or Dekyn), who originated from Lindon-in-Craven, was making a good living growing and selling flax, or hemp, which he stored in his barn. The money from the sale was kept in a strong box under his bed. Two robbers planned to hide in the hemp and at the dead of night, emerge and rob Squire Giles. Whilst making their plan they were overheard by the local innkeeper, who decided to warn the Squire of the plot and whispered 'Strike Daykin, the devil's in the hemp'. The Squire acted, roused the villagers, the villains were captured and tarred and feathered. So was created the motto of the Deakins, 'Strike Dekyn – ye De'ils in ye Hempe'.

Linstock

The village of Linstock, or as formerly spelt Lynstock, lies two and a half miles east of Carlisle, near the banks of the river Eden and within a short distance of the line of the Roman wall. The village today consists of 60 homes and about 150 inhabitants, and also includes a small castle.

During the 16th century ancient Linstock Castle was still intact and was a good defence against border reivers; mainly the Armstrongs who were a Scottish clan, and who tore the castle to ruins until their capture and death. The castle was altered in 1790, when the flat roof was removed and gabled over. In 1863 the castle was sold by the Ecclesiastical Commissioners, modernised and repaired by John Nicholson who was lessee of the estate. The present owners are the Wannop family. It is said that the ghost of Bishop Irton, who died in 1283, roams Linstock Castle on the anniversary of his death.

During the early days of the 20th century many women in Linstock worked as laundresses, and washing was collected by donkey carts from Carlisle and returned later. There were also several traders in the village, including a tailor, shoemaker, joiner and blacksmith. At one time there was a school in Linstock, but when a new one was built in Crosby-on-Eden the children were transferred there. The village has lost some of its picturesque quality by the drying up of its ponds. In the olden days the cattle would be watered there night and morning, but these days troughs of fresh water have taken their place.

Employment in the village today consists mainly of farming, a local joinery and funeral directors, market garden, lawn mower repairers and pottery. The majority of the inhabitants work in Carlisle and district. Entertainment in the village mainly consists of the Women's Institute, indoor bowling and whist drives. A church service is held in the Women's Institute hall about four times a year.

Little Salkeld

On the east bank of the river Eden, halfway between Appleby and Carlisle and six and a half miles east of Penrith, is the village of Little Salkeld. The main part is built on a south facing hillside, and on a winter's night the house lights scattered across the rising ground give it an alpine appearance.

After crossing the stone bridge over Sunny Gill beck the ground rises again, and over the hill are nine dwellings situated near the old railway station and the paper mill. The station, on the Carlisle-Settle line, was built about 1874 and finally closed in May 1970 – it has since been converted into a private residence. The mill, which had previously been a manure factory, began manufacturing cardboard from waste paper about 1900, and is now the main source of employment for the immediate area. Returning over Sunny Gill beck the old corn mill is on the right. A mill was in existence on this site in 1345, and until 1974 had been in the ownership of the Atkinson family for most of 300 years. It is still water powered and today produces wholemeal flour.

The two small village greens are separated by the approach road to Salkeld Hall, which was originally the seat of the ancient family of Salkeld. It was built before the Civil Wars, but in the 1940s it became an hotel for a while before reverting into private use. Now it has been made into holiday flats. Colonel Lacy who purchased the hall in 1790 had a batman who deserted the army and came here, and rather than give his faithful servant over to the military the Colonel gave him the task of hewing out of the solid rock some caves on the river bank about a mile north of the village, which are known as the Lacy Caves and are now a tourist attraction. This batman also built a bridge over a rivulet which divides the parishes of Hunsonby and Glassonby.

In 1847 there were seven farms in the village, but now only four remain plus a small training stable.

A short distance from the Lacy Caves an alabaster mine was opened in the 19th century, and in 1953 it was reopened for the mining of anhydrite, so 14 houses were built near the vicarage to accommodate the influx of workers. The mine closed at the end of 1975 and the houses have been let or sold to other workers in the area. During the last 40 years many more dwellings have been erected so that now the red sandstone houses are being interspersed with houses and bungalows of modern materials and designs.

Before the Second World War the village was only half the size, the population consisting mainly of families whose ancestors had been in the area for generations, but today the population is more mobile and as there is no pub, chapel or shop there is nowhere for the people to meet so that most residents only know their immediate neighbours.

Public transport began declining in 1970 and now the only public service is the 'Fellrunner' mini bus, which is organised by a committee and staffed by voluntary drivers. This has been in operation for over ten years and is much appreciated by the senior citizens and mothers with children.

Long Marton 🐏

Long Marton is situated three miles north-west of Appleby, with the Pennine fells rising behind it to the north-east and the Eden valley lying westwards.

The early Norman church lies well to the south of the village and has many interesting features. It is thought to be the only church in England dedicated jointly to St Margaret and St James (the Greater), and its position probably indicates that it was built to serve the two hamlets of Long Marton and nearby Brampton. In the north-east corner of the churchyard are several graves of gypsies who happened to die while in the area for the Appleby Horse Fair, still held every June. These graves are well tended and still visited by surviving friends and relatives.

Over the beck from the church is the site of the old corn mill, and at the top of the hill approaching the village on the opposite side is the spacious Marton Hall. This was built in the early 18th century and subsequently much enlarged, and was the home of many former rectors of the parish.

One of the rectors, Rev Erskine, was a particular benefactor of the village, and it was he who initiated and financed the construction of the Institute in 1893. This dominant sandstone building stands at the junction of the roads to Dufton and Appleby, on the site of the old pinfold where the stray animals used to be kept. The bell hanging at the west end was rung when there was a fire in the village, to alert the members of the local fire brigade. Many of the cottages had thatched roofs then, and fire was a constant hazard.

The building of the Midland Railway company's Carlisle-Settle line, opened in 1876, provided employment locally, increased communications with the outside world and changed the face of the village. The road was diverted opposite the public house, the Masons Arms, and goes through the railway embankment under a bridge to rejoin the Milburn road a little further on. This made the northern part of the village, with

Town Head Farm at the top, into a cul-de-sac. Long Marton station was closed in 1968 and the building now belongs to a school.

Until the turn of the century the life of the village was largely based on agriculture, and was fairly self-sufficient. In 1880 the population was 709, and there were three grocers, two shoemakers or 'cloggers', two clothiers, two butchers, two blacksmiths and farriers and a washing agent. Nowadays the village has a post office and general store, and a butcher's shop. Other local businesses include a joiner, a wrought-iron worker, a furniture restorer, a market gardener and a plant hire firm. There is now only one farm in the village and most people earn their living elsewhere.

Longsleddale ✑

Longsleddale runs west off the A6 for six miles to the pass over to Haweswater. Very good slate was quarried from mines on the pass worked by Italian prisoners during the war. It was abandoned suddenly when they were sent home – tools laid down, jobs half done.

The first St Mary's church was probably built in the 13th century. The third building was rebuilt in 1863, as were the parsonage and school. Yewbarrow Hall incorporates an old pele tower. Kilnstones was once inhabited by monks, and in the 1600s provided hospitality for pack-horses and travellers on their way to Scotland. Two old packhorse bridges still exist.

In the 1930s a huge pipeline was laid the length of the valley, bringing water from Haweswater to Selside for Manchester. Traces of the work-men's camp can still be seen near the head of the valley.

The last few years have seen the amalgamation of farms with farm-houses being sold. There are now only seven working farms in the valley, while the resident population is just under 70.

Longtown ✑

Longtown's name first appears in 1584. Netherby, the home of the Graham family, lies two miles north of the town and Arthuret church half a mile to the south. The attractive five-arch bridge built in stone in the 1700s spans the Esk river, which is famous for salmon fishing.

The village was more important in the days of the stage coaches when the main route to Edinburgh passed through the village. There was then a cattle market which was a rival to Carlisle. The Graham Arms is an old coaching inn. The houses were built mostly in the 1700s by Dr Robert Graham, who also planned the town.

Longtown is situated in the parish of Arthuret and has long laid claim to connections with the legendary King Arthur. In 1669, the rector wrote in the parish register: 'Arthuret has its name from the famous King Arthur, King of the Ancient Britons, in whose time there was a battle fought here, probably on the moor of the same name.' The battle took place in the 6th century and according to legend 80,000 were slain. A further battle involving Arthur's mentor, Merlin, took place just north of Longtown, at Carwhinley. As a result of this battle Merlin is thought to have lost his mind, and wandered the forests for 40 years. Arthurian expert Dr Norma Goodrich has named Arthuret as the last resting place of the legendary monarch.

Arthuret church of St Michael was built in 1609 and an interesting gravestone can be seen erected to Archie Armstrong, who was born in Longtown and who was jester to Charles I. He was, appropriately, buried on 1st April 1672! Just beyond the walls of the church lies St Michael's Well, a holy spring for many centuries.

Dr Graham helped bring the Carlisle-Edinburgh railway line through Longtown, which was a great asset. From 1802 many people became weavers for the mills in Carlisle and many sheds were built behind the houses. One road now called 'The Shades' was originally 'The Sheds'. In 1851 the bobbin mill was built by the English Cotton Co, along the Brampton Road; this provided much employment especially for women. By 1860 Longtown had become a prosperous community with eight bootmakers, seven grocers, seven tailors etc. There were also eight public houses, one of which on Esk Street, was reputedly visited by Robert Burns. Some of these have been converted to houses and businesses but the names have been perpetuated.

Longtown then saw a period of decline but new ventures have brought more prosperity to the area, although agriculture remains the main occupation. The cattle mart is thriving and becoming one of the largest in the country. The nearby ponds attract a wide variety of birds, including the rare smew, which is an attraction for many bird watchers. The Catholic church, which is associated with Dr Rutherford, was built in the 1940s. Few people are now employed at Netherby. Sir Charles and Lady Graham now live at Crofthead and Netherby Hall has been sold.

The community centre offers a focus for sport and recreational facilities. Longtown unfortunately lost its historic Waverley Line, but communications are now much better generally. The rugged independence of the people has not disappeared and the strong sense of community was evidenced by the tremendous support given to the successful struggle to retain Lochinvar School.

Lorton 🦋

'Lorton, a little village lying in a fruitful valley, surrounded by high mountains, the sides of which are covered with grass and woods, and the bottom watered by two small rivers.' So wrote John Wesley in 1752.

Today, the countryside remains much the same – perhaps a little less wooded. The village itself retains its traditional character with slate-roofed houses mostly between 150 and 300 years old, although a few modern bungalows and conversions have appeared.

The 'roaring stream' had greater significance in the past in that it provided the necessary power to run a brewery and a thread mill. The well known Jennings brewery originated in Lorton in 1828. As the business grew it moved to Cockermouth in 1887, where it still operates at the Castle Brewery. The original brewery maltings still exists as the village hall. A slate building with a slate roof and the original slate floor, it has changed little over the years.

Apart from the brewery and thread mill, there were also two corn mills, a saw mill, two smithies, a grocer and post office, baker, joiner and cobbler. All have long since vanished, though a post office plus shop provide a much needed service and meeting place for many of the local inhabitants. Farming has always played and continues to play an important part in Lorton's way of life. Redundant farmhouses and barns in the village have been converted to holiday cottages, with tourism becoming a significant aspect of the village.

The village hall was named the Yew Tree Hall in recognition of the large yew tree behind. Reputed to be over 1,000 years old, the tree was immortalised in 1803 by William Wordsworth in his poem *Yew Trees*.

This tree has played an important role in the history of Lorton. George Fox, the great Quaker preacher, preached here in 1652, noting that the 'tree was so full of people that I feared they would shake it down'. It is thought that a guard of Cromwell's soldiers, stationed at Lorton, kept the meeting in order.

Lorton church, dedicated to St Cuthbert, is an early 19th century Gothic building. It is still used for a service each Sunday and also frequently hosts musical concerts with artists from the Northern Sinfonia and local choirs. The Methodist chapel, once called the 'Wesleyan Preaching House', is a tiny, one-roomed building where John Wesley preached to a 'large and serious congregation' in 1752, 1759, and 1761. Today, the chapel is only used for one annual service.

Until recent years both High and Low Lorton boasted a local pub, the Horseshoe and the Wheatsheaf respectively. The Horseshoe was called the Blacksmith's Arms but the name was changed when the smithy operating beside it was demolished and the inn extended. Sadly, it closed in 1990.

Low Row 🌀

Low Row, in the parish of Nether Denton four miles east of Brampton, was originally High Row, Middle Row and Low Row. Until the 1960s it could be called a 'family village', many residents being related by birth or marriage. Today the village is enlarged and there has been an influx of newcomers who commute to work to Brampton or Carlisle.

Until 1970 most of the working population of the village was employed by Carricks, in their factory on the south side of the Carlisle to Newcastle railway line which runs through the centre of the village. Carricks started as a creamery making butter and cheese and progressed to sausages, pies and a laundry. They built houses for the workers. Dairy Cottages was also a blacksmith's shop, pub, post office and school until a village school was built in 1874 – now closed. Today the cottages are homes with only the post office still there, but at the opposite end.

The church of St Cuthbert is outside the village. Rebuilt in 1866 there used to be a door at the back (now bricked in). It is said that every Sunday before service, the vicar opened this door and chased out the devil. One Sunday school the vicar closed his eyes for the closing prayer, the children opened this door and silently crept out, leaving the vicar to wonder, when he opened his eyes, if his congregation had been spirited away by the devil!

The village shop was built a century ago – made of tin and completely lined with wood. The interesting feature is that today it is exactly as it was then, complete with rows of small drawers for dried goods. The old scales and coffee grinder are still on view in the shop. The house was built on in 1910 and the present owner, Isabel Burn, is the third generation of her family to run this business.

There is in Low Row a charitable trust known as The William Hodgson Trust. This was formed in 1856 when William Hodgson donated a field to the parish whereby the rent be given to the poor. The field was sold in the 1980s and the yearly interest on the money is given to pensioners and widows of the parish.

Low Row started as a hamlet, grew to a village and practically died with the closure of Carricks, the railway station and the school. Now with more houses, the younger generation and their children and new families joining into village life, the village has come alive again.

Loweswater ✺

Looking over Crummock to Buttermere is said to be one of the loveliest views in the North of England.

The village of Loweswater is very scattered, it extends for three or four miles along the road which winds along the narrow strip of comparatively flat land between the fells and past the lake of Loweswater. The only two adjacent buildings are St Bartholomew's church and the Kirkstile inn. There are in addition, one hotel, many farms and several houses, some of which were once working farms and some now used as holiday homes. The former little school was altered in 1956 into a village hall, which now provides Loweswater and surrounding districts with many amenities.

Apart from fell walking and tourism, the two main things for which Loweswater is noted are the Melbreak Foxhounds and the local Agricultural Show. Loweswater lies in the heart of the Melbreak country and takes a lively interest in the various hunts.

The Loweswater Show is held on the third Thursday in September and come rain, hail or shine all roads lead to Loweswater on that day. Set in the magnificent setting of the school field it boasts one of the finest industrial tents in the county and has many added attractions including a craft fair, hound trails and sheep dog trials.

Thackthwaite lies along the back road which joins Lorton to Loweswater. It is a straggle of houses and farms which have almost all changed hands in the last 30 years, resulting in a great change of population. Mockerkin is a tiny hamlet, which has as its main characteristic a sense of continuity, its farms remaining in the same families.

The whole area lies within the precincts of the National Park and much land is owned by the National Trust.

Lowick ✥

Perhaps the most spectacular view of 'The Vale of Lowick' can be obtained from the A5092 road (leading to Whitehaven) about three quarters of a mile past its junction with the Coniston road. From this point, a panoramic view of the whole valley opens out with Blawith and Torver fells behind and, in the distance, Coniston Old Man, Dowcrags and Wetherlam. The area consists of farmsteads and cottages, but the main consolidation of houses fall into the villages of Lowick Bridge and Lowick Green, with a small group at Woodgate.

The church, situated in a magnificent setting, is dedicated to St Luke and was rebuilt in 1818 and 1884/5, but records indicate that a chapel existed prior to 1577.

On the first Saturday in September, locals and visitors alike enjoy the 'Laal Royal' – the agricultural show, established in 1857 and still going strong.

The village of Lowick Bridge forms a ribbon of houses on the road leading to the church, and contains the Red Lion inn. Formerly the village housed a smithy and a joiner's shop, also a corn mill, which dated back to 1250 and operated until after the Second World War.

Lowick Green, on the other hand, forms an attractive triangle encompassing the village green. Its varied early industry included two tanneries, a spade and shovel factory, a smithy and several swillers, who fashioned coracle-shaped baskets, woven from strips of oak which were boiled to make them supple. These baskets were supplied in large numbers to the Lancashire mills amongst other customers.

Perhaps the most unusual cottage industry was carried out from

Beckbottom, where a family, enjoying common rights, bred geese. These birds, with their feet tarred, were walked some 20 miles to Kendal market to be sold at the Martinmas fair, following which the family returned, laden with whalebone, which they proceeded to convert into corsets. Although it would be impossible to top that, the village still boasts a small screen-printing workshop situated adjacent to Lowick House.

Lowther 🖋

Lowther is synonymous with the Lowther family, which is of great antiquity in the old counties of Cumberland and Westmorland, now known as Cumbria.

Lowther is also the parish name, with the villages of Lowther, Lowther Newtown, Hackthorpe, Melkinthorpe and Whale within its boundary. The river Lowther is the westerly boundary to the beautiful park, with the magnificent facade of the castle to the south and the church to the north.

The 18th century Lowther village, as known today, is situated between Lowther Newtown and Hackthorpe. The houses are in three groups, and housed estate workers. This village is now owned by the Lowther & District Housing Association who modernised the houses inside, reducing the number to 26. The old village of Lowther was pulled down in 1682 by Sir John Lowther as it was in front of Lowther Hall, the site of the present castle, which he wanted to enlarge. The village of Lowther Newtown was built afterwards, including a laundry and a carpet factory.

Between Lowther village and Hackthorpe on the A6 there is Lowther endowed school. This was founded in 1635 by Sir John Lowther, his uncle Richard Lowther, and John Teasdale, rector of Lowther. Opposite the school is the parish hall, built 1932/3, where community events are held.

The local public house, the Lowther Castle Hotel, has a bar named the Court Lounge to mark the days when the room was the venue of fortnightly sittings of the West Ward Justices on alternate Mondays. These were transferred to Shap in 1963.

The house named The Hermitage was where Jacob Thompson, the artist, lived. He was a student of the Royal Academy, returned to Westmorland in 1840, and was provided with the Hermitage by the then Lord Lonsdale. Jacob Thompson painted landscapes of the Lake District and portraits. He died in 1879 and his tombstone is in Lowther churchyard.

Melkinthorpe is about three miles eastward from Lowther church with houses either side of a cul-de-sac, which now has a garden centre. The family name of Kendall goes back a very long way, being yeomen farmers; the last heir lives at the end of the village. Whale is a small

St Mary's Church, Mallerstang

hamlet at the southern end of Lowther Park, mainly concerned with farming.

The old home of the Lowther family was Lowther Hall, the main part of which was burnt down in 1720. The family lived in the west wing until in its place the magnificent castle was built in the early 19th century designed by Sir Robert Smirke. A mammoth 22 day sale of the treasures of Lowther Castle was held in 1947, and another one in the 1950s.

Lowther church is a very ancient building with pillars and arches dating between 1175 and 1300. On the mound to the left at the entrance to the churchyard where the 5th Earl of Lonsdale is buried, Norse hog back gravestones were found which date from about AD 950. These are now on display in the church porch. The mausoleum on the left is where some of the Lowther family were buried, and the church itself is full of memorials to the family.

Mallerstang

Mallerstang is a very quiet and remote unspoilt valley. The sheer cliff face of Mallerstang Edge dominates the eastern side of the dale and the dramatic outline of Wild Boar Fell the western side. The last wild boar in England was killed here in the 16th century.

The famous Settle to Carlisle railway line runs the whole of the western side of the dale and often throughout the year there is a touch of nostalgia when one of the great steam locomotives pounds through the dale. Many hundreds of men lost their lives building the line and some are buried in the churchyard at Outhgill.

This is the centre of Mallerstang, a small hamlet that not so long ago had a village hall, school, shop, post office, chapel and church. Sadly only the church has survived, with the post office only open so many hours a week. The father of the great scientist Michael Faraday was the blacksmith here 200 years ago.

The charming little church of St Mary was built in the 14th century. The first things to catch the eye on entering the church are the kneelers, these are displayed on the hymn book racks for all to see, each depicting some aspect of local life; hand embroidered and designed by the late Miss Betty Rothwell. The simple interior includes a stained glass window dedicated to the saints of northern England and an old coat of arms of Lady Anne Clifford. Next to the door there is a set of shelves which used to hold the loaves of bread for the poor of the valley. The bread is still distributed today under an 18th century charity.

The church was restored by Lady Anne in 1663. She often travelled between Appleby and Skipton making an en route stop at Pendragon Castle. This is now a ruin which lies just below Outhgill. According to legend it is named after Uther Pendragon, King Arthur's father.

Modern day Mallerstang is still mainly a farming community but in the last few years has seen many changes, with houses falling empty and new people moving into the dale, many of them travelling to their work; there are several holiday homes, a tea room/craft shop, two hotels and two bed and breakfasts.

Matterdale ✍

Matterdale, a parish that runs the length of a peaceful valley from the main Penrith to Keswick road to Ullswater, is famous for Wordsworth's daffodils. It is a dale of scattered farms and cottages. At one end lies the hamlet of Matterdale End and at the other the attractive village of Dockray. Matterdale, derived from 'Madderdock', was named from the madder, a red-rooted plant that was used to make a dye.

At the turn of the century Matterdale could boast its own butchering house, blacksmith, shoemaker, sawmill, cornmill, dressmaker and two general stores. There was no running water in those days, water was carried in buckets from the spring on the common and the farmers took it in turns to water cattle at the beck on the village green. There was no electricity either and tallow candles or paraffin lamps were used for lighting. 'Peats' were used for heating and every homestead had a right to cut peat on Birks Moss.

The children went to school on foot and many had several miles to cover, carrying their packed lunches with them. The original school, on a one and a half acre site on the fellside above the church, was erected by Rev Robert Grisedale.

The present Matterdale church, built in 1686, replaced the original smaller church and is a typical Cumbrian building of greystone walls, low pitched slate roof, ancient beams and small oblong nave windows. The only stained glass window is the deep set east window depicting the Holy Nativity. The wide bench by the door is still used for coffins at burial services as in the old days.

The Royal Hotel in Dockray was built in the 16th century as a small coaching inn. It has been extended and renovated several times. It has been said that Mary, Queen of Scots stayed there, and also William and Dorothy Wordsworth. The Royal is still the meeting place of locals and visitors alike and many a good 'sing-song' can be heard following a meet of the local foxhounds.

Farming and tourism are the two main occupations in Matterdale today but whereas there used to be 37 small farms there are now only seven larger ones. Many of the smaller farmers also worked at Greenside lead mines and walked to Glenridding over the fells on Monday morning staying for the week in small stone built huts known as the shops.

The famous huntsman Joe Bowman was born at Matterdale in 1850 and he died not far away at Glenridding in 1940. He came of hunting stock, his mother Mary Dawson being a direct descendant of no fewer than seven generations of huntsmen. 'Auld Hunty' as Joe was commonly called has been immortalised in a famous hunting song written by Dr Walker who lived at Southport. The Ullswater pack of hounds was the product of an amalgamation in 1873 of a pack based at Baldowe, Matterdale, with the Patterdale hounds. These hounds are still boarded out in the summer at some of the local farms.

Melmerby

Melmerby is situated on the A686, ten miles east of Penrith on the edge of the Eden valley. It is a picturesque village with almost every house overlooking the green, which is some 14 acres in area. It nestles at the foot of Hartside Pass, originally a turnpike road leading over the Pennines to the old lead mining area of Alston Moor. The Penrith to Alston toll road was one of the best managed in the district and was eventually taken over by the County Council in the late 19th century.

The population of the village was 191 in 1891 and today it is 177. Many trades and businesses flourished in the late 19th century, supported by passing travellers using the turnpike road. The village had three inns, two blacksmiths, tailors, shopkeepers, a shoemaker, a miller, a carpenter, a stonemason, post office, seed dealer, many farmers and a lead mine at Melmerby scar. At the present time there are still several small businesses although some residents commute to Penrith. There are now nine farms in Melmerby Parish, an inn, bakery and restaurant, printer, caravan site, sawmill, post office and shop, agricultural contractor, and holiday accommodation.

The extensive village green is dissected by three becks with varied woodland and wild flowers. Each householder has grazing rights; horses are grazed more commonly now but earlier this century it was more usual to see large flocks of geese grazing, and there was once a cottage industry making pillows and mattresses from goose feathers.

May Day at Melmerby takes place on the second Saturday in May each year. The custom began in 1925, originally sponsored by the vicar and the village schoolmistress. The format has changed very little over the years although there is now no Morris dancing, and the elm tree under which the ceremony took place has sadly been cut down.

The parish church of Melmerby dedicated to St John the Baptist is situated on the edge of the village, close to Melmerby Hall, the first known rector being presented in 1332. The school was built around 1860 and is unusual in having a church-like clock tower. It was eventually closed in 1974. The residents of Melmerby Hall, the manor house, also own several properties, farms and sporting rights in the locality. There has been a record of a lord of the manor here since the reign of Henry III.

Melmerby has changed considerably over the years, with many small farms being absorbed into larger units. Closure of the school and Methodist chapel, road improvements and the demise of public transport have resulted in most households owning at least one car, and travelling many miles for school, work and shopping. Fortunately Melmerby is still a working village with a community spirit. During the summer months there are many visiting holidaymakers but, despite this, the village still retains a peaceful atmosphere.

Middleton

Middleton is bounded on the west by the river Lune, with Middleton Fell rising to the east. The northern boundary is Rawthey Bridge, where the Lune and Rawthey meet. Scattered farms, houses, two inns and the church are set in beautiful countryside. The main road, completed in 1778, leads to Sedbergh six miles to the north, and to Kirkby Lonsdale six miles to the south. Apart from farming the only industries are the joiner's workshop, the fish hatchery and a bottled gas depot. Young people who are not employed on the farms, mainly go to work at Kendal, twelve miles away.

A Roman road ran through Middleton and a fine Roman milestone stands on a hill near the church. This was ploughed up and re-erected in 1836. The inscription 'MPL 111' is thought to be the distance in Roman miles to Carlisle. The other Latin words were added on the instruction of Giles Moore of Grimeshill and mean 'Restored from the soil by Giles Moore'.

The church of the Holy Ghost was built in 1878 and was preceded by two earlier buildings erected in 1634 and 1813. There are two stones bearing these dates built into the churchyard wall. Inside the church are many fine stained glass windows, including one with the artist's error giving the blind beggar two right feet!

Middleton Hall, now a family farm, was once the manorial residence.

It was for centuries the home of the Middleton family and is a splendid example of domestic architecture of the 15th century, the huge curtain wall being a spectacular feature. Grimeshill, later the manorial residence, was demolished in 1938. The original gardener's house has been extended and renamed Grimeshill and is now the home of the present heir to the Middleton estate. In days gone by nearly all the cottages were occupied by those who were employed at Grimeshill, such as the laundress, gamekeepers, cattlemen and coachmen.

There are two attractive old inns; near the church is the Swan and two miles along the road is the Middleton Fells. The latter was originally the Railway Inn, so called because a farmer who lived there during the 1860s began selling beer to the men employed in laying the new railway and it has been an inn ever since.

Ever since the monasteries established flocks to graze the fells, centuries ago, sheep farming has played a significant part in the life of the area. Some years ago the annual sheep clipping held at Middleton Hall was a great social event. Over 300 guests were invited and after the work was completed, there were sports followed by feasting, music and dancing in the great banqueting hall. The invention of electric sheep shears was largely responsible for the demise of these great gatherings on the farms.

Milburn 🌿

Milburn is a classic example of a medieval fortified village, with houses built around the ancient village green. Outside the village to the southeast, but still within the boundaries of Milburn parish, is Howgill Castle, the former manor house, dating from the 14th century. Although the castle has undergone a number of architectural changes during the past centuries, much of the interior of the two pele towers has been lovingly restored by its present owner, as also was the adjoining watermill, which is now in regular use driving the machinery for sawing timber.

The village green has been used as common land for centuries and some of the present inhabitants still retain their grazing rights on it. Near to the middle of the green is the maypole, sadly no longer used as such, but believed by some to have been erected on an ancient Celtic burial site. The present maypole, replacing a long line of similar maypoles, was erected quite recently and is about 50 ft high and topped by a weather-vane.

The village shop/post office, regretfully, is no longer part of the village scene but the village pub, the Stag, situated just outside the village at Gullom Holme, has a name for good food and is well patronised. The main occupations remain centred on livestock and sheep farming, with local farmers having extensive grazing rights for their sheep on Milburn Forest. The nearby gypsum mines and plaster works at Kirkby Thore no longer provide work for as many employees as they once did, so villagers find employment in the nearby towns of Appleby and Penrith.

Cross Fell, Milburn

St Cuthbert's, dating from Norman times and built of red sandstone, was set apart from the village because, as some believe, it would have been safely hidden away from the marauders from the north, who would cross the borders to descend upon the fellside villages to rustle cattle and to plunder.

An ancient custom occurred on Saturday nights, known as 'Butt hill nights', when lads of the village would remove gates and set them round the Butt hill. They would then gather together other people's household goods – brooms, buckets etc, even washing from lines, and set them round the maypole to be retrieved by their owners the following day. That custom, thankfully, has died out but children do still remove gates on Hallowe'en night which often need to be rescued from the bonfire before the annual bonfire party held on Guy Fawkes' night. The green is also the scene of the annual village sports which culminates in the exciting 'round the green' race. Schoolchildren have the freedom of the green as far as the maypole during playtime, and it is a pleasant sight to see them taking lessons under the shade of the horse-chestnut tree on hot summer days.

Milnthorpe 🌿

Milnthorpe is an 'in-between' sort of place; a town by population and size, but a village by nature and character. It sits astride the A6 between Kendal and Lancaster and the Arnside to Crooklands road, and where the two roads meet at the traffic lights is its busy hub.

A market town since the 14th century, it has always been a 'work-a-day', down to earth place. Trades and industries have come and gone with the changing times; Libby's factory on the outskirts of the village near the station presently provides some employment. It is now owned by Nestle's and no longer processes milk, instead fruit canning and sauces are the main products. Houghton's Coachworks on Park Road manufactures bodies for lorries and is now building a huge extension behind the row of houses at the lower end of Church Street. The river Bela skirts the south-west corner of the village, running past the comb mill (still manufacturing combs today, though of synthetic material not ivory, horn or tortoiseshell), and through Dallam Tower park on its way to meet the Kent at the estuary. Until c1880 the Bela was navigable as far as the Strands, now an attractive river side walk.

Interesting architectural features of the village are the folly at St Anthony's Hill, known as St Anthony's Tower or the Summerhouse, and now almost surrounded by brash new housing; and the Market Cross on the Square. There is not, in fact, a 'cross' but a weather-worn column with ball finial set on limestone steps. The Cross was the village crying-stone for proclamations and the like, and also served as a whipping-post for wrongdoers. At the opposite end of the square is the fountain, once the main village well, and the spring can still be seen underneath the grating today. Also on a corner of the Square, but not an architectural feature, are often to be found little knots of men, known locally as 'the standers'! Possibly the oldest corner of Milnthorpe and one of the most attractive, is Harmony Square, with cottages set around a green.

There are several greens dotted around the village, the largest one in front of the Victorian church of St Thomas and adjacent to the Square, where markets and fairs were held from the 14th century. The existing Friday market was revived in 1966.

Monkhill 🌿

This small hamlet situated at a crossroads approximately four miles west of Carlisle, is approached on three sides by a hill which causes cyclists to dismount and pedestrians to be pleased when the hilltop is reached!

The east/west road would have been the basic route of the early Roman settlers to the coast. Later came the men who drove cattle, sheep, pigs and even geese to and from Carlisle and Silloth docks via the coastal road of Burgh Marsh, where the river Eden broadens out to become the Solway Firth. The north/south road would have been one of the routes used by the invading Picts and Scots and later it too would be used by the drovers who brought their animals across the narrowest, shallowest part of the river Eden, from the Scottish Borders to the western area of Carlisle and Wigton. That they paused for rest and refreshment at Monkhill is evident by the name of the local pub the Drover's Rest.

At the edge of the crossroads are two well known landmarks, a small but well supported Methodist chapel and the remains of a windmill (complete with grinding stone) soon to be developed into a house. A few hundred yards away once stood a water-mill, powered by water from Monkhill Lough. These have both now disappeared; of the mill nothing remains, while the lough, once a popular venue for ice-skating and curling, has been drained into the swift running Monkhill beck. Water from the lough has been used on two occasions to put out fires at Monkhill Hall, the first in the early 1930s when a human bucket chain was formed and again in 1971 when firemen's hoses were used.

In 1940 there were six dwellings, a public house and three farms. While the public house and two farms remain, there are now 14 dwellings, nine of which are bungalows, and 35 residents.

Moor Row 🍃

Moor Row is a small village situated off the A595 between Whitehaven and Egremont. The first early settlers were farmers, who occupied three or four surrounding homesteads. Late in the 19th century, the land in this area was found to be rich in iron ore deposits and, in the development of the iron ore mines, many Cornishmen with their particular knowledge of mining, came to the area with their families. The village developed resulting in terraced houses being built. In fact one of the streets, Penzance Street, is a reminder of the Cornish influence.

Early in the 20th century Henry Bonney MA, the school's headmaster, became renowned throughout the area. Many students later became famous in their own right as professors and lecturers in various universities and colleges.

With the Cornish influx, the chapels were numerous and services were held on Sundays and often mid-week by the Wesleyans, Primitive Methodists and what was then called the Free Church. Many activities centred around these establishments, especially for the younger generation.

The decline of the railways and the iron ore mines left a large gap, to be filled by the advent of the Sellafield nuclear complex. Nowadays there are just two shops remaining – a post office and a general store.

Unfortunately the three chapels are no more. One was converted into a garage, one divided into two houses and one has been demolished and a bungalow built on the site. The Church of England hold a service on Sunday evening in the village hall, originally constructed over a hundred years ago by the then contractor in the village.

The latest development on the old railway tracks is the landscaping and construction of pleasant walks and nature reserves. All the old mining shafts have been filled in as a safety measure.

Moor Row is mentioned in the first section of A. Wainwright's Coast to Coast walk. The hikers all walk through the village and inhabitants marvel that our small and rather insignificant village is a source of interest to those who come from all over the world in their eagerness to follow the Wainwright walk.

The latest development is the establishment of a science park at Ingwell, where the government and the nuclear power establishment have taken over the pleasant site of an old mansion and woods near Moor Row.

Moresby 🌿

To the Roman soldier of the Second Thracian Cohort climbing the steep track which led inland from the fort at Gabrosentum, the countryside in the 3rd century AD would have looked very different from today. Over the brow top, what is now an open, windswept, and at times rather bleak area, was then and for many centuries afterwards, thickly wooded. The fort was for a time the last in a chain of forts, a day's march apart, running along Hadrian's Wall and down the Solway coast, and built to keep at bay the Picts and the Scots who 'greatly infested these parts'.

Moresby Hall was built on the site of the old Roman civic settlement alongside the fort, and is one of the many places at which that unhappy lady, Mary Queen of Scots, was said to have stayed. A priest's hole, known to have been used at the time of the Reformation, still exists in the Hall, and the story goes that the Squire hid a Roman Catholic friend of his here, but then had to make a hurried and unexpected departure from home. As no-one else knew of the presence of the fugitive, the unfortunate man died from starvation.

During the course of the following centuries other mansions appeared nearby – the homes of members of the 'big' families in the district. For generations they mined the coal which lay under their land and exported it from the tiny harbour at Parton. For a time this trade competed in volume with that from nearby Whitehaven, to the alarm of the Lowther family of that town.

These early mines were shallow day-holes, also known as 'bell-shafts', but in 1876 the Moresby Coal Company opened up the Walkmill mine and the centre of gravity of the parish changed from the site of the old Roman fort to the higher ground, a little inland, when 'Moresby Parks' came into being. Eighty stone cottages were built to house the miners

173

who were to work the new mine, and in the early days the mine manager lived at No 1. As befitted his position, his house was equipped with an indoor tap – his neighbours had to share the two or three outdoor taps to each row of houses.

The present parish church, St Bridget's, built on the site of the Roman fort, has existed since 1822. Other earlier churches have occupied the same ground, and the chancel arch of the old church, left standing alongside the new building in 1822, appears to date back to the 13th century.

Today, due to the continuing presence of coal beneath the surface, the hand of the National Coal Board can still be seen in opencast mining in the Moresby area. The worst scars in the village have healed, however, and what was a deep hole is soon to be a brand new municipal golf course on the outskirts of a village whose residential area is growing fast.

Morland

The village of Morland is a delightful 'picture-postcard' village in the Eden valley, eight miles south-east of Penrith.

In 1362 Morland obtained a grant to hold a weekly market and an annual fair, and was an important coaching centre. Morland has the only 11th century Saxon tower in Cumbria still in use today, at the west end of the parish church of St Lawrence.

Morland beck and mill race once turned the wheels to power the small mills that stood on the banks of the beck some two centuries ago. One of these mills produced coarse linen goods and another tape, thread and other small wares, thus providing employment for some of the local people of that time.

The main street, aptly named Water Street, follows the beck and mill race. Two small footbridges and a ford lead to the small village green. Across the ford at South View a barn has been converted to a music room where concerts are held with professional musicians taking part. Also on that side of the beck stands the old Quaker meeting house, now a dwelling, as is the Methodist chapel opposite. Over the hump-backed bridge, passing the cricket field on the right, can be seen several old lime kilns, the lime from which was used in the rebuilding of Morland. Today Morland is a living, thriving community. In the square is the Crown inn with its mounting block and opposite are two local companies, namely Travelling Light and Survival Aids.

The village has many farms, mostly dairy and sheep. The oldest farmhouse, dating from 1709, lies over the bridge and waterfall and has a semi-circular horse engine house or ginn gann, where a team of horses walking round powered the earlier threshing machines.

Bell Lane is where, to celebrate the defeat of the Armada, the churchwardens ordered the founding of a new church bell. At the end of Bell Lane is 'Little Appleby', a lovely old house with a pretty cottage garden.

174

The name is derived from the story that in the Middle Ages the plague struck Appleby and a grant was given for the Appleby gipsy fair to be held here, Morland at that time being the third largest settlement in Westmorland after Kendal and Appleby.

Annual events in Morland include a Choristers Camp, a Scottish Dancing week and a Folk Dance week. At one time there were three cloggers, five joiner's shops, a bell foundry, two mills, a lemonade factory, post office and several grocer's shops. Now there are haulage contractors, coach proprietors, garages, cabinetmaker, builders, a light engineering workshop and two public houses.

There is an abundance of birdlife. Red squirrels, though not plentiful, still breed in the Morland area and deer are occasionally seen.

Mungrisdale

When travellers ask the way to Mungrisdale, one needs more precise information before giving directions. To the stranger Mungrisdale is a 'village', to the locals it is a beautiful, unspoilt Cumbrian valley which includes the main village of Mungrisdale, the smaller hamlets of Bowscale and Mosedale and a number of scattered fell farms.

The village blacksmith's forge once stood on what is now the car park of the inn but it was demolished in the early 1970s. During the dismantling of the building there was a shout followed by a great deal of chuckling. What was the cause of the merriment?

A gaff, used by poachers to stun salmon, had been cunningly concealed behind the old fireplace; it had probably been concealed there for generations. The water bailiffs had often searched along the river for poachers but had never traced anything to the forge.

Next door to the Mill inn is the internationally known Mill Hotel. During the tourist season this can cause confusion as they are two different establishments. It has been known for visitors to book into the inn and be enjoying a relaxing drink at the bar before someone has realised that they should have been next door. As they both provide an ambience of warmth and hospitality no-one usually takes umbrage.

Although sheep are still important in the economy of the valley, farming is now more diverse. Most of the farms have herds of either beef or dairy cattle and of course the tourist provides another source of income.

Tourism in the valley has changed over the years. In the 19th century Bowscale was considered to be a 'must' on the itinerary of the gentry visiting the Lakes. They travelled by carriage along the gated road from Keswick to the hamlet and then walked, or continued their drive, up the long track above the valley to view Bowscale Tarn. The tarn is set in a wild and rugged place surrounded by majestic crags. It has been said that because of its position, surrounded by high quarry-like ridges and its great depth, it is possible to see stars in the tarn at midday. This however is only possible if the sky is clear, the air stable, the water still and the spectator stands 200m above the tarn! The tarn was also famous for the two immortal fish which were said to live in its waters.

It was on these fells on a summer evening in 1744 that a spectral army was seen marching. The previous year two horsemen and a dog were seen galloping along the side of Souther Fell in a place which was so steep no horse could possibly have kept its footing. When onlookers spoke of what they had seen, they were not believed. The next year at 7pm on the 23rd June a troop of horsemen was seen marching on the same fellside. This time the phenomenon lasted for several hours and was observed by most of the inhabitants of the valley. The only explanation ever given was that the atmospheric conditions on that summer evening had caused a mirage of the troops of Bonnie Prince Charlie, who were at that time on the west coast of Scotland.

So the village has stood for centuries, its rustic church and variety of dwellings show the march of time, its tales and legends provide stories for winter evenings and the warmth of its people gives Mungrisdale its heart.

Musgrave 🌿

Musgrave is a parish situated in the upper Eden valley and is divided into two townships of Great and Little Musgrave. One mile to the east is the A66 trunk road, a main trans-pennine route between the North East and Scotland over Stainmore Pass. The village stands on a hill and commands fine views of the Eden valley, the Pennines or fells as they are known locally, and the lakeland mountains in the distance.

The parish church, dedicated to St Theobald, was built in 1845. It is the third to be built on the same site. The tower at the west end contains two pre-Reformation bells supposedly cast early in the 15th century and bearing Latin inscriptions.

Each year on the first Saturday in July a Rushbearing festival is held. A procession of girls carrying crowns of flowers and boys bearing crosses made from rushes march to the church led by the Kirkby Stephen Silver Band, for a service of thanksgiving and praise.

This small community with a population of only 124 also runs and maintains a village hall, which boasts a snooker room and large function room.

It is believed the old manor house stood in a field next to the farm now known as Hallgarth. The field contains some of the best examples of the pre-historic cultivation terraces, known as lynchets, to be found in the country. The manorial rights granted by William the Conqueror were dissolved in 1914.

The Eden Valley Railway line which passed through the village was closed along with the station in the 1960s as a result of the Beeching policies. The station has been tastefully converted into a private dwelling.

The tiny village school was closed in 1980 when there were only twelve pupils on the roll.

The village is primarily a farming community with ten working farms; other residents are employed in local services and some light industry in the nearby market town of Kirkby Stephen.

In recent years one large house has been converted to act as an annexe of the Outward Bound School, which has its base at Ullswater. Course participants clad in track suits are a familiar site orienteering and jogging in the early morning.

At the beginning of September each year Musgrave holds an Industrial and Horticultural Show attracting entries from a five mile radius. The exhibits are of a high standard illustrating that an old Westmorland village can still produce some very good cooks, knitters and gardeners.

Nateby & Wharton 🍃

Nateby and Wharton lie in the upper Eden valley and although very different have always been closely associated. The compact village of Nateby, one mile south of Kirkby Stephen, is on the east side of the river Eden and the scattered farms of Wharton on the west. It was only a short walk across a footbridge for Wharton people to share the school, chapel, inn and shop at Nateby. The link is less strong since everyone has a car, but all societies are joint affairs.

Nateby's 35 or so dwellings are built of brockram and many have buildings attached and a small garth or large garden indicating that they were once smallholdings. There are now only four farms in the parish. They each have a flock of heafed Swaledale sheep and three of the four also rear suckled beef calves to be sold at the local autumn sales.

The original water supply for the village was a spring appropriately called 'The Wells'. It still bubbles up through gravel and flows away in a stream to join the Eden half a mile away. This spring has never been known to fail, even in the driest summers. There are two ancient clapper bridges and a ford crossing it and an abundance of waterside plants.

At its centre the village has a small green with a shady sycamore, commemorating victory in 1918, and a copper beech to mark the 1953 Coronation. Facing the green the Black Bull inn wears its old AA plaque informing motorists that it is 266¼ miles to London. The village has a shop, garage with filling station, a builder and a haulage contractor. The Methodist chapel, built in 1873, is still in use but the village school closed in 1970 and was then used as a village hall until 1990.

Wharton at the present time consists of ten scattered farms and has many historical associations. The oldest building is Lammerside Castle, now a ruin, built in the 13th or 14th century to guard the pass between Wild Boar Fell and High Seat. It was built by the De Quertons. Through time the family name changes to Querton, Werton to the present Wharton. They built a second stronghold on a well chosen site further down the Eden, high on its west bank. This is Wharton Hall, begun in the 15th century by Hugh De Querton, and it has had a chequered history. Now it is a farm, privately owned and not open to the public, a very fine example of a fortified farmhouse, with a gatehouse and courtyard.

The most colourful of the Whartons was Thomas, who prospered in the turbulent reign of Henry VIII. In 1560 Thomas made himself a deer park by enclosing land from Wharton over to Ravenstonedale and turning out his tenant farmers. They had to build the surrounding nine ft high wall to keep the deer in and people out. The old deserted village of Wharton disappeared. The wall survives nowhere at its original height, stones having been removed to build or repair later walls, but after over 400 years is still a distinctive feature of the landscape.

Natland & Oxenholme ༄

The parish of Natland, only a short distance south of Kendal, embraces the two villages of Natland and Oxenholme. They share St Mark's church, the village hall and the village school, all situated in Natland, and are dominated by Helm, a hill of Silurian rock 605 ft above sea level. A Wishing Tree stands alongside the footpath bordering the western side of Helm. For countless numbers of years, those passing under this tree made their wishes, at the same time placing a small stone in the wall under the tree. Tradition tells that, having done this, a backward glance at the tree invalidates the wish!

Natland, once a small cluster of houses round a village green, has grown considerably in recent years to become an outpost of Kendal. St Mark's church was built in 1910 replacing a former church on the same site and Canon Miller, who was its vicar from its consecration until his retirement in 1949 was one of Natland's great characters. The school, which stood next to the church until it was demolished and replaced by houses and a new school in 1967, doubled as a village hall and was in much demand for village 'hops' and as a meeting place. St Mark's Boys Home for 'Waifs and Strays' was an important feature of the village at one time and is now run as a holiday centre for disadvantaged children under the auspices of the Childrens Society.

The Lancaster to Kendal Canal on the west side of the village is now filled in, but some folk still remember the horse-drawn barges bringing coal to Kendal and returning to Lancashire with local limestone. In summer the Kendal Sunday schools organised trips by boat to Levens Park and in winter the canal was much used by skaters.

The village of Oxenholme has a much shorter history, although its name, meaning 'place where oxen came to drink', dates back a long way – one of the fields being called Watery Pasture. It made its debut as a village with the opening of the main line railway to Scotland from the

South and was, indeed, a very busy rail centre with houses built by the railway company for its employees, the stationmaster occupying one of the larger of these houses.

It has been administered by Kendal since the 1930s when it was incorporated into the then Borough of Kendal. There is a shop/post office and a garage, and a good bus and train service, but the cobbler and village joiner no longer ply their trades and the district nurse, once a valuable member of the community, has gone.

Near & Far Sawrey 🐚

The two Sawreys are half a mile apart and two miles from Hawkshead. On a good day, the exciting way to get there is by ferry across Windermere.

St Peter's church in Far Sawrey was built in 1869 and is a good viewpoint. From there, it is worthwhile to walk to Esthwaite, the quiet lake so loved by Wordsworth in his boyhood.

Near Sawrey attracts visitors from all over the world as Beatrix Potter lived there from middle age until she died. Hill Top, owned by the National Trust, is kept much as it was in Beatrix Potter's day. Many other cottages in the village together with the Tower Bank Arms feature in the watercolour illustrations she made to accompany her famous stories.

Nenthead 🐚

For centuries this was the centre of a thriving lead mining industry, and the area was also valued for the associated finds of silver and zinc. Strange humps and hollows on the hillsides bear witness to the work of thousands of unknown miners, as do the many mine entrances, arches of stone, built with pride and care, which have outlasted the workings.

Early in the 19th century the mine owners, the London Lead Company, designed and provided facilities for its workers including a school, chapel, miners' reading room and library, market hall, clock tower and dwellings with land for smallholdings which were usually worked by the women to provide a vital source of food to supplement the miners' wages. Some of the buildings have now disappeared and many outlying smallholdings stand abandoned on the higher hillsides, but the school building has become the village hall – the biggest public hall on Alston Moor, and the highest in England.

When the Belgian company, Vieille Montagne, took over the mines in 1895, Nenthead was 'invaded' by foreign workers: Belgian, German and Swedish engineers managed the mines, occupying and maintaining most of the larger houses, such as Nenthead House, Wellgill Villas and Ivy House. Three hundred Italian miners worked under them, reopening the old miners' shops and fraternising with the village population, making Nenthead a truly cosmopolitan village, which at times must have sounded like the tower of Babel! Their presence helped preserve industrial and domestic buildings a little longer. Now visitors come from all over the world looking for their roots.

For almost 400 years lead was the sole industry: thousands worked in the valley, and with the powerful influence of John Wesley the area became such a stronghold of Methodism that the Quaker mine owners built the Methodist chapel. They also built the school for 200 pupils. Nenthead was the second village to have electric street lighting and had one of the earliest Co-ops. Now, in the centre of the village, the local bus company, Wright Brothers, occupies a large building built by Krupp, originally part of a lead crushing mill which dominated the village. Some think it an eyesore but it has interest as a part of the village's industrial history and serves a useful purpose in the life of the community today.

In 1988 the county considered closing the school and the whole population united successfully to save it. A lively Brownie Pack meets in its own hut and a new children's playground is being created. The lead mining has gone but the people are surviving and making a future.

New Hutton

New Hutton is a rural parish, three miles due east of Kendal. It lies a short distance from the main Kendal to Sedbergh road. There is no village, only scattered hamlets and somewhat isolated farms. The parish consists of the church, the vicarage and the school. There are no shops, no post office and no inn. No buses run here.

The Gin Shop, on the main Sedbergh road, was once a stop for the carrier's cart, which travelled between Kendal and Sedbergh. It is now a cottage. The vicarage was sold in the 1980s and is now a privately owned house. The present school building was built in 1873. Owing to the lack of numbers of pupils, this building closed about 1946 and is now used as a snooker club room.

The first record of a church goes back to 1739. It was built by the efforts of the parishioners. In 1829 the church was almost rebuilt, and enlarged. The music was then provided by an orchestra of fiddles, which was in turn replaced with a barrel organ, then a harmonium, and lastly a pipe organ by Willis, the gift of John and Helen Rankin, as a memorial to the three parishioners who gave their lives in the First World War.

A mansion with lodges at Raw Head, once the home of the Sleddall family, has now entirely disappeared. The crest of the Sleddall family, two stone greyhounds, which was removed from the old mansion, is to be seen on the gates of the old school, and the church. It had been the intention of the Sleddall family to build four almshouses in New Hutton, but it is said that Mr Sleddall took offence over a call at the vicarage, and he took the almshouses to Kendal instead.

Situated on the main Sedbergh road is the 'Toll Bar' with a stone staircase inside. This can be remembered as a working toll bar with a wheel in the living room which was used to open the toll gates.

There used to be a joiner's shop and a smithy at Gill Mill. These have now been replaced by private houses. The old corn mill situated at Mill Holme was burned down in 1927 and has been replaced by houses.

Newbiggin-on-Lune ॐ

Eight hundred ft above sea level, 18 miles from Kendal and in the shadow of the beautiful Howgill Fells, lies the small limestone village of Newbiggin-on-Lune. A spring of clear water, known as St Helen's Well, gushes up beside the village and local tradition has it that this is the start of that great river, the Lune, which meanders through the Lune valley to join the sea in Morecambe Bay.

The main employment of the area is in farming, as it has been through the centuries, with hill sheep playing the most important role. A knitting gallery in the centre of the village is a reminder of the hundreds of pairs of stockings which were knitted here and sent to Hawes and Kendal for distribution. Close by is a small, single-storey building, once the communal bakery, where housewives brought their bread to be baked in the village oven, whilst Low Yard was the venue for a small market held twice weekly, when farmers' wives gathered to sell their chickens, eggs and butter.

The little church of St Aidan overlooks the Square, but it is no longer a place of worship, having closed several years ago. It is now converted into a family home. Methodism has always had a strong influence in the village, and its members are served by a chapel.

The village has seen many changes over the years. At one time there were 14 tailors supplying local needs, a candle house where all the candles for the dale were produced, a wine merchant, corn merchant, joiner and undertaker, grocer, pot shop, general store and snuff mill, two visiting banks, a post office, a school and a daily bus service! As a result of social changes, most of these amenities have gone, including the school which, when it was built in 1872, offered Greek and Latin (to boys only) as part of its curriculum.

But Newbiggin remains an active, thriving community, still retaining its strong links with agriculture through farming, its animal feed merchant, the Weasdale tree nursery (one of the highest in England), a garden centre, a fish farm and an agricultural contractor. With a good mixture of old and young, working and retired people, the community spirit of the village remains alive and well, strengthened perhaps by its relative isolation in this lovely corner of Cumbria.

Newby 🦢

One of the townships of Morland parish, Newby, or as it was once called, Newby Stones, is situated about one and a half miles from Morland. The name could relate to several old limestone quarries to the west of the village on Stonehills. The sites may be clearly seen along the narrow Lansmere Road.

Newby Hall is now an hotel and contains many original features including a grand fireplace and Jacobean windows, some with original glass.

At Cross House a plague stone has been set into the garden wall. During the plague in the late 16th and early 17th century vinegar was put into the plague stone to wash the coins.

The small hamlet of Newby consists of several farms, pretty stone cottages, several new properties, a dairy engineer and electrical contractor, with their shop selling farm supplies, post office and grocery shop, a riding school and a haulage contractor. Quite close to the village there is an old Quaker graveyard. A short distance further on is a farm which breeds alpacas.

Long ago a seam of coal was worked here at Newby for use in the lime kilns at nearby Towcett. Also of interest is that when the foundations were being dug for a bungalow in the village, Roman remains were found.

Newton Arlosh 🦢

Newton Arlosh, or Longnewton as it is sometimes called, being a long straggling village, owes its origin to the misfortune of Skinburness, which was swept away by violent storms in the 14th century. The inhabitants moved to a safer spot which became known as Newton Arlosh, meaning 'New town on the marsh'.

Newton Arlosh is situated on the B5307 road between Abbeytown and Kirkbride, bordered on one side by moss (peat) land, and on the other by tidal salt marsh. In years gone by, 'peat rights' were owned by farmers, who allowed villagers to cut and dry peat for household fuel. The majority of this land now belongs to the Nature Conservancy Council, who plan to restore it to a 'raised bog' condition. Farmers also held grazing rights to 'stints' on the marsh. These were defined areas of the marsh where they could graze their livestock, and originally benefited only the farmers of the parish. At various times over the years some of these rights have been sold, and some present owners are not resident in the district.

The main architectural feature of the village is the church of St John the Evangelist, erected in 1303, and noted for its pele tower. The church door is only two ft seven inches wide, and it is said that, at a wedding, the first of the bridal pair out of the church will be the boss.

A joiner's shop, blacksmith's, post office, public house and school were all features of the village until comparatively recently. Today we still have a post office (in a council house) and a public house. Sadly the school closed in 1978, and the children now travel by bus to the next village.

Agriculture sustained the village at the beginning of the century, farmers' wives and daughters going to market at Wigton or Carlisle by pony trap, and later by bus, to sell butter, eggs and poultry, returning with the week's provisions.

Over the years the scattered nature of the village has been partially filled in by the inclusion of 16 council houses, some of which are now owned by the tenants, together with the building of a number of new houses and bungalows, from which the residents mostly travel elsewhere to work.

Nibthwaite 🌿

The setting of High Nibthwaite is idyllic, situated on the quiet south-eastern shores of Lake Coniston. Small wonder, therefore, that it was to inspire the writings of Arthur Ransome, who, even in his old age, could never resist the thrill of dipping his hands in the cool water just to prove that he was 'home'.

The village has been important even from early times. The monks of Conishead used the lake for fishing from the 12th century. In later centuries various commodities were transported down the lake, including charcoal from the woods which flanked the lakeside, slates from the Coniston hills and gunpowder from Elterwater. There were many landing places stretching from Water Park down to the fields below Allen Tarn, and several buildings which housed the various goods overnight before they continued their journey down to the port at Greenodd, carried by every farmer who had a horse and cart. Needless to say, disputes were many and landing places changed with regularity. The carts often returned with other goods – pig iron for the forge at Langdale and saltpetre for the Elterwater gunpowder works.

There was a tanyard which did a considerable business. At the turn of the century its tall brick chimney could be seen from the lake. The building has now vanished, the adjacent house enlarged and the tanpits filled in and turned into lawns and gardens.

A little lower down the valley towards Lowick Bridge is the hamlet of Low Nibthwaite. The village consists of a group of six or seven houses, Nibthwaite Grange and its adjacent farm and buildings. Again, its sleepy appearance is in direct contrast to its earlier bustling years. In 1735 a smelting furnace, foundry and forge was set up here; the situation was ideal – near the swift flowing water of the river Crake, and in close proximity to the charcoal-burning operations. It was from here and from Dixon Ground in Coniston, that cannon balls were made for the Duke of Cumberland's use in the '45 Rebellion. On the site of the furnace, the first of two bobbin mills was erected, and bobbin manufacture continued here until the 20th century. Later the mill was used as a joiner's shop and sawmill, but now all the buildings are converted to residential use.

Nicholforest

Within the parish of Nicholforest are several small hamlets but no settlement, with the exception of Kershopefoot, which could be called a village; Catlowdy, Warwicksland, Scuggate, Stoneygate, Penton and Bushfield are all part of Nicholforest.

The area is historically of great interest. In the 16th century the Borderland was divided into six Marches; three on the Scots side and three on the English side, and Nicholforest was part of the West March. Kershopefoot, which is in the northern corner of the parish, right on the Border, was a recognized venue for the feuding Scots and English reivers to meet on days of truce, and reference to this can be found in the fine Border ballads, which recount the deeds of these men.

Probably the oldest building in the area is Stonegarthside Hall, an impressive ancient Border stronghold; at one time it was the seat of the Forsters. It is now a listed building. Below the massive edifice are dungeons; and in one of the four ft thick walls is a heart-shaped aperture through which one can see almost the whole extent of Liddesdale.

The railway, originally the North British Railway, ran through Nicholforest until 1968, when the Beeching axe descended on the 'Waverley' main line route to Edinburgh. Penton and Kershopefoot stations fell victim, and as one local farmer said, regretfully, 'the life went out of the parish with the closure of the railway'.

Between the wars, the Forestry Commission planted thousands of conifers on the surrounding fellsides, covering the bleak moorland like green knitted blankets. Now the rail link has gone, and the forests are being cropped, huge lorries, some in tandem, thunder their way across the countryside, churning up the roadside verges, and dominating the winding country roads. Those forests still owned by the Forestry Commission are open to the public for hikers and ramblers, but those sold off in recent years to private concerns are now padlocked and entry is forbidden.

At Stoneygate there was a blacksmith's shop until about 40 years ago, Jobby Turnbull being the blacksmith. Nearby at Drakemire, Wat Cowan plied his trade as a clogger. The parish was plentifully supplied with inns and alehouses, many of the latter now dwelling houses or farms. Probably the most famous of these establishments was the Huntsman, or the Corner House, known locally as 'Annie Jane's'. Annie Jane Potts was the proprietress of the Huntsman, and her premises were the centre for a variety of entertainments. Every Easter Sunday night she made traditional mulled ale, with eggs, stout, ginger and spices, to her own recipe, and people came from all parts – especially from over the Border, where Sunday drinking was forbidden, to enjoy a convivial evening.

Farming, mostly sheep and cattle, is the chief occupation of the local people; very few crops are grown, and most of the land is under grass or forestry. Nowadays, farmers are diversifying; farming and tourism in some cases taking equal shares. Tourism has, in recent years, become an important earner in this unspoilt corner of England.

Old Hutton ✍

Old Hutton, approximately five miles south-east of Kendal, consists of five small hamlets and covers an area of 3,924 acres with a population of approximately 280.

No-one sees the picturesque scene at Beckside with its lovely waterfall without coming away full of admiration. The waterfall is part of the river running through the village known as Peasey beck and below Old Hutton is called the river Bela. This is fed by small streams, but its flow is partly controlled from its source at Killington Reservoir and when the British Waterways need water to keep the Lancaster Canal full, a siphon is opened at the reservoir for the amount of water required.

Many years ago Old Hutton was practically self reliant, with two grocer's shops, joiners, blacksmiths and a few mills, which employed a number of villagers. There was a corn mill at Beckside, The Ghyll in Holmescales hamlet where there was a mill which made billycock hats and at Bridge End a mill which was the oldest one recorded for spinning and wool combing. There is still a joiner's shop in Bridge End, which has been in the Nelson family since 1628.

In St Johns View hamlet is the school, public hall and St John the Baptist church. The church was rebuilt in 1873 and possesses a silver chalice which dates back to 1495. It is the only piece of medieval church plate in the diocese. The chalice is kept in a bank for safe keeping.

A house in the hamlet named Church View has a plaque on the wall telling all who pass by that John Wesley slept one night in the house as he rode on his way from Leeds to Whitehaven.

Holmescales Farm seems to be the oldest house in Old Hutton and has been in the Robinson family since 1904. In January 1955 a special service was held in the farmhouse kitchen to mark 50 years of Methodism in the Robinson family. Until very recently services were still held there and at Strickley on alternate Sundays.

Bleaze Hall was of the Jacobean period. It was built about 1600 by a Mr Roger Bateman, who made his money as a cloth manufacturer in the nearby town of Kendal. In one of the attics there is a 'dobbie stone' which is a charm to prevent evil spirits or ghosts of the house disturbing the household. Believe it or not.

History records the parish had its own brewery and had three beer-houses. That was in 1642, but now people who want a beer have to travel about three miles.

Ormside 🦢

Some four miles from Appleby-in-Westmorland and eight miles from Kirkby Stephen lies the picturesque village of Ormside.

On the river bank, high on an artificial mound, stands the ancient church of St James, one of the oldest in the Carlisle Diocese. Relics of early Christian burials and a Viking sword have been discovered in the churchyard, but the most exciting find was the Ormside Cup. A fine example of Anglo-Saxon metalware dating from the 8th century, it is of gilded silver, richly decorated with vine scrolls, birds and animals. It is now on display in the Yorkshire Museum, York.

South-east of the church is Ormside Hall, built as a place of defence with its 14th century pele tower. The Hilton family lived here for over 100 years from 1620. Nearby stands a large sycamore growing in steps, known locally as the Cross Tree. It is believed that this was the place of a preaching cross and when the cross was broken and removed to the churchyard the sycamore was planted in its place. A cheese and butter market was held here in bygone days. One mile east, passing the Old Rectory, at Little Ormside are two farms. In the Lodge garden is a magnificent cedar tree said to have been brought back from Lebanon in General Whitehead's hat, kept alive with part of his water ration.

There are fine examples of traditional Westmorland farmhouses to be seen, where an entrance to the house was gained through the adjoining barn. Two bear the dates 1683 and 1687. During the last two decades bungalows and a new house have been built as new people come into the village. A Victorian letter box is set in a dry stone wall. At the turn of the century, the majority of the population was involved with agriculture. Other trades included a coal merchant, station master, signalman, plate and brick layers, plus a school mistress. Following the national trend, the number concerned with farming today has decreased. In 1987, Rectory Farm was converted into a public house, Dexters, named after a local trotting horse. The village had been dry since the old alehouse closed early this century.

The Hospital for Infectious Diseases was opened in 1899. This later became a TB, then a geriatric hospital. Since its closure, the site has been developed into a tourist centre, The Wild Rose Caravan Park, with modern facilities and an outdoor swimming pool. There are timber-framed chalets which provide permanent living accommodation for 50 weeks of the year, so another community is growing here.

Orton 🌿

Orton or Overton as it was once called, is a lovely village situated in the northern part of the former county of Westmorland, on the Appleby to Kendal road. The background of Orton Scar is a pleasant setting for the village. Approaching from Appleby you have a magnificent view of the Howgills and Lune Gorge, with the hills of Fawcett Forest and Shap Fells in the distance.

Orton lies at the foot of the hill and overlooking the village is the beautiful old parish church of All Saints. The large tower can be seen from outlying parts of the parish and dates from about the year 1504. The present church was erected in the early 13th century. In the baptistry are some relics of past ages; one is a large box said to have been hollowed out of a tree grown in Lowther Park, probably the original parish chest, another is the old bread charity chest, into which loaves were put for the poor of the parish and distributed by the church.

A War Memorial commemorates the names of 18 from the parish who fell in the First World War.

Orton was granted a Market Charter in the reign of Edward I and, after being obsolete for many years, this was revived in 1863. A market hall was erected two years later by public subscription, mainly for the sale of farm produce. The building now serves as the parish hall and part of it is used as a doctor's surgery. The old school in the centre of the village, built about 1730 by private subscription, closed in 1963 when a new church school was opened.

The Wesleyan chapel bears the date 1833. A Sunday school was built in 1922/23 and was the first to be built in the village. The Temperance hall is now used as a joinery shop. At the northern end of the village is Mill House which had a water-wheel which was the largest in Westmorland with four stones for grinding. There is a date of 1693 on a cupboard in the house, which also served as a post office, the mill having closed in 1919.

In the year 1658 Oliver Cromwell, at the request of the Countess of Pembroke, granted to the inhabitants of Orton a licence to hold fairs. Fairs were held during the year, one on the 3rd May for horses, cattle and sheep (this ceased early this century), and a pot fair with side shows, gypsy caravans and horse trotting around the village. A tup fair held in October survived the longest.

Orton at one time had four inns and the George Hotel, formerly called the Fleece inn on Front Street, is the only one remaining. The Duke of Cumberland, a quaint old inn, dating from 1632, is in the centre of the village and it is reputed that a Duke of Cumberland stayed there. Orton Hall, at the southern end of Orton, built in 1662 and the residence of the Burn family for 150 years was recently made into holiday apartments.

Petty Hall, an Elizabethan house at the lower end of the village, has a date of 1604 over the lintel. There is a large open fireplace in the kitchen with a rannel bulk, an oaken bar which slides into sockets, still used to fasten the door.

Just before the turn of the century, there were in Orton four joiners, seven grocers and shop keepers, three boot and shoe makers, three slaters, two masons, three tailors and drapers, two blacksmiths, two resident doctors, a carrier and a policeman. Several of these carried on well into the present century. There is only one shop now in the village, which is also the post office.

Papcastle & Belle Vue 🎐

Papcastle and its twin Belle Vue are built on and around the Roman fort of Derventio. The hilltop site sweeps down to the river Derwent and overlooks Cockermouth and the northern fells. Derventio was a garrison of considerable size and importance, set at a junction of the defence and supply road system from the west coast to the Roman wall.

Sadly, little remains to be seen of the Roman occupation. Stones from the fort have been plundered over the centuries for building in the surrounding area – in Cockermouth castle for example. The fort has never been fully excavated and keeps its secrets, although many artefacts have been unearthed during rescue digs before building work. Castle Gardens, sheltered housing for the elderly, now stands on the main fort site. A mile off the line of the Roman road to Maryport is a waymarked footpath. Not for nothing is it known locally as 'Wet Lonning', and wellington boots are essential walking equipment.

Papcastle village retains the same basic shape, and many of the big houses and cottages (listed buildings) that it had 200 years ago. A wall sundial dated 1772 is a feature of The Grove. One old house, The Mount, was demolished in recent times, and a modern housing estate built in its grounds. The edges of this incongruous development are gradually softening as its gardens mature. There is now only one public house, at Belle Vue. The old 'Bird in Hand' keeps its name as a dwelling house. The railway station has become someone's home and likewise the corn and linen mill complex on the Derwent at the south-east corner of the village has been converted into dwellings.

The population today consists mainly of business, professional and retired people. Only one farming family remains, keeping sheep and dairy herds in the surrounding fields. The sub-post office, after several moves, has come to rest in outbuildings opposite the old east gate of the fort. It incorporates a small shop, and in the summer is surrounded by a colourful blaze of flowers deservedly commended in the 'Britain in Bloom' competition.

Today Papcastle and Belle Vue form a peaceful island in a sea of continuing change. A new bridge over the Derwent leads the A595 to

Carlisle past the western edge of the villages to meet a new roundabout and realigned section of the A594 to Maryport. Papcastle still stands at a junction of the main road system just as it did in Roman times.

Patterdale 🌿

Amongst the fells, high above Ambleside and Windermere lies Patterdale, or to give it its ancient name, Patricksdale. Tradition has it that the saint, having been wrecked on the Duddon Sands, made his way to this beautiful dale, staying long enough to baptize the local inhabitants. A well-head at Glenridding commemorates this.

Crossing the lake of Ullswater at Glencoin, the parish boundary continues for about 50 miles over fells. Down in the valley bottom, a road of roughly eight miles links the hamlets of Hartsop, Patterdale and Glenridding, together with Deepdale and Grisedale, each having its own little dale.

The Kirkstone Pass rises at the other extremity with Dovedale, Red Screes and Caudle Moor; Brotherswater at the foot. Hartsop shows evidence of its old importance with 'spinning-galleries' and lead-mining remains. Above this lies Angle Tarn and Hayeswater, which is a water supply for Penrith. It is a beautiful sight in the winter when ice forms in upstanding segments about its rim, the wind creating music as it lifts.

Both St Patrick's church and churchyard are kept in wonderful condition by local residents. A violent snowstorm in 1852 damaged the church so badly that it had to be rebuilt. One of its more recent rectors was John C. Rogers, of whom it was said, 'Just to see him made your day'.

Opposite the churchyard is The Butts, where archery was practised and the stocks once stood. It marks the beginning of the area where the annual Patterdale Fair was held, with all its sport and fun. Nowadays although hunting and hound-trailing continue, the sheep dog trials which take place in August are the big event.

The beautiful Grisedale valley is behind Patterdale Hall, which has played an important part in the dale. Above the valley is the famous Striding Edge, a knife-edge ridge leading on to Helvellyn, over 3,000 ft. This walk is 'a must' for visitors.

John Mounsey, 'King of Patterdale', lived at Patterdale Hall. His main claim to fame was when he led a party of dalesmen to Stybarrow Crag when Scottish marauders were expected. He deployed his 'troops', then left them saying, 'I'm a bit lame lads. I'm gan yam (going home)'. But Patterdale was still victorious.

John Mounsey sold Patterdale Hall to the Marshall family who were public benefactors. Pony tracks were created to provide work locally, and rare trees planted on the estate.

After centuries of lead-mining, Greenside at Glenridding became uneconomic and closed. A dramatic event took place in 1927 when the

The Village of Patterdale

dam burst. Floods swept into the basement of the local hotel where the maids were sleeping and their beds floated up to the ceiling. Fortunately the windows broke and they were saved.

Under 400 adults occupy this paradise, though many hundreds come in the 'season'. The locals have had to 'do battle' at times to protect Ullswater and the dale for those who care about its beauty. For many the glory of the beechwoods at Glencoin make an unforgettable memory.

Pennington

Pennington parish covers an area of some three and a half by one and a quarter miles, consisting of farms, small villages and hamlets. The earliest record of Pennington was in the Domesday survey in 1086. The manor of Pennington is situated in the centre of Furness with the A590 road from Ulverston to Barrow cutting through the lower edge. Land of almost every description is included within its boundaries. Gradually rising from about 175 ft above sea level to around 1,075 ft, the ground varies in character, becoming a wide expanse of moorland.

Villages and hamlets in Pennington parish include Harlock, Trinkeld, Carkettle, Walthwaite, Rathmoss, Horace, Holebiggerah, Cross-a-moor, Swarthmoor and Loppergarth. The hamlet of Loppergarth is said by many to have derived its name from a leper-house or hospital supposed to have stood at that place.

The iron ore industry brought work to the area with many men migrating from places such as Cornwall. Mining for the iron ore took place for over 100 years but declined after 1884 when there were many problems with water. However, the water in the area was put to good use with the construction of reservoirs; Poaka Beck in 1865, Pennington reservoir in 1879 and Harlock in 1897.

Pennington Church of England school was opened in 1876 and enlarged in 1885. A memorial of the First World War stands at Cross-a-moor in the form of a Cross of Calvary, with four steps instead of the usual three. It is made of Derby Dale sandstone and was dedicated in 1920.

A unique relic of medieval Pennington, the ancient parish stocks stand outside the churchyard walls. The two upright grooved stones have survived and were first restored in 1924, an Act of Parliament in 1837 having put an end to the use of stocks as a punishment.

The discovery of a tympanum with an inscription in Runic characters, a relic of bygone Pennington, is one of the most interesting remains of the manor. The stone was discovered during the reconstruction of the church in 1826. A quoin at the south-east corner of the church was taken down from near the roof and was found to bear on its inner surface a carving of a nude mannikin figure of extraordinary design. The carving is attributed to the Bronze Age and the figure is connected with pagan worship. Like many other stones from the building it was 'borrowed' and built into an outbuilding at Beckside Farm. It was noticed over a doorway of the building at the farm in 1902 and was restored into the church, being built into the west wall of the font. The inscription probably means that the stone belonged to Gamel de Pennington who was the donor of the church during the reign of Henry II (1154–1189). The stone is the only one of its kind in the country.

Penruddock & Motherby

The villages of Penruddock and Motherby are old Celtic settlements situated seven miles west of Penrith. All the surrounding land was at one time marsh and fell land and was reached by crossing the now somewhat diminished river by the ford which now forms part of the main Penrith-Keswick road. The villages are quite close, Motherby being built on a limestone ridge, and until 1972 the railway connecting Penrith and Keswick ran between them. The ruins of the station and stretches of the embankment and bridges still remain. Motherby is in the parish of Greystoke with a population of approximately 80 whilst Penruddock in the parish of Hutton numbers about 150. The actual village of Penruddock has about 50 houses and is within the National Park.

Penruddock school is in the centre of the village and was rebuilt by public subscription in 1872. Next to the school is the village hall, built of local stone in 1905, and opposite is the Norfolk Arms.

This area is largely a farming community, but with the advent of the motor car other means of livelihood can be followed in the neighbouring towns. Tourism is of course a feature in this beautiful part of England and guest houses and caravan sites are prevalent. There is no longer a village shop but groceries can be bought at the Motherby filling station and a busy sub post office operates in Penruddock. Opposite the post office is a strip of land, 'Bykeld', which is the old pound where stray cattle were kept until claimed by their owners. It was also the public watering place.

There are numerous farmhouses which were originally hay-lofts with living rooms below. One of the farms dates back to 1695 and is known as High Farm and belonged to the Kitchen family for many years. In one of the rooms a heavily padlocked chest was found. This chest is known as the Penruddock Kist and contained all the old deeds and documents relating to the village.

It is generally assumed that the Presbyterian or Puritan movement reached this locality in 1654 and the present church built in 1789, on the same site as the previous one, is reputed to be the third oldest Presbyterian church in England. There is an adjacent burial ground where many old tombstones bear the surnames of some of the village's present inhabitants. It is now incorporated in the United Reformed church.

All Saints church, designed by C. J. Ferguson, was built in 1901 on a piece of land presented by a native of Greystoke, Rev J. Hawell, who then resided in Ingleby Greenhow, Yorkshire. The land around the church is not used as a burial ground as the small church comes under the rectorship of Greystoke, all marriage and burial services for the extensive parish being conducted there. The Kist is now in All Saints Church and the documents held in the Carlisle archives.

Plumbland 🦜

Plumbland is an active working agricultural village, its farms busy providing milk, beef, lambs and other produce, as they have done for the past thousand years.

The site of a Neolithic settlement nearby indicates earlier habitation, and the Roman road from Old Carlisle to Papcastle passed within a mile of the village. Currently investigations are being made about the location of a Saxon village from which the medieval community grew.

On the gentle slope of the low hills between Lakeland Fells and Solway, Plumbland looks northward towards the Scottish hills. Just outside the Lake District National Park, it is off the tourist route and remains an essentially north Cumbrian village, with most of its inhabitants 'full-time' residents. The small caravan park brings regular visitors who are regarded as part of the community.

There are four 'manors' in Plumbland, often causing confusion to the visitor: these are Plumbland, Arkleby, Parsonby and Wardhall. This gives rise to the well-known local couplet:

'The greatest wonder that ever was seen
Plumbland Church on Parsonby Green'

Arkleby has its elegant Anglo-Baroque Hall dating from 1725, incorporating an earlier pele tower, with its spiral staircase. At one time the Rector of Plumbland lived in the Hall. Little remains of the old Wardhall, except a pair of gateposts standing forlornly in a field.

A glance around the village and its surrounds reveals a number of wooded patches which on closer investigation turn out to be abandoned quarries. When lime was extensively used agriculturally it was quarried here and taken down to the large kilns of Wardhall Lime Works – and from there distributed by rail. The old kilns can still be seen from the railway line between Aspatria and Maryport.

The present Victorian Gothic St Cuthbert's church was built in 1871, replacing the Norman church of 1130. There was probably a Saxon Christian community here as early as the 8th century. Two Viking hog-back grave stones can be accurately dated about AD 980.

As in any country village the village pubs must feature in any description of the place. Older residents remember the Royal Oak, which is now a private house, and which has been replaced by the 'Last Man Inn' – a reference to the cricketing prowess of the former landlord and his family. In Parsonby the Horse and Jockey caters for those at the west end of the village.

The people of Plumbland today have a diverse range of employment but the farming continues as always. Some of the old traditional crafts have died out, for example it is within the memory of many who live here that the village cobbler cobbled their clogs 'while you wait' – if you only had one pair of clogs and they were your main footwear, what else could you do? Another traditional craft still undertaken in Plumbland is the making of shepherd's crooks.

Plumbland 🐏

The village of Plumpton lies on the A6 four miles north of Penrith, a scattered community of some 300 adults and their offspring. The community is mainly involved in farming and its allied trades. Over the years the village has developed in a 'T' shape along the main road and west to the river Petteril, with outlying farms and houses. The main A6 road north and south is intersected by the east/west road from Lazonby to Unthank, and this forms the heart of the village where the church, school and village shop and post office are found. At one time the Packhorse inn stood with them, as did the smithy, but these are now dwelling houses.

Plumpton has a long history: Voreda, a Roman fort, stood a mile north of the present village and was of some importance, garrisoned by a fully armed and mounted troop guarding the Roman road from Chester in the south to Hadrian's Wall on the Border. The church lane is said to stand on the line of the old Roman road. In medieval times the area was called 'The Manor of Plumpton Parks' and stood within the Inglewood Forest.

Plumpton church stands to the west of the main road. It was dedicated in 1907 and replaced a chapel of ease which was originally within the parish of Lazonby. The cornerstones of the old chapel can be found in the older part of the burial ground. Plumpton became a separate parish in 1873. The present church was designed by Sir Robert Lorimer and is correctly called 'The Church of St John the Evangelist, Plumpton Wall'.

Plumpton has seen its share of crime over the years. Thieves and footpads were commonplace on the high road. On an October evening in 1885 Constable Joseph Byrne, having been alerted by the local signalman, set out to arrest the notorious 'Netherby Burglars'. These three violent criminals had broken into Netherby Hall on the Scottish border and made their escape down the railway line; they were spotted near Plumpton by the signalman. When the constable intercepted them he was overpowered and shot at close range, the men dumping the dying man over a wall, where he was found sometime later and carried by villagers to the Packhorse inn. He died before a doctor could reach him. The criminals were caught, tried for the constable's murder and were hanged in Carlisle Gaol in February, 1886. A memorial to Constable Byrne can be seen in the wall on Brockleymoor. In 1920 Percy Topliss, the 'Monocled Mutineer', an army deserter and murderer, was cornered by police at Romanway Farm at Plumpton and was shot and killed resisting arrest.

Pooley Bridge

Pooley Bridge is situated at the foot of Ullswater within the National Park and although it appears to be quite small, this is not so, combining as it does with the parishes of Barton and Martindale and the many farms which reach out to the surrounding district.

The river Eamont which flows out of the lake runs through farmland to Eamont Bridge and eventually reaches the river Eden. A very attractive 16th century bridge crosses the river Eamont and leads to the square which is the main part of the village. Prior to the existing bridge being built, a weir was erected with a fish trap. This gave rise to a fish market being held in the square in front of the Crown Hotel. At one time a cross marked the site but in 1859 this was removed, no doubt to make way for so-called improvements.

Away from the square stands St Paul's church. It is not so old (1868) but possesses many fine features. Next to the church is the village hall, erected in 1912 to the memory of Colonel Parkin, a much respected soldier in this area. Opposite stands a row of two or three very old houses, one of which was a blacksmith's and there are traces of a stand for the grindstone and a well for the cooling of irons.

On the northern side of the river is the hill Dunmallet; the name means 'hill of slaughter'. On the summit is an Iron Age fort; the ditch is still visible but not the well that was on the south side. At the lakeside, about a mile from the village, is the site of Tristamont. This is thought to have been the home of Sir Tristram, one of King Arthur's knights.

The oldest building in the village is a house dating from 1691. Being in the National Park very little development is allowed, although some dwellings have been built in the surrounds of the village.

Pooley Bridge is now a very popular tourist village and attracts many visitors in the summer months. Apart from the many farms around, tourism is the main industry, catering for the influx of visitors with hotels, guest houses, tea rooms, post office and general store. Out of the tourist season, approximately 250 people live and work in the area, which stretches from Barton to Martindale, an area of about six miles. One could not find a lovelier place to live and work in.

Portinscale

Situated at the northern end of Derwentwater, a mile from Keswick, it is a village of some 300 adults and 35 children.

In common with so many villages, Portinscale has lost its bus service and post office, but it still has a well-stocked village shop where most necessities can be bought, and this is a place where news is exchanged and the owner keeps a friendly eye on everyone.

Tourism obviously provides most employment in the village, but farming is still in evidence, and there is a family-run joinery business and a garage and taxi business, started in 1920 and now run by the son and grandson of the founder. Where the village shop now stands, there was a blacksmith's forge, and during the first part of the 20th century the blacksmith was a busy man, shoeing horses for the farmers and for the coaching horses kept by the Derwentwater Hotel. Extensive nursery gardens covered land from the centre of the village to the Farmer's Arms pub which grew, amongst other things, the first tomatoes in the district. All this land is now built on.

The Derwentwater Hotel, the largest hotel in the village, started as an inn, the Black Dog, changing its name to the Blucher Arms after Wellington's victory in 1815, and finally, as extensions were made, to its present name. Today the village inn is the Farmer's Arms at Low Portinscale.

During the 1960s, an estate of semi-detached houses and bungalows was built at High Portinscale, on what had been the football pitch, and the character of the village subtly changed, becoming largely a place of retirement. From the handful of those who were born and still live here, stories of life in their young days tell of barn dances, May Days, whist drives, Bands of Hope, football and cricket teams, a public reading room and lending library, the lady who took in washing for the gentry, the mistress of a private school who rode a tricycle ... all past and just a memory. Some have lived on in the folklore, one such being John Graves, the Cumbrian boy who rose to be three times Lord Mayor of Manchester. Retiring to Portinscale, he decided to build a mansion of Gothic grandeur on the edge of the lake, ignoring all local warnings that the ground was too boggy, only to have his plans of glory defeated when the ground sank, taking his 'folly' with it.

Preston Patrick
& Preston Richard 🌿

Preston Patrick and Preston Richard together form one ecclesiastical parish, but formerly were in the parishes of Burton-in-Kendal and Heversham respectively.

Preston Patrick consists of the hamlets of Gatebeck, Goose Green, Millness and Nook, and other scattered houses, and was referred to in the Domesday survey as a manor of Torfin. Preston Richard is also mentioned as Preston Uethred, getting the 'Richard' later, and comprises the hamlets of Crooklands, Milton and Low Park, and the village of Endmoor.

St Patrick's church stands on a hill to the west of the M6 motorway, and at Christmastime an illuminated cross shines out. Parishioners have enacted the Bethlehem scenes in the church for very many years. There is a Friends' meeting house and burial ground, and also an old burial ground nearer to Kendal. Camsgill Farm has connections with the Quakers.

On the various roads there are old milestones and boundary stones – examples of cast iron milestones, believed to have been made at Gatebeck around 1826, can be found on the Kendal to Burton road. A house at Cow Brow, near to Nook, still bears the name 'Toll Bar'.

The canal was opened in 1819 and enabled the transport of coal from Wigan to South Westmorland, and stone from Westmorland to areas south: hence the saying, 'Black one way, white the other'. There were coal wharfs and cinder ovens at Crooklands, and also stables; the old coal wharf at Millness is now a garden centre. The canal is culverted due to the motorway.

Once there were gunpowder works at Gatebeck and in the area of the river an old tramway used to run from Gatebeck, down to Crooklands and onwards to Milnthorpe. Retorts used for charcoal making now form the gateposts to caravan sites along the Gatebeck Road.

Coopers, blacksmiths, wheelwrights, and corn millers were once employed in the area and Staintons' Ploughs were made at Milton. Occupations now, whilst principally farming, are very varied. There is an antiques shop, printing works, garages, caravan parks, bakery, builders, joiners and undertakers, to name but a few. Once there were quite a number of public houses but now there is just the Crooklands Hotel, much enlarged since its former small beginnings.

Rampside ✣

On entering Rampside, a lovely seaside village situated five miles from Barrow-in-Furness and nine miles from Ulverston, one can see an unmanned lighthouse on the shore; this is a leading light for vessels entering Walney Channel.

George Fox, the Quaker, who married Margaret Fell of Swarthmoor Hall, came and preached in St Michael's church. Today's church, built in 1840, stands on the site of an older chapel of rest; this in turn stood on the site of a Saxon burial barrow. Vikings too knew Rampside, proved by artefacts found in the churchyard.

Folklore connected with Rampside Hall tells how, in the early 16th century, a young man wished to marry, but the lady's father would only give his permission when the lad built a house having twelve chimneys. The building was completed with the chimneys perched in line along the roof ridge. Each wedding anniversary saw smoke issuing from all chimneys – a reminder of the young man's tenacity. Until recent times the act was repeated, but on Christmas Day.

Concle Inn is built on the site of a gravel pit – known as 'Conk Hole'. This pit, filled with saline water, was used for therapeutic bathing.

On Roa Island lived the Trinity House pilots. Still there are the lifeboat crew members. There has been a lifeboat station at Roa for over 100 years, with an outstanding list of rescues.

Between Roa and Piel Island runs Walney Channel to the port of Barrow. Piel is famous for its castle, built by the Furness monks in the 13th century. It is said that an apparition of a monk still walks his domain. Nearer our times is the Knighting ceremony performed by the King of Piel (landlord of the Ship inn). The Abbot's chair is used, and the person being honoured is seated, wearing oilskins, a Viking helmet with a Viking sword to hand. After reading an old charter, the King pours a gallon of beer over the Knight (or Baroness if a lady). The Knight's first duty is to buy a round of drinks! His 'perk' is that he can claim a night's free lodging if shipwrecked on Piel!

A spur of land off the embankment – Foulney Island – is a bird sanctuary, like South Walney. In Walney channel is a small island known as Sheep Island; here are remains of an isolation hospital. According to old seamen's tales, in sailing ship days when yellow fever was commonplace, captains had to fly a yellow flag if infection was aboard. The sick were taken off the ship and into hospital.

One of the largest gas terminals in Europe is half a mile outside Rampside. From rigs in the Irish Sea, gas is piped across Walney, under the channel and into the terminal.

Raughtonhead ⚜️

Raughtonhead (pronounced Raftonhead) is the name of a parish covering some twelve square miles, and a telephone exchange covering many more. The map will lead you to the top of a windy hill looking eastwards to the Lakeland fells, north to the hills in Scotland across the Solway estuary and westward to the Pennines. You will see a church and a school, and a working farm and six houses. That is all.

The other parishioners are scattered, about 50 in Gaitsgill, another 50 in Stockdalewath, the remainder in twos and threes, some along the river valleys, some high and exposed. Back roads and muddy lanes (or lonnings, as they are known in these parts) lead off in every direction, each with a few isolated farms and houses. One homestead is well over 400 years old.

A mile north, across the river Caldew, is Rose Castle, the home of the Bishops of Carlisle for seven centuries. It is a magnificent building of red sandstone set among fine specimen trees and open parkland.

In 1884 there were four public houses in the parish. At Raughtonhead, the Duke's Head was run by Mrs Lennox. To the south the Traveller's Rest was appropriately named on its isolated crossroad between the fells and Carlisle. A mile up the river Roe from Stockdalewath was a humble beerhouse at Highbridge. A pleasant two mile walk down the Roe would bring the drinker to Gaitsgill and the Royal Oak. Today the parish is 'dry'.

The 20th century has seen great changes, not least in these rural parishes. Stockdalewath used to have four farms grouped round its handsome bridge, in those days a family could live off a few acres. There was no electricity, ten cows would be milked in the time it takes to do a hundred by machine now. Every task was done by hand, with horses to provide heavy transport and power. A farmer's wife would earn her housekeeping money selling eggs or butter at the market, supplemented by bunches of snowdrops (which grew freely here) or surplus vegetables. Water might be piped from a spring, or carried from stand pipes in the village. There was little further education for rural children, who would probably start working on the farm at 14. Now the small farms have gone, the land sold or let to bigger units and the buildings used for housing.

Ravenglass 🎐

Ravenglass is an ancient and delightful Cumbrian coastal village. Neolithic flints can be picked up on the sand dunes, and in AD 79 the Romans arrived. Their general, Agricola, built an extensive fort on the bank of the estuary and called it Glanoventa. The bath house, situated in Walls Drive, is one of the highest Roman remains in Britain, and has not yet been fully excavated. It is thought by some to have associations with King Eveling and King Arthur.

Ravenglass is situated at the junction of the rivers Esk, Irt and Mite. Here, they form an estuary flowing into the Irish Sea. Up to 20 years ago, the men of Ravenglass used to wade in the estuary with three-pronged forks and with a bag on their backs, fishing for flounders. The salmon-garth on the shore of the river Esk was constructed by the Muncaster estate, and has been in use for many years. There are also large and ancient mussel beds, which have been left undisturbed for many years. They are now being removed for sale in fish shops.

Ravenglass is under threat of flooding in times of storms and high tides. Flood gates have been built at the end of the street, which can be closed in times of danger. In addition, the village green and the ford have been banked up against the high tides. Stone walls have been built across entrances to the shore with steps across for access.

The original village was one street ending in the sea. One house at the sea end of the street was 'The Old Thack', a cottage with a thatched roof. Joe Farren, a boatman, lived and brought up a large family on his own here. The cottage was demolished in the early 1920s. In the 1980s a housing estate was added to the village. There are two hotels, a general store and post office and also a butcher's shop.

Muncaster Castle is just three quarters of a mile from Ravenglass and has been occupied by the Pennington family continuously since 1208. The castle and gardens are open to the public. The Norman church was probably built in 1160, and is in the castle grounds.

Behind the village is the main BR station, car park, and the Ravenglass and Eskdale Railway, 'Lal Ratty'. This attracts thousands of visitors yearly. A small caravan site has been built in the trees behind the village, and fortunately is not too intrusive.

Half a mile from Ravenglass is Muncaster Mill. After some restoration, this is still in full working order and produces flour and oatmeal, which can be bought from the miller. The mill race is fed by the river Mite. Flour was first ground here in 1455.

Ravenstonedale 🦚

The village of Ravenstonedale is five miles south-west of Kirkby Stephen. The dale is surrounded by hills, with the Howgill fells to the south-west and Wild Boar Fell rising to over 2,300 ft to the south-east. The river Lune rises in the Howgills, whilst other becks from the surrounding fells unite within the village to form the Scandal beck, which then runs down Smardale Gill to flow into the riven Eden. A noticeable feature of the parish is the extensive use of dry stone walls – there are few hedges but many small tree plantations, and there are trees near the houses and on the village greens. The houses and cottages are mostly built in the local limestone.

Ravenstonedale has been occupied since prehistoric times, as witnessed by the old dykes and mounds (known as giant's graves) in the fields. About the year 1200, the Gilbertine monks came from the priory of Watton in Yorkshire and settled in Ravenstonedale – they built a small establishment adjacent to the old church and they administered the manor of Ravenstonedale. The ruins of the small monastery in the graveyard of St Oswald's church have recently been excavated, and they were rededicated in 1989 by the Archdeacon of Carlisle.

The Lowther family acquired the dale in the 18th century – in 1744 the present church of St Oswald's was erected on the site of the old church. It contains a fine three-decker pulpit and oak pews facing into the aisle.

Ravenstonedale Village

200

Farming has always been the prime occupation with several farm houses within the village. It is mainly sheep farming because of the extensive common grazing on the surrounding fells, but beef and dairy cattle are also reared and there is a local milk delivery. There are three residential hotels – two within the village and the other just a short distance away – which attract many visitors, and there are a number of villagers who offer bed and breakfast services.

At one time there was a water mill beside the Scandal beck, which long since has become a private dwelling. In living memory there was a railway service, a daily bus service, a blacksmith's forge, a shoemaker, a tailor, two village stores and a post office. A district nurse lived in the village. A small stone building on the green housed a communal pig – all who fed it expected to get a 'cut' at killing time! There was no piped water until about 1890, when a tap was installed in a small shelter on the Main Street.

Builders and joiners still provide a most useful service; there is a slaughterhouse, a secondhand book business, an antiques and craft shop as well as an artists' studio. There is no general store, but a small sub-post office which is opened on two days a week. In 1982 a bypass on the north side of the village was completed – this road takes the heavy east and west-bound traffic, and is of great benefit to the peace of the village.

Renwick ✑

The village of Renwick is situated on the east fellside of the Eden valley, twelve miles from Penrith and twelve miles from Brampton. It is a quiet, working village off the tourists' route, nestling in the shelter of the Pennines in beautiful, dramatic scenery.

Since the 14th century, the manorial rights of Renwick have been held by Queen's College, Oxford.

The little church of All Saints has an ancient foundation, probably Celtic, but it has been burned, sacked, neglected, rebuilt and repaired over the years. It was while the rebuilding of 1733 was underway that an incident occurred which led to the legend of the Renwick Bat! It is said that those engaged in the rebuilding were startled by the appearance of a cockatrice in the foundations. Terrified, they fled, all except a man called John Tallentire who attacked the monster with a rowan branch; after a fierce struggle, he overcame it and slew it. For this act his estate was enfranchised to him and his heirs forever. Both church and chapel are beautiful in their simplicity, and are lovingly cared for by their members.

Most of the buildings in Renwick date from the 18th and 19th centuries (only five houses have been built in the village in this century), and there are some interesting features, including beehive shelters built into garden walls, and some fine barns.

Records show that in the 19th century, Renwick, like many other villages, was largely self-sufficient. The coalminers, the millers, the blacksmith, the tailor, the innkeepers, the general dealer, the clockmaker and the limeburner have all gone now; but the farmers and the builders remain, and other craftsmen and women have made their homes in the village.

Sadly, the village school, once the focus of much village activity, has been closed; but there is still a good balance of age groups in the parish, and community spirit flourishes. As well as the usual activities associated with church and chapel, and fund-raising events for various charities, traditional customs are observed and seasonal activities continue. Residents and visitors can enjoy pancake races, pasche egg and Easterbonnet competitions, sheepdog trials and the village sports in the summer, turnip lantern competitions at Hallowe'en and carol singing and Christmas socials in December.

Rockcliffe

Rockcliffe, with its miles of windswept marshland, must be one of the most peaceful villages in Cumbria. Yet warfare, smuggling, commerce and ship-building have played an important part in its history.

Records of the parish and surrounding area date back to 1185 but long before that the site was an important crossing point of the river Eden. The Solway influenced the development of the village to a great extent and at the beginning of the 18th century it became an important port and ship-building centre. Wharfs and quays stretched for 500 yards along the tidal reaches of the river and a great deal of timber and Welsh slates were imported. Today there is little evidence of the village's maritime past: only a few rotting remains of wooden jetties and the ship weathervane on the church spire.

The smuggling of salt and whisky from Scotland was carried on at Rockcliffe on a large scale, the men of the village using a variety of means to outwit the Excise officers. The contraband spirit was brought across a famous ford to the north of the village where the Boathouse still stands. For centuries the building served as an inn for travellers but the licence was allowed to elapse in 1889. A well-kept wooden plaque on a wall of the Boathouse tells, in verse, of the history of the ancient ford.

Like every other Border village, Rockcliffe was always on its guard and suffered several times at the hands of the Scottish raiders. At one time the village had its own castle, one of the earliest fortified defences built on the Border. It was erected early in the 16th century, could garrison 200 men, and served as a prison for the notorious Border clan of Grahams. The building became a ruin by 1683 and today there is no trace of the castle, which stood on the red cliffs overlooking the marsh and the Eden and Solway fords.

Rockcliffe's most ancient relic is the 1,000 year old weathered Norse cross which stands near the church. The present church of St Mary was built in 1848 and was rebuilt after lightning destroyed the spire and a large part of the roof in 1899.

The village has changed considerably over the years. The 1841 census reveals that 145 men, women and children worked in the local farms. Now only a handful of people work on the land. At one time there were eight public houses to serve the port of Rockcliffe. Now, sadly, there is only one.

Rosley

The name of the village comes from 'Ross Lea' which means a place where horses grazed, and it was the site of a very old horse and cattle fair, older than Appleby. In earlier times there were three inns, all grouped round the Fair field, now enclosed. The only one left is the Hope and Anchor, always referred to as 'The Camp' by local folk.

Around 1940 there were three farms, one manor house, three cottages and one inn in the Top Rosley area. Now there are 17 new homes along the 500 yards, and more planned. Two of the farms have been broken up and their buildings converted, and Rosley House has lost its private chapel and there are three new houses there. Round the church, in the centre of the scattered village, there are more new homes. The old school is now a pleasant dwelling and the playground a spacious garden. The church of Holy Trinity has no special features but celebrated its 150th anniversary in 1990. The plain windows are unique as the glass is pale green, which gives a peculiar light inside!

Once there were a number of village characters, the best known being Maggie Wilson who lived in Rosley Cottage. She was 'old-fashioned' even in 1940, and wore clasped clogs, hand-knit black stockings, a cover-all pinafore and a round knitted hat. Her door was always open, literally, and very few people got past her door without her popping out, like the old woman in the weather house! Most people called in anyway, to enjoy the comfort of a bright fire in the black-leaded grate, with shining brass knobs and a polished steel fender, and her rocking chairs! She is long gone but we do have Kitty Charters at Sandybrowe. The cottage she lives in was originally built round two old trams from Carlisle. She helps, supports, and belongs to, everything in village life, and is indispensible to the community. 'I'll get Kitty' and 'Ask Kitty, she'll know' are bywords. Rosley has no spectacular scenery, no architectural wonders, but it has kept the true essence of rural life.

The Rusland Valley

This beautiful and secret valley runs from the renowned Rusland Beeches through to Satterthwaite and the Grizedale Forest. The valley lies between Coniston Water and Lake Windermere with large portions being National Park or preserved by the Lake District Special Planning Board so it retains its natural beauty. Ashes beck drops down from Devils Gallop to Rusland Pool and then on to the river Leven.

The monks of Furness Abbey owned all the valley in the Middle Ages and when Henry VIII closed the abbey the monks left a small chapel at Satterthwaite. This little chapel was rebuilt several times and in 1840 was finally rebuilt and consecrated as a church. At the same time the villagers acquired their own vicarage and parish room. The monks exploited the natural resources of the valley with great thoroughness; farming and operating 'bloomeries' or smelting hearths. The valley is now mainly agriculture and forestry, held together by many winding roads that often defeat the tourists. There are many excellent examples of its industrial past left; the best preserved tannery in England, pitheads, pot ash pits and copwood kilns. No mills remain but the sites can be seen.

Rusland Hall, dating from the turn of the 17th century and built by the Rawlinson family, stands with a commanding view of the valley. Whitestock Hall just beyond the church is also still occupied but Grizedale Hall was demolished in 1952.

Rusland church occupies the most enviable spot in the vale of Rusland. St Paul's stands high on a rocky eminence that overlooks the whole valley. Many pilgrimages are made to the graveyard to visit the graves of the author Arthur Ransome, and his wife Eugenia. He had written that the churchyard was one of the most peaceful places on earth and as you stand by his grave you understand why. Several of the Romney family are also buried here, the painter at one time having lived in Whitestock Hall.

Moving back up the valley we pass the tiny post office and shop at Force Forge and nearer the village the school built in 1848. It stands in a most agreeable setting and has 30 registered pupils. Past the pub, the Eagle's Head, and on to Grizedale Forest. Here is the largest site-related 'Sculpture in the Forest' exhibition in the country which, in 1986, was awarded for 'the most outstanding contribution to art in a working environment' and in 1990 it won the £100,000 Prudential Award For The Arts. The project was started in 1977 by the Grizedale Society and the imaginative use of natural materials is varied and exciting.

Rydal

Rydal lies on the main Ambleside to Keswick road, one and a half miles north of Ambleside. In the 18th century, with the development of the turnpike road along the valley bottom, cottages and farms grew up and the village had three inns, a fulling mill, corn mill, smithy and school.

Historically and visually, Rydal Hall is the outstanding building in Rydal, and can be seen in its beautiful setting, with a backcloth of hills, from the main road. The le Fleming family came to live at Rydal Hall in 1575. In 1963, it became the Carlisle Diocesan Conference and Retreat Centre.

The chapel of St Mary was built by Lady le Fleming. She herself laid the foundation stone in 1824 and until this time Rydal relied on the local parish church at Grasmere, and a well-known walk is still called 'the coffin trail' where coffins were carried over the rough road under Nab Scar to Grasmere. The gallery in the church was reserved for the private use of the le Fleming family and Wordsworth occupied the pew in front of the pulpit.

The Rash Field next to the churchyard was famous for its daffodils and was bought by Wordsworth originally to build a house. The house never materialised, so the field was renamed 'Dora's Field' by the Wordsworth family. The wild daffodils which grow so abundantly give pleasure to thousands of visitors from all over the world every year. Further up the hill another old house dating from the 16th century with later additions, is Rydal Mount. Wordsworth lived here from 1813 till his death in 1850. It is now open to the public and is visited by thousands of visitors every year.

One of the oldest houses in the parish is Cote How, which lies on the other side of the river Rothay. It has a spinning gallery and dates from the 15th century. Fox How is another beautiful house, built by Dr Arnold, headmaster of Rugby School, with advice given by his friend, Wordsworth.

Beside the turnpike road was David's inn, now much enlarged and renamed the Glen Rothay Hotel, and farther on beside the lake is Nab Cottage with '1702' over the door. This is a typical Lake District farmhouse, and the writer, journalist and one-time editor of the *Westmorland Gazette* Thomas de Quincey lodged here and married the farmer's daughter. Harriet Martineau lived in Ambleside at this time and many interesting conversations and debates must have taken place between these literary celebrities in Rydal drawing rooms.

St Bees 🐝

St Bees is a small seaside village on the west coast of Cumbria, lying five miles south of Whitehaven. It looks out to the Irish Sea, and on a fine day the outline of the Isle of Man can be clearly seen.

St Bees has a fine Norman church with a beautiful carved door on the west side. The Public School, which now takes girls as well as boys, is a magnificent building, built originally in the latter part of the 16th century, and added to over the years. The village Main Street has many ancient houses of considerable interest, and there is an extensive sandy beach when the tide is out.

A few years ago, a house on Cross Hill, off Finkle Street, was discovered to be the birthplace of Archbishop Grindal, founder of the school, and a lot of work has been done to restore this lovely house to its former appearance. A plaque on the wall marks the spot.

In the 1980s, when excavations were taking place outside the library next to the Priory, a remarkable discovery was made. A lead coffin, in perfect order, was unearthed. It contained the mummified remains of what was considered to be a knight of the 13th century. The body was so carefully preserved that the blood was still viscous. The body was then removed to the pathology department of West Cumberland Hospital for a post mortem, and later re-interred. The shroud covering the body has since been on display in Whitehaven Museum.

The old Victorian station of St Bees has, for some years, been run as a restaurant, called The French Connection. The former waiting room is now a compact and comfortable residence.

Several housing estates have been built over the last 50 years, the most recent being the Seacroft Estate in the grounds of Seacroft Manor. One large house on that estate is used as a temporary holiday home for deprived children in the area.

There are three pubs on the Main Street, the Albert, the Queen's Hotel, and the Manor House. At the top of the village nearly opposite what used to be Fairladies Farm, is the Oddfellow's Arms, and near the beach is the Seacote Hotel. Each has its own character. Of the five farms that used to flourish in St Bees, only one, Fleatham Farm, on High House Road, still works full time.

The walk by the side of the beach and up Tomlin is still very popular, and provides people who like to get away from the crowds a chance to climb above the throng. A bird sanctuary, now officially sanctioned, is situated at the top of St Bees Head, and guillemots, puffins, terns and other sea birds can be studied.

Scales 🐾

Scales is a pleasant Furness village with only one street. The houses and cottages are of all shapes and sizes. The name of the village itself is of Norse origin, and means a shepherd's hut or cattle shed, so it is quite likely the invaders penned their sheep or stabled their cattle at Scales.

It has been a farming community for centuries and there are still three farms left. Over a hundred years ago there used to be a blacksmith, shoemaker, tailor, builder, threshing machine owner, coal merchant, shopkeeper, postman, post office, resident policeman, joiner and a maltster who lived at a fine residence called Dale Garth and owned the malt kiln. When the malt kiln was sold it was bought as a parish hall. At the rear of the malt kiln there are two or three stone huts used for cattle shelters, but said to have been used for cockfighting. They have a hole in the top to look down on the proceedings. The village has a school believed to have once been a tithe barn.

At one end of the village there are two greens. The larger is a play area with swings and slide and seats. The smaller green used to have a reading room in the middle for the men of the village for reading and games, but alas all this has gone and there is just a signpost and a few trees today. Adjoining the larger green is a pinfold – a pound for stray animals – used now as a builder's yard by the father and son of a longstanding family.

Scotby 🐾

Scotby, as its name suggests, has developed from an early settlement made by Scotsmen, clearing part of the ancient forest of Inglewood. It lies about a mile beyond the eastern boundary of Carlisle, on high ground well above the flood plain of the river Eden, and separated from the city by the M6 motorway. The centre of the village forms a rough rectangle, with railway lines forming the north and south sides, and streams forming the east and west sides. Around the green (a picture each springtime with its cherry blossom) there is a pleasing mixture of old and new houses. During the time of land enclosures, a very determined lady, Sally Routledge, saved the green for common land by uprooting each night the fencing stakes placed daily by a Mr Hodgson, until he admitted defeat. Most of the houses beyond this area have been built in the last 100 years.

By the end of the 17th century, Scotby had become one of Cumberland's earliest Quaker villages; the house opposite the pub being the farmstead of their leader, William Bond. A Friends meeting house was built in 1718 on the Wetheral road corner, with an adjoining graveyard. Recently, the 'broken pillar' tombstones have been moved to the side, but can still be seen around the new lawn.

Until 1781, farming, market gardening and milling had occupied the villagers, but in that year, Elihu Sutton, a local landowner and prominent Quaker, established a tannery opposite the Newcastle station, beside the stream and coal vaults. This became the major employer of labour, producing top grade leather of international reputation until its closure in 1930. Mr Sutton provided housing and gas power for his workers, and a well-stocked reading room for the community. The parish church of All Saints, founded in 1855, presides over the north end of the village green, with a war memorial by the gate.

Despite the ghosts that haunt the oldest houses, and a phantom horseman who races the road to Wetheral, Scotby is a lively village; the hall fully used by youth organisations, indoor sports, child welfare, play-school and the Women's institute (whose members had been instrumental in raising funds for its erection). An excellent village shop-cum-post office, the Royal Oak noted for good food, a large progressive primary school, and extensive playing field bequeathed to the community by Mr Hartly with facilities for tennis, cricket and football, recently equipped with an infants play park, plus a very ecumenical parish church, all combine to give the village an active life. From supplying Carlisle with food and goods in the days of yore, the Scotby villagers at the end of the 20th century now provide the city with a professional and skilled workforce, whilst still being able to enjoy the assets of a small community.

Seascale 🦢

Seascale is not a typical Cumbrian village. There were two distinct stages in its development. The first was with the coming of the Furness Railway in the 1850s when Victorian Seascale began, the hotels and large houses were built and it became a popular holiday resort catering for respectable middle class families.

There were bathing machines for hire and in the summer services were held on the beach, ice cream was sold from a stall in front of one of the shops in South Parade and some shops hired out deck chairs. People would take their tea pots to houses in Railway Terrace to be filled with hot water and a man from Gosforth used to bring his donkeys down to the beach for 'donkey rides'.

In 1897, soon after Seascale became a separate parish, the Council asked the Furness Railway to discontinue the cheap day excursions as these 'bring into the place a class of people who by their language and manners drive the visitors from the beach and to the streets'.

The foreshore was then wild and unspoilt and people living on the front used to put their washing out on the grass and stones to dry. Farmers had stints on the shore and the underpasses under the railway were for them to take their cattle through.

The beginning of the war in 1939 brought an end to the holiday trade and after the war the second stage of the village development began. The Ministry of Defence set up the first atomic station at Sellafield, then known as Windscale. The village was chosen to house the staff and the population doubled. Now it was the Windscale workers and their children who enjoyed the use of the beach. The day trippers still came and bought their buckets and spades in the shops and the pupils from the two boarding schools used to bathe in the sea. Then the Windscale fire made national news and started the decline of the schools which led to their closure.

As Sellafield expanded the beach declined in popularity and early in the 1980s the contamination of the sea and shore by BNFL occurred. The most frequent daytrippers now were journalists and TV crews. The attendant bad publicity emptied the beach, and it has remained almost deserted ever since. The beach huts which once lined the shore between the two railway bridges – reminiscent perhaps of the 'skales' or houses of the early Vikings – were abandoned and destroyed by gales.

Nature as well as man has had a hand in changing the scene. The sea has encroached and the grassy stretch beyond the Herding Neb, where smugglers were once supposed to have operated, has gone. The 'cinder track', once used by those cycling to Sellafield, is being eroded and another stretch has recently fallen away. The railway which once carried the holidaymakers now carries Sellafield workers and nuclear waste. It, too, is threatened by the advancing sea, though work is being done by BNFL, who now own the beach, to prevent further damage.

Seaton

Seaton is the largest village in Cumbria, having almost 5,000 inhabitants. Originally it was a small mining community with a brickworks and a few farms, so most of the menfolk were either colliers or farm servants. Later, a few people carried on their trade within their own homes, having no purpose-built shop. These included butchers, drapers, grocers, cloggers, bakers and blacksmiths. Until quite recently there were still six of these 'front-parlour shops' in Seaton, where a large variety of articles could be bought, and people very seldom left the village to buy goods. One old-fashioned 'real' shop sold groceries, medical requisites, linoleum, carpets, vegetables, ironmongery, wallpaper, confectionery, paraffin oil, pig food, hen corn etc, all from the same counter. How times have changed! We still have six farms, but the mines and brickworks have disappeared, and the modern shops are mostly self-service. Gone is the helpful shopkeeper, in his brown twill shop-coat, who always found time for a few minutes chat.

Though Seaton has grown quickly, over the years, there still remains a village atmosphere, and many of the old traditions are still upheld, such as the village carnival procession, always held in June.

Many years ago, a charter was granted to the people of Seaton, giving them permission to hold a market each Thursday, also a fair, of three days duration, on the feast of 'St Peter in Chains'. The charter is signed by the Bishop of Norwich, also the Earl of Lincoln, and is dated 24th May 1270. Though the market has long ceased to function, there is still an occasional fair. Villagers are also proud of the fact that in 1752 John Wesley, the founder of Methodism, preached a sermon on the village green, and proclaimed that he was standing on the greenest turf in the country. Methodism still flourishes in Seaton. In the centre of the village stands the parish church, St Paul's, which celebrated its centenary in 1982. It is built of local stone, in Gothic style.

There is one factory on the outer edge of the village, called Ectona Fibres. Though most people work outside Seaton now, at such places as the Thames Board paper mill at Siddick, and British Nuclear Fuels at Sellafield, they still have time for hobbies. Pigeon racing is a great favourite. So are the local hound-trails, and many people enjoy walking. There are some lovely places, and views worth seeing. Seaton Mill Farm is situated on the banks of the river Derwent, and has an old mill wheel. Though not working, it adds interest to a typical Cumbrian rural scene, and the local woodland areas, though not extensive, are popular with evening strollers, and provide a wildlife habitat.

Sebergham 🌿

Sebergham is not large enough to be called a village, but is rather a hamlet, although in the 15th century it had more inhabitants than the nearby town of Penrith.

There has been a community in the area since the 12th century, when a monk journeying through Inglewood Forest decided to settle near the river Caldew. This monk made a clearing in the forest and built a chapel on the spot where now stands St Mary's church.

In the 13th and 14th centuries Sebergham grew, as more people found the area ideal for milling, with the swiftly flowing Caldew providing the necessary energy, so that in the 14th and 15th centuries there were six mills on the banks of the river. Only one of these has disappeared altogether.

The valley through which the Caldew flows after leaving Hesket Newmarket is thickly wooded, with steep sides until it widens into pastureland on the outskirts of Sebergham. At this point there is a huge boulder with a crack across it about a foot deep. The story is that a young man was courting one of the Miss Dentons, daughter of the local landowner. She refused to marry him, until one day he vowed to saw through this boulder, and would not stop until she consented to marry him. After sawing a foot deep she must have relented and given her consent.

Anyone wishing to leave Sebergham, unless they follow the narrow road which runs by the river, must climb a steep hill. To the south is Sebergham Brow, 1 in 8, and to the north is Doctor Brow, 1 in 6. Doctor Brow is so named in memory of the local doctor, who was coming down it in his pony and trap when the horse shied, turning the trap over and the poor doctor was killed.

Only five houses in Sebergham have been built this century. Most of the others were built in the 17th century, and on the same plan. There are two rectories, the second one was built in the early 19th century because the rector's wife, who had quite a large private income, objected to the smells coming from the nearby farmyard.

It was in Sebergham that the internationally known civil engineering firm of Laings had its beginnings. David Laing and his younger brother had travelled from Dumfries, found building work in the district, and prospered so much that he married Jane Mason and moved into the Old Rectory. In 1867 the family moved to Carlisle and the business grew to what it is today, but some members of the Laing family continued to live in Sebergham until the 1960s.

Sedbergh ✤

Sedbergh was incorporated into the new county of Cumbria in 1974. Although this means that administratively it forms part of South Lakeland, the main bulk of the population still feels a sense of identity with Yorkshire. Sedbergh is within the Yorkshire Dales National Park, an area that has little in common with its neighbour, the Lake District.

Little is known of the early history of the town, and the Roman occupation of Britain has left virtually no traces. Sedbergh seems to have been a place that people passed through on their way from west to east. The main occupation of the natives was hill-farming, and tradesmen sprang up to service the agricultural community. The Industrial Revolution saw the development of several mills, for water power was freely available, as was the wool for spinning and weaving. One by one the mills closed, and the last viable one, Millthrop Mill, was burnt down in a spectacular fire in 1967.

Perhaps Sedbergh's main claim to fame is its public school, founded in 1525, which today is a thriving establishment with about 500 pupils. It owns a quantity of land, much of which is used as sports fields, resulting in plenty of open space within the boundaries of the town.

The Parish church of St Andrew is in the heart of the town, surrounded by its graveyard, with spectacular rhododendrons. Sedbergh also has Methodist and United Reformed churches, as well as a very old Quaker meeting house at Brigflatts. Roman Catholic services are held in St Andrew's church – a development that would astonish our ancestors who endured the bitterness of the Reformation.

Sedgwick ✍

Sedgwick is situated by the river Kent some four miles south of Kendal. Before the A6 was built Sedgwick must have had a lot of traffic and the coaching inn, now the post office, must have been a busy place as the road through the village formed part of the main highway from Kendal to the south. Visitors to Levens Hall would turn off into the park and approach the Hall through the lovely avenue of oak trees. Nearer to the village, where the road bends away from the river, coaches would splash through the ford taking their passengers to Sizergh Castle. These two great houses are still easily accessible from Sedgwick. Sizergh, now in the hands of the National Trust, with its 14th century pele tower has been the home of the Strickland family for 750 years and members of the family are still in residence there.

However, it is the smaller Sedgwick House, built in the village by the Wakefield family in 1869, that altered the life of Sedgwick. The Wakefields brought the gunpowder industry to the area and built many of the cottages for estate and other workers including the smithy and the schoolhouse, now both converted to living accommodation. Most of this building was probably done by Francis Willacy, joiner, builder and wheelwright. It is interesting to note that the builder operating in the village today is still a Willacy.

The original village buildings are mostly gathered round the area of the post office and along the main road, but newer houses have been built on the Drumlins roundabout and have increased the population if not the picturesque quality of the village considerably. It was on Sedgwick House tennis court that the now firmly established Mary Wakefield Music Festival (the first competitive festival in the country), now held biennially in Kendal, had its beginnings. At a later date a hall was erected in the village to house the festival and this has now become the club room or village hall to be found behind the post office.

The site of the gunpowder works on the West Bank of the river is now used by the Caravan Club but a stroller in that area will come across many examples of industrial archaeology.

One of the most interesting pieces of architecture in Sedgwick is the canal bridge or skew aqueduct built by John Rennie. Sadly now the canal carries no water beyond Hincaster but there are still pleasant walks to be had along the line of the old tow path, passing other remaining bridges which now just straddle fields.

Selside 🦢

North of Kendal lies Selside, a hilly area with scattered farms and houses and green fields bounded by grey walls and dotted with cattle and sheep. Most buildings are old and many farmhouses have been split and barns converted or rebuilt to provide homes for local families. Selside's one hamlet, Watchgate, has twelve houses and a blacksmith's combined with a post office, worked by the Tallon family for over 60 years. A Roman road ran through the parish and over notorious Shap Fell. It can still be traced where it diverges from the A6. Watchgate, Gateside, Leagate and Hollowgate were old settlements along it. The new line of the turnpike road was marked by a milestone in 1825, while half a mile away Toll Bar cottage was built to collect the tolls.

Half a mile down a winding lane stands St Thomas's church surrounded by churchyard yews, tall trees, wild snowdrops and daffodils. It looks down on Selside Hall, a fine Elizabethan farmhouse which started as a 14th century pele tower. Selside Hall, like Forest Hall, combines successful farming with taking in visitors.

The church school and school house, now private, is half a mile further down a dead end lane by a stream. In 1730 John Kitching gave land and money for a Whitwell and Selside school, long before rural education became general.

Watchgate Water Treatment Plant is tucked away on the old Roman road. Built in 1972 it is the biggest water treatment plant in Europe, supplying a large area from Manchester to Barrow. It draws water from Haweswater, Ullswater, Thirlmere and Windermere. Selside's population is under 200.

Shap 🦢

The village of Shap winds snake-like along the A6, almost mid-way between the towns of Penrith and Kendal. One hundred years ago Shap was a stop-over place for the weary traveller on horseback, and indeed the steps, where stagecoach passengers alighted, are still standing at each end of the village.

Until 1971 the A6 was the main trunk road and carried a vast amount of heavy traffic through the village, and the notorious Shap Fell earned a reputation countrywide. With the coming of the motorway Shap became a much quieter place, going about its business with almost no outside intervention – in fact Shap can be regarded as a perfect example of a working village community. Employment is high – the famous granite and limestone quarries to the north and south of the village provide work for the men, whilst the K Shoe factory, on the site of the old co-operative store, and the newly erected and fast expanding 'sausage factory' employs many women.

When Shap Abbey was plundered in the 17th century stone was brought to the village to build the market hall and a charter was granted. The arches of the old hall have long since been filled in and from being a dame school and the parish rooms, it now houses a library. A plaque on the outside wall commemorates the tercentenary of the granting of the market charter, which was celebrated in style in 1987.

The closure of the railway station in the 1960s and the severe cutbacks in the bus service means that travelling out of Shap can be a problem. However locals have tried to solve this by organising their own rural bus service. For this reason Shapites fiercely guard and take pride in the village amenities which they have. Not many truly rural villages can boast their own church, chapel, fire station, police station, post office, doctor's surgery, bank, library, and also newsagents, butcher's, baker's, Co-op superstore, general stores, antiques shop, fish and chip shop, launderette, betting office, garages and farm supply shop. Recently the parish council was able to install a bottle bank which is very well used.

Silecroft

Silecroft village lies on a long street between the main coast road and the sea. Cobble walls line the street between the houses. It still boasts a railway station, and if you live 'below the line' you have to run the gauntlet of three level-crossings to do your weekly shop in Millom, three miles away.

The oldest house in Silecroft had a well in the kitchen; the newest are set in a square and fit in happily with the rest of the village architecture. Not one style here, but a variety of stone houses and farm buildings, bungalows and terrace homes built originally to house the railway workers and the employees of the small local iron workings. The family who own the 'big house' established a brickworks on what is now the caravan site; the bricks were stampled 'W. J. Walker Sylecroft', and can still be found in and about the village.

Although Silecroft is a working village, there are still plenty of opportunities for play! There is a golf course right beside the sea, well run and popular with visitors and locals alike. The shore here is a wonderful place, especially when the sun is shining and the tide is out; it is very safe for children, and the local sport of 'wrecking' or beach-combing, can turn up some wonderful finds. Sadly, a lot of plastic and other rubbish also washes in on the tide, and the parish council, with the National Park wardens, organises a great beach-clean in the spring to tidy it up before the summer visitors arrive.

Visitors often ask about the long line of cars outside the village hall on a Friday night; that is when the whist drives take place – part and parcel of Silecroft life for as long as anyone can remember. They are always well supported, and people come from all round the district to join in.

Best of all in Silecroft is its own hill – Black Combe, which lies to the north and shelters the village from the worst of the winter weather. It seldom snows here but the winds can be devastating! Black Combe is a beacon hill, where great events are celebrated with a huge bonfire on the summit. The views can be spectacular on a clear day. The WI don't neglect it – they climb it every year on St George's Day!

Skelton 🐚

Skelton, a place on a hill, as its name suggests, lies six miles north-west of Penrith off the B5303 Wigton Road.

With a population of 330 in the 19th century the village boasted a smithy, a tailor, a butcher, a cobbler and clog repairer as well as a draper and general stores. In the early part of the 20th century a post office, general shop, garage and cycle shop served the community. One villager recalls the custom of giving 'luck money'; when he bought a bicycle from Mr Simpson he was given back a small amount of money for luck. Today, with a population of 270, the needs of the village are met by a sub post office, a small but well stocked shop and a veterinary practice. Records show that a succession of doctors practised in Skelton from 1829 to 1923. The last one, Dr Mortlock, died while visiting a patient! Originally the village had three inns but only one remains today, the Dog and Gun, once known as the Sportsman.

The church in Skelton dates back to the 13th century. King Edward I, probably on a hunting trip north, took communion at Skelton church in 1299 and left seven silver shillings in the offertory. In 1794 St Michael's church was restored and rebuilt, with further rebuilding in 1879.

At the heart of the village is the Toppin Memorial Hall, the meeting place for local associations and village celebrations as well as for the play group and indoor and outdoor bowling. The hall was built in 1923 by a generous benefactor, Mr Fred Toppin of Musgrave Hall, Skelton. Mr Toppin was the chairman of the New York Dock and Harbour Board and villagers still remember the boxes of lovely red American apples and grapefruit which he delivered to each household in the village.

Skelton Show, which has been held on the third Saturday of August for 100 years, is the largest horticultural and agricultural show in the north-west of England. Still very much a village show it is held at Hutton in the Forest park. Hutton in the Forest is the historic home of Lord Inglewood MEP and in the Middle Ages it was held direct from the King by money rent and the duty of holding the King's stirrup when he mounted his horse at Carlisle Castle. The earliest part of the house is the pele tower which dates from the 14th century.

Approaching Skelton from the north-east no one can fail to see the vast forest of aerial masts which mark the BBC radio station. Since its formation in 1942 Skelton Station has transmitted foreign news broadcasts daily throughout the world.

Skelsmergh

The gently rolling countryside of Skelsmergh lies a short distance to the north of Kendal. It is bounded on three sides by the fast flowing waters of the rivers Mint, Kent and Sprint and has lovely open views towards the Lakeland fells. Its unusual name is derived from the personal name – Skjalmar – of a Norse settler.

Now, as in the past, sheep and cattle are reared on the scattered farms, most of which are several hundred years old. Coppice How farm still retains its early cruck construction, and Burton House, where the barn is set into the house in an unusual way, has impressively thick walls and round Westmorland chimneys. In the hamlet of Garth Row, along a lane which each spring is lined with thousands of snowdrops, nestles an interesting blend of old farms and modern houses.

Skelsmergh Hall, which was the home of the Leyburne family for over 400 years, has its origin in the 14th century and still retains its 15th century pele tower. The Catholic Leyburnes lost their property as a result of their support for the 1745 Jacobite Rebellion, but a strong Catholic presence has remained in Skelsmergh through extensive landholdings. Dodding Green, a fine residence first built by William Dodding, a shearman from Kendal, nearly 600 years ago, was extensively renovated in the 17th century by Robert Stephenson and later left by him in trust to provide a permanent home for a Catholic priest. Mass was celebrated here in secret in an attic chamber until 1791 when more tolerant times allowed a small chapel to be built. The Anglican church of St John the Baptist is of much more recent construction, dating from 1871.

A Roman road passed through the area en route from the fort at Watercrook, just south of Kendal, to the fort in Borrowdale, crossing over the river Mint probably at Laverock Bridge. This old packhorse bridge, now widened to take modern traffic, forms a lovely stone arch spanning waters where the heron fishes and dippers skim the surface.

There must have been more activity, more hustle and bustle here in former days than there is now. Then, flourishing watermills such as those at Oakbank, Beck Mills and Stocks Mill ground corn, sawed timber and produced bobbins and woollen cloth. The busiest millsite was the industrial village of Mealbank, just across the river Mint in the parish of Scalthwaiterigg, where at one time more than 500 hands were employed producing woollen cloth of international fame. These mills were not closed until after the Second World War and some of the buildings still stand and are now used for small businesses. Other mills, some with a long industrial history, have received a new lease of life by conversion into comfortable modern houses.

Slaggyford 🦢

In spite of its unprepossessing name, the village of Slaggyford is set in a beautiful valley of the South Pennines with the river South Tyne running through it, sometimes noisy and swiftly flowing after heavy rain, sometimes trickling through its stony bed inviting you to ford it. The name Slaggyford means muddy ford. The Pennine Way goes through the valley, part of the way along the old Roman road, the Maiden Way, on its way northwards from Alston to Greenhead. Walkers of many nationalities pass along during the summer months.

The area of Slaggyford is known as Knarsdale, taking its name from the Knar burn which flows from the western fells into the South Tyne. Knarsdale Hall, situated about a mile and a half south of the village, is a 17th century farmhouse with stone slab roof and mullioned windows, now falling into disrepair. It appears to have been built on the motte or mound of a Norman castle, with the remains of a moat around it or possibly old fish ponds. A more recent farmhouse now adjoins the old building.

There is a ghost story connected with the old Hall concerning a laird whose young wife fell in love with her husband's nephew. The young man's sister learned of the affair, and the guilty pair, fearful that she would betray them, seized her one stormy night and plunged her into the moat. The old man, being awakened by the howling of his dogs, saw his niece standing by the kitchen door wringing the water from her hair, but at the sound of his voice the apparition vanished. The young nephew disappeared and was seen no more and the young wife died of brain fever after revealing the guilty secret and her ghost is said to haunt the Hall.

About half a mile up the road from the Hall towards the village you come to the church of St Jude, built in 1838 on the site of an older church, the only remains of which are some Saxon memorial stones, a few of which are let into the walls of the present building. There is a curious epitaph in the churchyard commemorating a certain Robert Baxter who died on 4th October, 1796 which reads –

> 'All that please these lines to read
> It will cause a tender heart to bleed
> I murdered was upon the fell
> And by the man I know full well
> By bread and butter which he laid
> I being harmless was betrayed
> I hope he will rewarded be
> That laid that poison there for me.'

Immediately adjoining the church is the Kirkstyle inn, now the only pub in the village, although within living memory there were three pubs in the area.

The village of Slaggyford itself is about a mile northwards down the

A689, and most of the houses are grouped round the village green, on which it is still possible to obtain grazing rights. The post office and small general shop is on the main road and was at one time one of the old pubs. Higher up on the green is the Methodist chapel, which succeeded a smaller building at the top of the hill.

Smardale

Smardale is situated three miles west of Kirkby Stephen, a very small village consisting of two farms and six houses. There are a few farms in the surrounding area. It is known to be among the oldest inhabited parts of Cumbria, containing remains of prehistoric village settlements.

Smardale possesses a 13th century fortified Hall which is used as a farmhouse now. It is an unusual design, being a long narrow rectangle with round towers at the four corners, rather after the Scottish style of architecture.

There are two railway viaducts at Smardale, one in use and the other which is being restored. Smardale Viaduct is on the Settle to Carlisle line which is used regularly. The viaduct was built in the 1870s and it gave the contractors a formidable task. Its bed was not rock as was supposed and its piers had to go down 45 ft through clay to reach anything solid. During the five year construction period 1,000 tons of stones were being used every week. The viaduct stands at 130 ft above ground.

There is a heronry in Oxenbrow Wood and in springtime there is much activity when the young chicks are hatching. Scandal beck provides fish for the herons and some days you can see them catching them. Near the Scandal there is known to be one of the medieval settlements, near the ford which leads from Smardale to Crosby Garret. At one of the settlements shown on the Ordnance Survey maps there are some Giants Graves (a local name). Some authorities say these were artificial warrens made for rabbits as a food supply, others that they were platforms for drying bracken, all agree that they were not burial mounds. The proximity of those at Smardale to the village settlements, however, suggests some association with the culture of the villagers and therefore dates them to the same period of pre-history long before rabbits were introduced to this country.

Soulby

Soulby is a small but spacious village on the banks of the Scandal beck, a tributary of the river Eden. Its population in 1981 was 176, and it lies two and a half miles north-west of Kirkby Stephen. The name of the beck

Bridge over Scandal Beck at Soulby

must not be taken to imply outrageous deeds along its course, but is derived from two Old Norse words meaning 'short valley'.

About half a mile above the village stands the old water mill, disused since the 1950s and recently much altered, but remains of the mill race can still be seen.

On the wide village green in the centre of Soulby, close by the beck, stands the village pump in an ivy-covered limestone enclosure. A commemorative plate shows that it was erected in 1888, in celebration of Queen Victoria's Golden Jubilee. Until 1938, when a piped water supply reached the village, most residents were dependent on this pump for their drinking water. Nearby, the beck is spanned by a sturdy three-arched stone bridge, which valiantly carries much heavier traffic than could have been foreseen by its builders in 1819.

Farming has always been predominant in Soulby. For centuries it followed the Cumbrian variant of the traditional manorial system, having a large open 'infield', mainly arable, and an 'outfield' which had pasture as well as some ploughed land. From the early 15th century the manor was held by the Musgrave family. Each tenant had his share of strips in the 'town fields', while much of the land to the west and north was common pasture. An area of common waste land was Soulby Mask. By an Act of 1810 the enclosure of almost all the village land was completed, creating a field pattern very similar to that seen today. There are still 17 farms or smallholdings remaining in the parish.

As in most villages, the number of other occupations and trades which once existed has been greatly reduced, and many people travel out of the village to work. In the mid 19th century, Soulby had a typical variety of tradespeople living in the parish – carpenters, stonemasons, tailors, dressmakers, etc. Amongst the more unusual jobs mentioned in the census of 1851 we find that Soulby had a twelve year old labourer's son who was a 'gatherer of dung'.

Soulby contains no buildings of great antiquity, though several houses have door lintels or tablets bearing 17th or 18th century dates. The parish church of St Luke dates from 1663. A small but well maintained building, it was originally a 'chapel' of the church at Kirkby Stephen, for Soulby was a 'township' of that parish. It was not until 1873 that Soulby became a separate parish.

For a village as quiet as Soulby, there was one disturbing experience during the Second World War. One October night in 1941 a German aircraft dropped a bomb which fell about a quarter of a mile from the village. There was slight damage to some buildings but no casualties resulted. Local farmers later carted over 100 loads of soil to fill in the bomb crater.

Spark Bridge 🌿

Nestling along the banks of the river Crake, which flows from Coniston Water into Morecambe Bay, and situated five miles north of the historic market town of Ulverston, lies the village of Spark Bridge.

The peace of modern times is, however, in sharp contrast with the bustling industry of former years. As the name 'Spark' implies, there is evidence of early iron smelting in the village, and a bloomsmithy was erected here in 1710, although there is a strong possibility that this replaced an earlier enterprise. Converted to an iron furnace in 1761, it despatched much of its products to Scotland, Wales and Ireland by way of ships which sailed from the port at Greenodd. In 1848 the forge was demolished and rebuilt to form a bobbin mill, which, in addition to manufacturing a large range of bobbins for the textile industry, also made pillboxes, brush heads, spinning tops and a wide range of other 'turned' commodities. Sadly, the advent of plastic reels was to prove the death of the bobbin industry, and the mill finally closed its doors in 1983. Since then, several of the buildings have been converted into charming cottages, although the timber drying sheds still lie idle.

A little further up-river was situated Crake Mill, in existence as early as 1742. It is probable that it was originally connected with the woollen industry, but from 1774 onwards its business was that of a cotton mill.

In the 1790s the mill owners issued their own bank notes. It is likely that, in the absence of banking facilities, the money was used by the workers with the mill owners acting as bankers. The mill was extended in 1820, but had ceased cotton manufacture by 1867, when steam-powered Lancashire mills replaced local water power. Thereafter it continued its links with the textile and other heavy industries by the manufacture of swill baskets. It was finally demolished in the 1950s and a modern bungalow now stands on the site. The only evidence which remains is the row of mill workers' cottages alongside the road.

The village is still home to one of the last woodmen in the district, who carries out the business of coppicing, besom making and bark peeling started by his father just after the Second World War, although he admits that he will probably be last in his line.

The rise in popularity of the motor car contributed to the demise of the village store, but, conversely, has benefited the two local inns, the Royal Oak which is situated in the village and the picturesque Farmer's Arms, with its 'spinning gallery' and huge round chimneys, just a couple of minutes away up the hill. Nearby, the Methodist chapel holds regular services each Sunday.

Stainmore

Stainmore lies in East Cumbria bordering Yorkshire and Durham, where some of the most spectacular limestone fells in the Pennines give way to moors of millstone grit.

Stainmore's history is long and illustrious. During excavations weapons and tools have been found, dating from the Bronze and Iron Ages. Maiden Castle is thought to have been a small square Roman fort on the old Roman road north of the A66 and not far from the summit of the pass. A Roman signal station at Roper Castle or Round Table may have been built on a site going back 3,000 years and used for religious rites. Other areas of Roman antiquities are being investigated by archaeologists in advance of the upgrading of the A66 to dual carriage-way.

Of major importance in these excavations has been the remains of a stone cross, the Rere Cross (a stone reared up) or, the Scots call it, Roy or Rey Cross (King's cross). This cross has been removed but will eventually be re-erected at or about the boundary of Cumbria and Durham. Various theories have been formulated about the cross. One is that it marked the old boundary between England and Scotland agreed by William the Conqueror and Malcolm, King of Scotland in the 11th century. Or a popular theory is that it was erected to the memory of the last Danish king, Eric Bloodaxe, killed in a battle on Stainmore in AD 954.

Sir Cuthbert Buckle, Lord Mayor of London in 1593, endowed a school at South Stainmore with £8 per year in 1594. The school house was built by local inhabitants. Although the church, consecrated in 1608, is still in use, the school closed in 1970 and is now a residential outdoor centre. A school on North Stainmore was founded in the 18th century and closed in 1959. The building is now a parish hall. The church there was built in 1873 but closed less than a century later and was converted to a house.

Farming was and is the mainstay of a parish such as ours. Coal was mined up to the early 20th century. Some men and boys worked in the barytes and lead mines on the Middleton road, only coming home at the weekends. Children walked to school from all over the parish, and early this century each school had about 50 pupils. As the small hill farms became uneconomical and amalgamated or were sold, so the population decreased. At various times there have been as many as 13 public houses on Stainmore, today only two. The Punch Bowl Hotel on the A66 has, for centuries, been a welcome hostelry for those caught by snowstorms.

Stainton 🌿

Stainton village lies two and a half miles south-west of Penrith, bypassed by a dual carriageway, the A66 some years ago.

Venture down to the lovely old village green, little changed over the years. Adjacent stands the smithy, still with its large stone used for making iron wheel rims set into the pavement. Cross the road and you will find the sheep pens where farmers in the village could dip their sheep free of charge and still do to this day. Near the entrance to the pens are large stone animal drinking troughs, set into the ground with a small stream running through.

Echoes remain of the church, long since gone, in the name St Johns Road. Villagers now journey to Dacre church to attend services. A cottage in this road had floors paved with gravestones, but is now modernised. The Methodist chapel was built in 1877, and is still in use.

Stainton was the site of an old Roman settlement and is built on limestone. Pieces of limestone of the most curious and unusual shapes are frequently found buried in the soil just beneath the surface. Barons Cross Quarry atop the hill is no longer in use. Stone from the quarry was used to build village houses in the past. Owned by the parish council, it is now a haven for wildlife and flowers; the old lime kilns are also there. Tradition says that one of the Barons of Dacre was killed in a fall from his horse at this spot, and a cross was erected in memorial. The cross is no more but the quarry takes its name from the legend.

The Stainton Jury which consisted of twelve good men and true from the village, administered all the parish-owned properties and preserved them over the years. Their duties were taken over by the parish council in 1990.

The village inn, the Kings Arms, is in the centre of the village, and across the road is the Brantwood Hotel, once the home of a village lady, where villagers could go round to bowl on her own bowling green. The green is now the hotel car park. The old school overlooking the village green was converted into two houses, but the character and charm of the old building has been retained. The new Church of England School was opened in 1965 and is very popular.

Stainton with Adgarley ⚬

The village lies one and a half miles from Dalton-in-Furness and roughly midway between Barrow-in-Furness and Ulverston. As its name implies, there are in fact two small villages with no obvious boundary. Taken as one entity, Stainton with Adgarley is essentially a working village with one large and two smaller farms, and on the north side of the village is a working quarry. There are also two inns, the Farmers Arms and the Miners Arms. Each of these show Stainton and Adgarley's connections with farming and iron ore mining in the past. The largest building is a Manor House dating back to 1658.

Stainton green is owned by the parish council and Adgarley green is administered by the estates of Lord Derby. Grazing rights are in force for both greens and a stream runs along the south side of Adgarley green. The village green at Stainton was one of the centres for cockfighting and the remains of the cockfighting ring can still be seen.

The most impressive building both for size and historical interest is Stainton Hall, the manor house. It is still in use as two residences. It is rumoured that the Hall was built by the ancestors of George Washington but no documentary evidence has been found for this. The Hall is distinctive for its mullioned windows and high, huge chimney stack. It is understood that part of the Hall was demolished by cannon fire during the Civil War.

Old farm cottages are abundant in the village, several dating back to the first half of the 18th century. This is not surprising as it has been established that there were at one time six farms within the villages and eleven farms within the parish boundary. The oldest of these cottages is probably that adjacent to the Stainton Hall, which is thought to have been converted from the Hall's stables. Several buildings show the skills of the dressed limestone masons.

The old Mission, now a residence, is easily recognized by the small bell tower which has been retained, although the bell is kept in Urswick church. The Mission has had many uses from reading room, social room, working men's club, school and, immediately prior to its present use, was the Mission church to St Mary and St Michael's church, Urswick, being dedicated to that purpose in 1885.

Within the village boundary, evidence of Bronze Age burial grounds and both Bronze Age and Neolithic settlements has been found. Stainton's mention in the Domesday Book is brief – 'Stainton (Steinton) Kings Land. Two farms near limestone quarries'.

Stapleton & Solport ✑

'You can have it young man – if you can find it!' This was the advice given to a young clergyman who was considering the living of St Mary Stapleton.

The twin parishes of Stapleton and Solport are situated roughly 15 miles north-east of Carlisle and are separated geographically by the river Lyne, originally called the Leven, a tributary of the Esk; and united ecclesiastically in the benefice of St Mary. A study of a map of the locality will show that it is a community of scattered farms and cottages, none of which are sufficiently grouped as to form either hamlet or village. Confusion arises from the whole area being linked under the postal district of Roweltown, and letters passing through Carlisle with either 'Stapleton' or 'Solport' included in the address are frequently endorsed 'Not Known'!

Stapleton and Solport are typical of those country parishes where the population has drastically diminished over the past 150 years. In 1841 there were 1,170 people living in 224 houses; at the present time the population has been reduced by two thirds and the number of houses by one third.

In the south-west corner of Stapleton behind a group of houses called the Barracks, a relic of more unsettled times, there is a peat extraction works on Bolton Fell moss. For three decades horticultural peat has been dug here, bringing welcome employment for local people but also resulting in the loss of much of the wildlife and habitat peculiar to the upland peat moss.

The parish church of St Mary, built in 1830, stands on an ancient site, replacing what appears to have been a sadly neglected edifice. Nearby is the 'Brides Well' which may have been one of the reasons for a holy place being established here in the first place, it being dedicated, some believe, to a popular Celtic saint, St Bridget or St Bride. Less than a mile to the south is another watering place, probably named after St Patrick and known locally as Paddies Well, giving its name to the present-day farm known as Patties Hill.

The public hall built in Stapleton at the beginning of the century and recently renovated, provides a meeting place for the WI and the other organisations of the two parishes. There are also two and a half public houses to satisfy the thirst of locals and visitors; the Drove inn and the Crossings, with the parish boundary running through the centre of the Pointer Dog!

Staveley 🌿

The village of Staveley, meaning 'a wood or glade where staves were cut', lies midway between Kendal and Windermere, nestling at the foot of the Kentmere Valley.

Lying between the rivers Kent and Gowan it has always been a village of small industries which in past centuries made use of the fast flowing waters to power their mill machinery. There is evidence of two fulling mills in Staveley being in full operation before 1135 and at Barley Bridge there was a working corn mill in the 14th century. It seems there were probably eight working mills in Staveley at one time, two of which were smelting mills for the lead mines, the others being corn, wool and bobbin mills. To this day there is a woodturning mill employing local workers.

Staveley was also a market town with the charter being granted to William de Thweng in 1281. He also held a fair in the village on the 17th, 18th and 19th of October each year. Sir William also founded the chapel of St Margaret, the tower of which still stands today and is well preserved as a popular tourist attraction. In 1864 it was decided to build a new church dedicated to St James.

In the centre of the village stands a rather imposing late Victorian building, The Abbey, built at the end of the 19th century to serve as an hotel when the railway was brought through Staveley to Windermere, giving tourists easier access to the Lake District. It was later used as a children's home and is now a residential home for the elderly. Opposite this building is the village hall.

The post office is not only the place to get your pension and stamps but it supplies us with knitting wool, patterns and anything that may be needed to replenish the needlework basket. There is the baker, the butcher, a grocer and a newsagent's shop which is a veritable Aladdin's Cave. There is also the greengrocer's and a quaint little craft shop which also serves afternoon teas. The three public houses provide a meeting place for all the locals to have their pint and a crack in the evenings.

Staveley also boasts its own doctor's surgery, chemist's shop, fire brigade, furniture restorer, upholsterer's and cabinet makers. There are even two undertakers but alas no longer a village 'bobby'. All in all it is a very self sufficient village.

Swarthmoor 🌿

The expanding village of Swarthmoor is in the parish of Pennington, situated astride the A590 Ulverston to Barrow road.

Prior to 1850 there were no houses in Swarthmoor, just a few farmsteads. A Mr Tom Town owned a small triangular field of a few acres, which he set out in proposed streets, to be named after local people. A few cottages were built and the place grew to accommodate the workers from the iron ore mining industry, the Lindal Moor Mines (Messrs Harrison, Ainslie & Co). Some houses in Fox Street were built by John Bolton ('Old Daddy Bolton'), who was a surveyor and geologist. The village has now grown to join up with the hamlets of Cross-a-moor and Trinkeld. There is a Co-op shop, a post office, hairdresser's, launderette and garage as well as two public houses, the Red Lion and the 'Miners'.

The mission room and institute now known as the Reading Room was opened in 1883 by Lord Muncaster as a place for the local miners to read the newspapers. It is now used extensively by village organisations. The upper floor is the church of St Leonard.

Much of the land in Swarthmoor is owned by the Society of Friends, the Quakers. George Fox came to the area in 1652 and was later allowed by Judge Fell to use Swarthmoor Hall as a meeting place. They became good friends and after Judge Fell died George Fox married Margaret, the widow of the Judge. The property later changed hands and at sometime became little more than a farmhouse. Since 1954 Swarthmoor Hall has been owned by the Society of Friends and can be visited by the public.

Not far down the road from the hall is the meeting house, bought by George Fox to be used by the Friends for worship. His instructions, 'Slate it and pave the way to it and about it, that Friends may go dry to Meeting' and 'Let it all be for the Lord's service to the end of the world' have been followed and the building has been used for worship for nearly 300 years.

In the post office wall in Fox Street can be found a quern, a stone used for grinding corn by hand, probably used in the Bronze Age; there are also some pieces of fossilised tree to be seen.

The Red Lion and the Miners, the public houses, were 'watering places' for the miners. Across the road Rufus Lane leads away to Low Greaves and Loppergarth. A one time a locked gate barred the path, the key being obtainable from the Red Lion. Rufus Lane is said to get its name from 'Rough House' lane, from when the miners walked from Swarthmoor to Loppergarth on pay day and met men from Loppergarth on their way to the Swarthmoor pubs. Very often a 'rough house' ensued, the men not being on the best of terms. A peaceful stroll and a friendly 'Hello' is what you will get these days.

Talkin

The village stands where the land, rising to 600 ft from the Irhing valley, flattens out before rising steeply to the fells. Though the Domesday Book gives no information for the lawless Border counties, quarrying in Gelt woods indicates early Roman influence in this area.

There were regulations for the protection of the community in 1552 when, from October to mid-March, twelve men were required nightly to guard a point where the river Gelt could easily be crossed by mosstroopers intent on stealing cattle and laying waste crops and homesteads. A record of these watchmen made during Elizabeth I's reign numbers 19 men from Talkin, ten of whom were Milbournes.

The name Milbourne – in 1224 spelled Milburn – may originate from Mill Burn which flows through the village, though now piped under the road. The Hayton register gives ten Milbourne families living in Talkin between 1639 and 1733. Elizabeth and Margaret Milburne are the last known, Elizabeth dying in 1939.

The village as we know it grew up between 1790 and 1900 when the stone houses now standing were built. Most have been modernised. Outhouses and barns have been converted into houses.

Talkin is within easy reach of the M6 motorway and the A69 Carlisle-Newcastle road, and the proximity of Talkin Tarn and Geltsdale make Talkin popular with holidaymakers. The Hare and Hounds inn and the Blacksmith's Arms attract many customers.

In bygone days, agriculture was the main occupation. Coal was mined in the fells during the 19th century and miners lived in the village. There are also disused limestone and stone quarries in the area. Farming, though no longer labour intensive, remains the most important activity. A research farm employs technical and office staff drawn from Carlisle and the surrounding area.

The church was built in 1842 by T. H. Graham of Edmond Castle. The Hayton vicar officiates at most services. For many years Mr Francis L. Wood was organist and is remembered with affection.

Though Talkin has many modern amenities, including street lighting, it remains a rural community. With magnificent views of the fells, where sheep graze peacefully and stone walls bound the fields, the village and its surroundings provide a safe haven for plants, birds and small mammals. From the trees and shrubs growing in the hedgerows it is possible to estimate that many are over 300 years old.

Tebay 🌿

Tebay is a long rambling village, with a population of about 700. It is situated midway between Penrith in the north and Kendal in the south, near the junction of the river Birkbeck with the river Lune.

Although it was at one time a sheep-farming area and railway village, now it owes its importance to the fact that the M6 motorway runs through, giving rise to employment in the service stations and maintenance depots. After the railway station was closed in 1973 local men were without work, so the coming of the motorway was a great asset.

The church, built in 1880 and dedicated to St James, is an attractive Gothic edifice of Shap granite with a roof of pitch pine. A Methodist chapel was built in 1865, and before this members of that body conducted services in farmhouses in the district. The old school, which was endowed by Robert Adamson in 1672, is now closed, and at the present time has been made into a County Venture Hostel, where countless visitors enjoy its facilities.

The hamlets in the parish of Tebay are Ellergill, Gaisgill, Redgill and Roundthwaite. It is said that at Redgill there once lived a person called William Farrer, who combined the two-fold profession of surgeon and magician (wise man). He could read the stars, cast horoscopes, and possessed the power of circumventing witches and casting out evil spirits. If anything was stolen it was believed that Dr Farrer could, by the mysterious knowledge he possessed, infallibly detect the thief.

There are several places of historical interest in the neighbourhood of Tebay. In the Galloper Field (Old Tebay) is the Brandery or Brandreth stone, where it was customary, before lands were enclosed, to brand the cattle. Near Low Borrow Bridge are the ruins of a Roman Fort, which appears to have been a place of considerable strength. In Old Tebay, close to the motorway is a rounded hill or mound, called 'Castlehow'. Whether a castle ever stood there, we cannot prove. If so all record of it has long since been obliterated, but the name is also perpetuated in 'Castle Green' a field nearby.

Thornthwaite 🌿

Thornthwaite lies at the foot of Seat Howe and the scree slopes of Barf, on the northern fringe of Thornthwaite Forest, and a short distance from Bassenthwaite Lake. It is in the parish of Thornthwaite-cum-Braithwaite, but is the smaller village.

Most residents are happy that it is now bypassed by the A66 road, as they only hear the rumbling of traffic in the distance. There is a cluster of converted farm buildings in the centre of the small village, together with a small amount of more recent housing, and Thornthwaite reaches out to include scattered farm developments and isolated houses in its area.

Within a short distance is the very small hamlet of Seldom Seen, most of the houses now used as holiday properties. This small hamlet is dominated by the roaring Chapel beck which crashes over large boulders. In days gone by, it was harnessed and produced enough power for working the Rachel Mine and driving the plant at the saw mill. Apart from the farms, the lead mine used to be the chief source of employment in the area, and the miners were housed at Seldom Seen.

The mother church of the parish of Thornthwaite-cum-Braithwaite is St Mary's, built in 1746 near to the site of an earlier church. It is a lovely church and stands amidst pastoral scenery, with the main door approached through an archway of yews. The churchyard is the burial ground for the parish, with old tombstones with many recognisable local names.

Thornthwaite Gallery is a great attraction for tourists. It is an attractively converted 18th century barn which deals in fine arts.

A prominent landmark high above Thornthwaite on the steep scree slopes of Barf is the whitewashed Bishop Rock. There are many versions of the legend of the Rock. In 1783, the newly appointed Bishop of Derry was travelling to Whitehaven en route for Ireland. He broke his journey at the Swan in Thornthwaite and, over a few drinks, bet his fellow guests he could ride his pack pony to the top of Barf and Lord's Seat. He reached the rock, now known as 'The Bishop Rock', where the pony stumbled and killed the rider and itself. They were buried at the foot of the scree at the rock known as 'The Clerk'. The landlord of the inn had the rock whitewashed and it is still done annually by Keswick Mountain Rescue Team. The payment used to be a shilling and a quart of ale!

Thursby

Lying to the west of Carlisle, Thursby, on the old Roman road from Carlisle to Old Carlisle and now bypassed by the main road to West Cumbria and the Lake District, takes its old name 'Thor's by' from Thor, the Thunder god of the Saxons, whose temple was reputedly nearby at Kirksteads.

The village skyline is dominated by St Andrew's church, a Victorian building which replaced two earlier ones, the first a 7th century wooden church and the second built by David I of Scotland. In the graveyard lies the Rev Mason, who was rector of Great Orton when he died and curate of Thursby as a young man. His granddaughter was Mrs Beeton who wrote the classic book on 'Household Management'.

Earlier travellers could not fail to see the old school which stood on a triangular green where the roads divided. A native of Thursby who died in America in 1802, Thomas Tomlinson, left money the interest of which was to go to the teaching of ten poor children in the parish. After 1903 it was used for extra amenities in the school. The curriculum in 1838 was wide ranging; reading, spelling, writing, geography, grammar, arithmetic, book-keeping, trigonometry, algebra and Euclid were offered and for an extra ten shillings and sixpence the student could learn navigation, nautical astronomy and the use of maps!

Two customs which were once familiar to all pupils were the 'barring out' of the headmaster at the approach of the hay harvest to secure holidays, and the giving of the 'Christmas goose' to him. The latter always provided an amusing incident. As Christmas approached a neighbouring farmer would be asked to keep the chosen bird until the last day of term when two senior pupils would collect it, tie a bow of ribbon and a card round its neck and put it through one of the windows of the school, so the goose would be seen walking round the classroom much to the amusement and delight of the younger pupils.

Now the new primary school has been built on one of the housing estates. The old school bell is still kept there as a reminder of those earlier 'calls to school'.

Since the 1970s race horses have been trained by the Dixon family. Many winners have been saddled at both local and national courses and it is a familiar sight to see them in the village and training over the jumps.

At one time there were several public houses in the area, a butcher and numerous travelling 'shops', first with horse and cart and later vans. Now with the advent of supermarkets there is one general shop, a post office and a public house.

Thurstonfield

Thurstonfield is a village in Burgh-by-Sands parish, two miles inland on the English side of the Solway estuary, five miles west of Carlisle in Cumbria. It was a thriving farming and business community from 1870 to 1930, with most people living and working in the immediate area.

The Stordys, a Quaker family from Moorhouse, owned most of the land, the industries and houses. The villagers were self sufficient with water from their own wells and grew vegetables, corn and wheat with the latter being ground by the farmer at the mill until it closed in the 1920s.

There were seven working farms, a corn water mill, a tannery employing 20 workers, a wine and spirits merchant and the Greyhound inn. Around 1900 the Stordys built several large brick houses, bringing the total housing to 25. Mrs Stordy at Red House, kept the famous 'Thurstonfield Harriers', a pack of hounds known from Silloth to Caldbeck and Carlisle. Cockfights, although illegal, still took place at the cock pit beside the Methodist chapel, which had been built in 1861 to accommodate 100 and still has a practising congregation now. Other social life was provided by summer swimming and winter skating on the Lough. The Lough was the millpond, surrounded by woods, owned until the 1980s by the Stordys. A business consortium bought the Lough and built fishing lodges, tidied the wood and created a private fishing holiday centre.

In 1895 the tannery sold one of its houses to a Kirkbampton stonemason, W. R. Purdham, who developed a building company with his family which survived into the 1970s. The Carlisle and District State Management Scheme, set up during the First World War to combat drunkenness among munitions workers, forced the closure of the pub and the wine and spirits business, while the tannery shut in 1927.

The 1914–1950 period saw 'Nannie' Rickerby running a village shop. She sold everything, except to those who annoyed her! Luckily pony and cart 'mobile' shops visited bringing goods from Carlisle. Great Orton's Hannah Jane wore 16 skirts and sold flat cigarettes. She carried them in her pockets and sat on them whilst driving along. Several mobile vans operated into the 1980s, but only the Wigton fish man now calls each week.

The village entered a new era in 1959. Pattinsons Joinery and Undertaking business moved in and the joinery side still thrives today. Building, barn renovations and infill housing have meant an increase to 86 houses. The one working farm left is a family concern and many of the old industrial and farm buildings are now houses.

Old customs have not survived these changes. When everyone was known all were 'bid' to a funeral, and tea afterwards. The quality of the funeral could be judged by the 'ham and currant cake' tea. Groups of neighbours still rally round to help when trouble strikes, but many don't know their neighbours well and social life takes place away from the village. The hundred years has brought prosperity to many in Thurstonfield, some who have moved here, and none feel the influence of a gentry-type landowning family on their lives as the villagers of 1890 did.

Thwaites

The parish of Thwaites, consisting of three hamlets – The Green, Hallthwaites and Ladyhall, is situated on the Duddon estuary, midway between Millom and Broughton-in-Furness.

This district has been populated for a very long time. Neolithic man lived here and most probably built the stone circle, still standing, at Swinside. There are also the remains of their round dwellings on Thwaites Fell.

From the Middle Ages until the beginning of the 20th century, whilst the district was mainly agricultural, there were several industries, deriving their power from either the river Duddon or the swift running Black beck, which flows from the fells, through the village and on to the Duddon estuary. There was a bloomery in the woods near Duddon Bridge, established in 1737, the woodlands providing ample supplies of charcoal for the furnaces. The buildings here are being preserved and are now open to the public. There were also corn mills, driven by water power, which are no more. Their memory lives on in the names of two small housing estates, Mill Park and Race Grove. There was a thriving woollen mill, said to date back to the 16th century, at Hallthwaites. Carpets, blankets, etc, were woven and dyed; there are some still in use in the district, although the mills are long gone.

On the hill above Hallthwaites is the parish church, dedicated to St Anne. The first church was built in 1725 as a chapel of ease for Millom. In 1805, as a larger building had become desirable, the older church was replaced by a grander one, complete with steeple and two bells, one of which still exists.

Until 1826 the parson was also the schoolmaster. The Rev John Ormandy, the last to hold the dual post, received a grant from Queen Anne's Bounty, which enabled himself and subsequent incumbents to manage without the addition of the small salary paid to the schoolmaster. Amongst the many stories told about the early days of the school is this – on 'Catechising Sunday' the children came to church and stood in a half circle at the front, the schoolmaster taking great care to arrange them so that the question each child had been coached in came to the right child. The story goes, that when one question was asked, a voice piped up, 'Please Sir, the boy who believes in the Holy Ghost has got measles.'

In the past, when the greater part of the population was engaged in agriculture, the district was practically self supporting, with its own blacksmith, cobbler, dressmaker, shop, public house, post office, and the corn and flour mills. The poor were cared for by charities giving coal at Christmas, flour and gifts of money. All that is left in the village is a post office on two mornings each week and the public house. Nevertheless, it is a very happy and go ahead community, with a splendid village hall.

Tirril & Sockbridge

Nowadays people tend to say Tirril-and-Sockbridge as if it were the hyphenated name of a single village. Perhaps this is because modern building lines have marched toward each other, although a small stream known as the Lady beck still marks a boundary between the two villages.

Sockbridge and Tirril both stand on the B5320 two and a half miles from Penrith and three miles from Pooley Bridge and the foot of Ullswater.

Sockbridge Hall is a 15th century manor house but is believed to stand on the site of the earliest dwelling in the area. Today it is a farm most concerned with sheep. In the village itself there is a house dated 1699 built for Reginald and Elizabeth Dobson. The property was later sold to Richard Wordsworth, who was Receiver General at the time of the Jacobite Rebellion. Richard's son John was William Wordsworth's father, but the family had moved to Cockermouth by the time William and Dorothy were born. It is now known as Wordsworth House.

A little way out of the village and on the banks of the river Eamont is Sockbridge Mill, which is now a fish farm where one can buy or catch trout.

The village of Tirril had its share of famous sons and visitors. Thomas Wilkinson, the poet and friend of Wordsworth, was very active in the Quaker movement. In 1733 a Quaker meeting house was built in Tirril and was in constant use for over a hundred years, but in 1861 the house was closed and subsequently sold as a private dwelling. In the graveyard attached to the house was the grave of Charles Gough who was killed in a fall whilst climbing Helvellyn. His dog stayed beside his body for three months until she was rescued. This incident is recounted in Wordsworth's poem *Fidelity*.

Little is known of the beginnings of Tirrel and Sockbridge but throughout history the two have kept their distinctiveness. By 1930 there were 56 houses, 12 of which were farms, in the whole area. By 1988 the number of farms had shrunk to five with sheep farming the main occupation. In the last few years both villages have become considerably enlarged through building. Tirril has a shop and post office, a garage and a public house. At one time there was a Wesleyan chapel. There is no church or school in either village.

Standing at the side of the road that leads from the B5320 to Sockbridge there is a stone bearing the inscription 'Big Jim, R.I.P. 1773'. Who Big Jim was has long since gone from memory: an old horse, a faithful dog or an old tramp who could go no further? He may remain for ever a mystery.

Torver

The picturesque village of Torver is situated approximately three and a half miles south-west of Coniston. Torver beck runs through the valley carrying the waters of a small tarn, Goats Water, into Coniston Lake and giving its name to the parish. The village centre consists of some 26 houses, a converted railway station, a church, two hostelries and a disused school, now the parish room. Other residences and farms, many of them very ancient properties, are scattered throughout the parish, which comprises some 3,120 acres of land, stretching from Goats Water in the high fells to the north-west, to Stable Harvey on the Low Common in the south and Coniston Water to the east.

In 1859 the Furness Railway came to Torver and made life easier for everyone as it carried the stone and slate from the extensive quarrying industry, iron from the bloomeries, and bobbins, swills and charcoal from the woodland crafts. The farming community also made use of the trucking facility on the market train to Broughton-in-Furness. In 1958 the railway closed and the disused goods yard is now used by a local agricultural machinery dealer, coalman and farmer, who is a resident of one of the Green Cottages. These were built by the Furness Railway Company at a cost of £50 each, and are so called because of the colour of their stone-faced front elevations, built from the local green stone to look attractive from the railway.

The original chapel of Torver came with the founding of the priory of Conishead, at a remote period between 1154 and 1189, but the dead of the parish had to be taken to Ulverston for burial , a journey of some 16 miles over mountain tracks. The chapel was consecrated as a church in 1884.

The mill is now an attractive residence, but was originally of great interest, being a corn mill and a fulling mill as well. In the past all the tracks led to the mill. The area is still criss-crossed with footpaths, making a walker's paradise right from the high fells to the craggy lake shore off Torver Common. Although the parish is adjacent to Coniston Water only a few properties have private lake access.

A farming tradition is kept alive by the formation of The Walna Scar Shepherds' Meet, the origins of which are lost in time. It is an organisation of local shepherds for the exchange of stray sheep: an annual meeting being held in July and an annual show each November. This is a social occasion with a show of hill sheep of the Herdwick and Swaledale breeds, sheep dog trials, fell races and hound trails. 'Tatie Pot' is obtainable for dinner at the local, and an evening singing contest rounds off the event.

Troutbeck 🦌

Despite the growing influx of tourists into the Lake District National Park, the village of Troutbeck remains relatively unspoilt. Nestling against the western hills which protected the early buildings from the prevailing westerly winds, it stretches along the valley at the level of a line of springs and never appears to have had a single nucleus. The houses are grouped in little hamlets such as Townhead, Townend, The Cragg, High Green and Longmire Yeat. The river, from which its name derives and which forms its eastern boundary, no longer abounds with trout and salmon as it did in the 17th century, but fishermen still cast their lines after heavy rain with some success. The Patterdale road, after passing the church, climbs up to the Kirkstone inn, reputedly one of the highest hostelries in England.

In the past, a lively social life centred on the many inns where cock-fighting was common and from which hunts regularly departed. Trout-beck is the only village in the area where the office of Mayor of the Hunt has survived for the last 200 years. He (or she) is appointed by their predecessor at the Hunt Supper held every year in February at the Queen's Head. The old hunting songs are rendered with great gusto by the local farmers singing unaccompanied. The village institute was built in 1869 to wean the youth of the village from drinking to more sober pursuits and is now not only the post office and village store but an important centre of village life.

Troutbeck is still essentially a working village, though its population now includes a number of 'offcomers'. Since its lord of the manor was for centuries the absentee Earl of Lonsdale, its social elite comprised the more prosperous 'statesmen' or yeoman farmers such as the Browne family, who lived at Townend for some 400 years. Little modern building has taken place, and the Troutbeck is now a special conservation area, containing marginally fewer residents than in 1560.

Many of the old buildings of Troutbeck remain, though in some instances, as at the Mortal Man inn, the old core has been obscured by later building. The church, with its unusual dedication to Jesus, was rebuilt again in 1736, and now has a magnificent east window which was the combined work of Burne Jones, Maddox Brown and William Morris. The schoolhouse, built in 1637, ended its original function a few years ago and is now a day nursery. Many of the houses date back to the 16th and 17th centuries and some still preserve their old spice and court cupboards. Townend, now a National Trust property, contains the library of the Browne family and much of their carved oak furniture, some of it dating from the 17th century. With its traditional round stone chimneys, it provides a rare insight into the surroundings of a statesman farmer.

Troutbeck Park farm was owned by Beatrix Potter and some of her work was done in a little study there. On bequeathing the farm to the National Trust she stipulated that her flock of Herdwick sheep should be preserved. The local Royal Academician, Caesar Ibbotson, who lived in Troutbeck 1801–3, painted the original sign for the Mortal Man inn. Unfortunately only a later copy of this survives.

Uldale ৰ৯৯

Uldale is a small village on the fringe of the Lake District, the population of 164 having declined since 1900 when there were 222 inhabitants. The village itself sits at the foot of a steep hill, which leads over the Uldale Common to Caldbeck.

On the outskirts of the parish, joining the fells, are the farms, where the livelihood comes mainly from sheep. Aughertree is a small hamlet where remains of Roman camps can be seen, and in a field near Orthwaite are the vestiges of another Roman camp.

A century ago the village boasted a post office, baker's shop, cloggers, smithy, joiner, cornmill, grocer's shop, several farms, a lace-maker, a school, a pub and two churches. Today there is the post office, pub, one church situated on the road to Ireby, a builder, a business of cane/rush seating and soft furnishings and fewer farms. There are several holiday homes and a sprinkling of bed and breakfast accommodation.

The first school to be built in Uldale was in 1726 when Matthew Caldbeck, a farmer from Ruthwaite, gave £100 and 42 other landowners in the parish matched this amount. The school was built on part of the village green and remained in use until 1895. The original building is now a private dwelling known as Dale House.

The shepherds meets are still held. Until some 20 years ago these meetings were held on the fells and the shepherds walked to the appointed place, gathering the stray sheep as they went. They met at Wylie Ghyll for the summer meeting and the autumn meeting was held at Black Hazel – this was of course for the Skiddaw range. The strays would be sorted out to their rightful owners. The valley meeting was held (and still is) on the first Monday in December at five different pubs in the area. The Blencathra Foxhounds always meet at the relevant pub on the same morning and hunt the district, the hunt staff joining the farmers in a tatie pot supper and sing song at night.

With all the hill farms there is the traditional right to graze sheep on the fells and these are termed as heafed flocks – this means that the sheep graze their own part of the fells regardless of the fact that there are no fences. The Swaledale is the predominant breed nowadays having replaced the Herdwick.

Underbarrow

The turnpike road from Kendal climbs westward over the windswept limestone escarpment of Scout Scar, with its far-reaching views of the Lakeland hills and the Kent estuary, to drop steeply past Toll Bar Cottage (1764) to the green and fertile parish of Underbarrow. This, lying as its name suggests below the Scar, is a widespread village of farms and gardens, damson orchards and whitewashed dwellings, covering an area about three miles square, and with a population of about 400. People have lived here from ancient times, but the village of today is largely of 17th century origin, with two or three houses of much earlier date. The climate of the district is notably mild, being sheltered from the east, and lying within the Morecambe Bay horseshoe. It is green here when all around is under snow.

A century ago Underbarrow was proud of its Agricultural Show, and boasted prize-winning ploughmen from contests outside the parish. The village still enjoys friendly rivalry in a good cause, and the annual Marrow Competition, held in August, raises money for the campaign against cancer.

The ancient packhorse road from Kendal, preceding the turnpike and probably known to the Romans, came over haunted Cunswick Scar and past the oldest house in the parish, Cunswick Hall, once a pele tower, now a farmhouse. Helpot, another farm, was traditionally an inn, to serve travellers and packmen alike on their journeyings to Ulverston or Kendal. The church of All Saints was built in 1869, replacing the old church of 1708.

The village hall, erected in 1904 and by very nature of its corrugated iron appearance a feature of Underbarrow, is affectionately regarded and well used. There is no longer a shop or post office, the children have gone to Crosthwaite to school since 1985, and the vicar now lives in Levens. But for all that, Underbarrow has won the Best Kept Village award several times, and the pride of the residents in their village can be seen in the springtime in the magnificent display of daffodils that they have planted on the roadsides.

Underskiddaw

Underskiddaw, as the name suggests, lies at the foot of Skiddaw and its associated peaks. Now a civil parish, it was formerly one of the five townships which made up the huge parish of Crosthwaite in Keswick. In the old churchyard of St Kentigern's, gravestones bear the names of former Underskiddaw residents who would have made their last journey in the horse-drawn hearse which was kept in the parish Hearse House. This building, though long redundant, still stands over Applethwaite.

Although strictly speaking a parish comprising the villages or settlements of Millbeck, Applethwaite, Ormathwaite, Brundholme and Thrushwood, Underskiddaw regards itself as one community. The focus of its activities is the parish room at Millbeck, built by the villagers when Underskiddaw became a civil parish under the 1894 Local Government Act. The most important parish get-together is the Parish Tea and Entertainment held, usually, in February.

Nowadays, the chief industry in the parish is farming: sheep and dairy and beef cattle. Tourism is important too, as most of the large houses have become hotels. Only Ormathwaite Hall remains a private residence. There is also a thriving garden centre.

It is hard to believe that this quiet district was once a busy industrial scene. Woollen mills at Applethwaite and Millbeck provided employment until the 1880s. Applethwaite produced blankets and Millbeck, once a corn mill, later turning to wool, sent blankets, cloth of many sorts, caps and bonnets to the rest of the country and also to many parts of the world. Mill ledgers show that payment was sometimes in kind, for example West Indies rum, coffee and sugar or wine from the Cape of Good Hope. Later, competition from the steam driven mills of Yorkshire caused the mills to close. The Millbeck mill was converted in 1903 into Millbeck Towers, now owned by the National Trust, and Applethwaite Mill is a private house.

Urswick ✤

The villages of Great and Little Urswick are one community. Urswick is in a valley and to the east above the village is Birkrigg Common, an ideal place for recreation and over which the road leads to the sea. The land surrounding the village is in agricultural use. Traditionally those born and brought up in the villages are known as 'Ossick Coots'.

Urswick Tarn covers 14 acres and is fed by Clerk beck and several springs. Its outlet is a beck flowing through Holm Bank and neighbouring villages to Morecambe Bay. It is an important habitat for water birds including coot, grebe, wild geese, mallard and water hens. Cormorants are regular winter visitors. There is a record of a pair of swans being on the Tarn in 1767 and from that date swans have continued to breed there.

The church of St Mary and St Michael dates from the early 12th century. A traditional stone stile still gives entry to the churchyard. In times past the vicar kept a cow in the churchyard to support his living and a chain was fixed to prevent it entering the porch.

The ancient ceremony of Rushbearing continues in the village to this day. This procession and service is held on the last Sunday of September, the Sunday nearest to St Michael's Day. The Rush Queen wears a crown of plaited rushes and carries a decorated crook, while the children carry bunches of flowers and rushes. After the service the flowers are placed on graves in the churchyard.

The village school is in Little Urswick. It was built in 1585 by order of Queen Elizabeth I, and its charter still exists today. It was originally built for the education of boys but is now a primary school. In 1985 HM Queen Elizabeth II visited the school as part of the quatercentenary celebrations. In front of the school is the village green. It is on a rise with several rocky limestone outcrops. In the past cockfighting took place here with many of the older houses having cock lofts.

As in most village communities people come and go but a high proportion of the population are 'Ossick Coots' or their families.

Waberthwaite ✤

Evidence of the early growth of Waberthwaite as a settlement is hard to find. There were certainly communities of hunter/gatherers making camp near the mouth of the estuary of the river Esk between 5,000 and 6,000 years ago, but they did not create permanent settlements. Many years later some historians believe that the Roman troops who established camp at Ravenglass (Glannaventa) came from the south and crossed the river at the ford where the church now stands. The name Waterthwaite is of Norse origin probably meaning 'Wyburgh's clearing'. A preaching cross was erected in the 9th century on what was a well-used route for travellers heading north, and the sandstone cross shaft still stands, now in the graveyard of St John's church.

The abandoned air of the former railway station contrasts with what must have been a busy scene at the start of the century. Quarrying had started at Broad Oak at that time, with granite sets of different sizes sent to Lancashire towns for tramline pavings. Later crushed roadstone was sent by steam wagon to Eskmeals and then by a bucket roadway to Monksmoors siding. The quarry employed about 50 men some of whom travelled from Leicester for employment. Their families later joined them to settle here. The most successful year for the quarry was 1926 when the main road through the village was widened. After that quarrying began to decline despite a slight recovery during the Second World War, and the quarry closed in 1946. Some granite was extracted for Ingersoll drills as it was exceptionally hard and some stone was taken to London Airport in 1979 to be used as cladding for the facade of a building. The quarry site is now a Site of Special Scientific Interest.

As one industry declined another has revived and continues to expand. The village shop was opened in 1828 by Mrs Hannah Woodall, who had been widowed and had seven children to support. The oldest boy went to work at a nearby farm and then returned home to start work as a pork butcher. Many local people brought their pigs to the shop to be slaughtered and the family business began to expand. Hams were entered in shows and exhibitions with prizes being won as far afield as London. The business has continued to expand and modern marketing techniques mean that their ham, bacon and sausage can be sent far and wide. The growing popularity of food prepared in traditional ways continues to bring visitors to Waterthwaite to buy from Woodalls'. The culmination of many years of effort has been the granting of a Royal Warrant for traditional Cumberland sausage.

Waitby ॐ

Waitby is a small village about one and a half miles south-west of Kirkby Stephen. It has three farms and a few houses. One or two barns are now being converted into houses. It has a small village green and also an overgrown village pond. Farming is the main source of employment.

It is said to have been an ancient market town, with a castle, chapel and cemetery, but no trace can be found now. The manor was originally held by a family named Wate after whom it was named.

The free school for Waitby and Smardale was situated on Waitby Fell and was erected in 1680 by a Mr James Highmore of London, a native of Waitby, who endowed it with £400. It was closed in the 1930s and the children transferred to Kirkby Stephen. There is a parish meeting to administer the income from the endowment.

Walton 🐚

> Walton on the Roman Wall!
> Fairest village of them all!
> Rivers three around thee flow,
> Clearer streams no man may know!
> Irthing, King and Cambeck sally
> Sportively to Eden's valley . . .

Thus did James Steele of Holly Garth, blind from his early youth, yet a poet, social reformer, teacher and musician, hail the village of his birth.

Since his death at the beginning of the 20th century many changes have taken place in his beloved Walton. The sapling limes planted around the central green to mark Queen Victoria's Golden Jubilee have grown into magnificent trees. The plodding horses have vanished and formerly dark corners have been brightly illuminated by street lighting. Most of the houses at the heart of the village have been altered almost beyond recognition and new building has taken place on the outskirts, the first of these projects being the Wilson Cottage Homes.

The 'Big House', however, Castlesteads, has by no means gone and is still inhabited by the Johnson family who built it towards the end of the 18th century. At the other end of the architectural spectrum is the beautifully preserved cruck cottage, Roman House. The clear streams, Irthing, King and Cambeck still flow although the corn mill formerly driven by the Cambeck has long ceased to announce its presence by the 'clock-clock' sound which the antique machinery made when working. The fourth generation of the Wilkinson family still live there.

There is still a church, chapel, post office, also a shop with petrol station attached and, of course, the inn. In addition there are two joiners and builders, an electrician and a farrier. The school, having been closed, is now the village hall. Despite the passage of 100 years with all its changes, Walton on the Roman Wall remains a beautiful and unspoilt part of England.

Warcop 🐚

Warcop parish, just off the A66, comprises the village and the hamlets of Sandford and Bleatarn, in all about 450 people. The Pennine range forms the eastern boundary and this also attracted the War Department, who commandeered about 4,000 acres. The Army camp and range are with us today. When the tanks are fired, doors and windows rattle in the village.

Warcop is a pleasant village with the river Eden, noted for its fishing, as a boundary. The ancient bridge connecting Bleatarn and Warcop is said to be the oldest in use over the river Eden. It is only eleven ft wide and has recesses for pedestrians. There is a well kept village green with a maypole and weathervane (made locally) and a well equipped playground. Corky beck runs through the village and has been known to flood into the adjoining houses. The road between Warcop and Bleatarn usually becomes impassable with flood water once or twice every year.

St Columba's church is in part Norman and was enlarged in the 19th century. The parish now is joined to nearby Brough and Warcop vicarage has been sold. St Peter's Day, June 29th, is a much anticipated day by adults and children. On that day the schoolchildren march in procession through the village to the church. The girls carry crowns of flowers, the boys crosses made of rushes. After a special service, tea and sports are enjoyed by all.

Sandford on the river Eden was mainly agricultural and is now almost wholly residential. The chapel there is well attended and the institute is suitable for larger functions. Bleatarn, over the river, consists of several farms. The small church and the chapel are well maintained and attended.

From 1862 to 1962, trains of the London and North-Eastern Railway stopped at Warcop station. Many milk churns were loaded on to the early morning train for delivery to Newcastle before the coming of the Express Dairy Company at Appleby. Trains ran every hour to cope with the sightseers on 30th September, Brough Hill Fair Day. This fair was held at nearby Brough until 1665 when a family there contracted the plague so that the fair was moved to Warcop, where it still is held to this day. It was a busy day for the cheapjacks, the fortune tellers and the horse dealers, but is sadly only a shadow of its former self now.

Warwick Bridge

To qualify as a village, perhaps, there has to be a school, a pub, a post office and a church. Warwick Bridge has all these and more. There are five churches – two Methodist, the parish church of St Paul and Our Lady and St Wilfrid's, the Catholic church designed by Pugin in 1841. The interior of this church has been faithfully maintained to the architect's design to this day. The fifth church is St Leonard's, hidden in a grove of trees at the top of Warwick bank. The present building is dated 1870 but its origins go back to Norman times.

The bridge, which gives the village its name, is three-arched. It was designed by Dobson in 1837 – but not with today's traffic in mind. This links Warwick with Corby Hill and Little Corby which together make up the village community.

One of the most interesting old buildings in Warwick Bridge is the corn mill, which is still operational. The present building is dated 1839 but it stands on the site of a much older mill – originally being a manorial one belonging to Corby Castle. The water wheel is 16 ft in diameter and is powered by a mill-race from the Cairn beck. The traditional lubricant is suet.

Further up the Cairn beck another mill-race fed the Waddell Otterburn Mill. At one time most of the people from the village worked there. Local wool was processed and goods sold worldwide. The Royal family used their famous cot blankets. This mill finally closed in the 1970s and now the site is occupied by an industrial estate and a small racing stable.

According to an old directory, Warwick Bridge used to have two smithies, several cloggers, a tin-smith, a surgeon-dentist, a thatcher and a butcher with a horse and cart. All gone now – on the site of the blacksmith's shop is an antiques shop. Howard Cottage was the last house in the village to be thatched. Mass was celebrated here until the Pugin church was built. It has an attractive stone plaque let into the gable end.

Warwick Bridge was one of the sites chosen for the Land Settlement Scheme. This was an idealistic scheme to help long-unemployed men and their families. Each family was settled in a small house with nine acres of land and a loan to buy seeds and equipment. The scheme was abandoned in 1968 and the houses sold off. The Club, which was formed for the wives 52 years ago, is still amazingly in existence.

Watermillock

On the north side of Ullswater, extending for three square miles, is the parish of Watermillock.

The protecting hills of Skiddaw slate and Devonian conglomerate create a micro-climate in parts of the parish, but the stony land is flooded in winter and baked hard in summer. Hay and silage are the predominant crops, while sheep, mostly Herdwick and Swaledale, are 'hefted' on the fells – the lambs learn instinctively their own pastures – though the obstinate few prefer the roadside verges!

In earlier centuries, much of the higher land was forest or deer park. Substantial stone walls – the 'fell' or 'moor' dyke, sometimes as high as five ft, marked the boundary between farmland and waste. The tenants had certain privileges, such as 'green hue' and 'fern bound', cutting brushwood as winter feed for cattle and bracken for bedding and thatching.

Cutting and clearing bracken by horse sled is remembered by some of the older farmers today. The forest was enclosed in 1816. Two thirds was converted to farmland, and the remainder left for the wild red deer. In 1904 the National Trust purchased 700 acres of Gowbarrow Park, and although the red deer have gone, roe deer, badgers, foxes, buzzards, hawks and herons make it a naturalist's paradise.

In 1891 the community boasted many trades, two schools, a post office, two pubs, and 46 farms. The last 100 years have seen some changes. The beauty of the district had been extolled as early as 1769 by

Thomas Gray, and in 1816 'never a greater run to the Lakes than this summer known' foretold today's outside pressures. Today over a third of the farms and buildings are holiday homes and tourist sites.

Welton ஒ௸

The name Welton comes from the existence in the old days of many wells – 17 are known at surrounding farms and cottages although not now in use. The water was said to be very pure and sweet, but piped water was laid down in the 1920s.

The village is eight and a half miles from Carlisle on the B5299 road to Caldbeck. Approaching Welton, the road drops slightly, swinging through the village in a sharp curve, past most of the houses, the pub and the village green before the climb up Warnell Fell.

It is a small agricultural village with several outlying farms; most of the inhabitants are either directly or indirectly concerned with farming, or the school, and several are retired. There is no industry except for the new factory producing steel prefabrications at the foot of Warnell.

The school, Stoney Cross, is along the Sebergham Road and dates from 1745. The church of St James was opened in 1873, built of local stone, probably from near Sebergham Hall.

At the beginning of the 20th century, life in Welton was very different from that of today. In the village there were, apart from farming, three shoemakers, two grocers, two joiners, a post office, a tailor, a petrol filling station and a blacksmith. He was still working in living memory, and that part of the village is still called Smithy Hill.

The Royal Oak public house has been here since the 18th century, and has hardly changed since it was first built. The famous brass band, with drums, trumpets, horns and cornets, used to practise on the grass in front of the Royal Oak. It played at all the outside events, at shows and picnics. These were local village parties, held on summer evenings in suitable fields or down by the river. Food was brought by the housewives, and people danced to the brass band, who were well fortified by liquid refreshment brought for them in a 'grey hen' – a large ceramic container. Many a romance must have started here!

Welton is best known as the home of Cumberland Farmers Foxhounds, who are kennelled along the Borrans Hill Road, and are counted in 'couples'. The opening meet is usually held on the first Saturday in November, and the village is crowded to watch the Master and two huntsmen in hunting pink, plus many other riders parading round the green, drinking the stirrup cup in front of the Royal Oak. Whatever one thinks of the sport of foxhunting, it is a very stirring sight and sound to see the start of the day.

Westnewton 🌿

Westnewton is a small rural village three and a half miles from the Solway coast at Allonby, and eight miles west of the market town of Wigton. The 60 or so dwellings are arranged in linear fashion along the wide road running through the village, and are a pleasing mixture of traditional houses and cottages dating from the 19th century and dwellings of this century. The oldest building is Yew Tree Farm, dated 1672, and recently most beautifully restored.

Historical records of the village prior to the 19th century are sparse. As late as the middle of the 20th century excavations for new houses revealed the path of a Roman road, and the remains of a Roman fort. At the western end of the village once stood a castle or manor house; remains of its tower were visible in 1829, but now only a rise in the grassy field gives evidence of former days.

It was with the return of a native of the village, John Todd, a Manchester merchant, that a new era began in 1856. Previously the village had no church, those wishing to worship probably travelling to St Mungo's church in Bromfield. John Todd provided funds not only for the building of St Matthew's church, but also the school and school house, a vicarage and four almshouses.

As new dwellings have appeared, so many of the cottages of the 19th century have been demolished to make way for modern day needs. Silver Row was one such row of cottages, and it was home to a village character still remembered by some residents from their schooldays. Coming to the village in the late 1920s, Willie Swails earned his living as a general dealer until his death in 1965. A tall man of over six ft, he made a remarkable sight as he walked down the village balancing his basket of pots for sale upon his head.

Westward 🌿

Westward is a scattered parish, not a village, although locally people tend to refer to the buildings on Church Hill as Westward, where recently a limited number of private dwellings have been built.

On Church Hill stands the church of St Hilda, the mother church of the parishes of Westward, Rosley and Welton. St Hilda's was preceded by a chapel near the river Waver, thought to be near Islekirk Hall, built by the monks from Holm Cultram Abbey at Abbeytown. Inside, at the entrance to the church, there is a brass memorial tablet to Gentleman Richard Barwise, late of Islekirk, thought to be a corruption of Hilda's Kirk. This man of great bodily strength was nicknamed Giant Barwise, and legend has it that he displayed his great strength by walking around the courtyard at Islekirk carrying, at arms length, his wife on one hand and a stone of a most prodigious size in the other.

In the ravine below St Hilda's, called Church Hill Farm, is a rebuilt dwelling which was once a farmhouse as well as an inn in the early years of the 19th century. During the days of the Resurrectionists the churchyard at Westward, being then somewhat isolated, readily lent itself to these ghoulish marauders, and the innkeeper and other volunteers formed themselves into a guard whenever there was a funeral, and kept watch for a least nine days after the burial – surely an eerie business at night in an age when many believed in ghosts and the supernatural.

The people of Westward were, and still are, good hard-working folk, and the parish boasts amongst its sons and daughters illustrious people such as the much honoured Sir William Henry Bragg (1862–1942), born and brought up at Stoneraise Place and educated in Wigton, who, along with his son, Sir Lawrence Bragg, shared the Nobel prize for Physics, awarded for their combined research into radioactivity.

Wetheral ❧

The river Eden flows gently through the Eden Gorge and meanders to the Solway Firth. Above its wooded western bank, five miles south-east of Carlisle, is to be found the village of Wetheral.

Benedictine monks from York in 1088 recognised the Eden as one of the finest salmon rivers in the country and built a priory, of which only the gatehouse remains. Their salmon traps can still be seen and nearby, cut into a sandstone cliff, are St Constantine's Cells.

The church of the Holy Trinity, St Mary and St Constantine is the only church in England dedicated to this latter saint and in 1988 celebrated its 900th anniversary. The anniversary coincided with the restoration of the Howard chapel, originally Roman Catholic, owned by the Howards of Corby Castle and annexed to this Anglican building. Within the chapel is to be found 'Faith', Joseph Nollekens' finest sculpture.

Before the railway viaduct was built in 1830, people crossed the river by ferry from neighbouring Gt Corby for a payment of one penny, children half-price, and villagers bought ice cream and were served teas in one of the cottages which used to stand on the west bank of the river. The viaduct must have been a great benefit to the local inhabitants when it was built for the Carlisle and Newcastle Railway by Francis Giles, the civil engineer who also built Southampton Docks.

The annual fete is held in June on the village green, weather permitting, to raise money for the maintenance of the village hall which, along with the church and Methodist chapel, plays a very important part in the lives of the villagers. Another popular annual event is the Flower Show which is held in September.

Windermere 🐚

Windermere village today is a busy tourist centre which has almost become entwined with the neighbouring village of Bowness-on-Windermere. It is hard to imagine that before the railway came to Windermere in 1847 there were only a collection of small hamlets with a few scattered farms.

The area became a favourite with the Manchester businessmen who used to catch the train to Manchester each day and return in the evening. Large mansions with substantial estates were built for them by local builders and Riggs Hotel was built by the railway company for the tourists. Today most of these mansions and estates which belonged to a few wealthy families have been turned into large council and private estates which now house many hundreds of people.

Windermere was a close knit community with plenty of shops to service the village but as the popularity of the village increased so the shops changed to suit the tourist trade, with many gift shops. Building societies and estate agents are also proving more popular than grocers, greengrocers etc. There used to be a police station and doctors' surgery in the village; both these have now moved and now serve both the villages of Windermere and Bowness-on-Windermere.

Some landmarks have disappeared. The drinking fountain which was situated near the old railway station has been removed and is now at the Brewery Arts Centre in Kendal, but the drinking trough for the horses can still be seen in the wall on the main Windermere to Ambleside road. A landmark which remains is the Baddeley Clock Tower, which was built in memory of Thomas Baddeley who was the first writer of guides to the Lake District.

During the Second World War Short Brothers built a factory just outside the village to build Sunderland Flying boats and after the war the workers were housed in Windermere. It was at this time there was a significant increase in the size of the village when the council estate was built.

Very few places have stayed unaltered throughout the years but Jordans Granary in the centre of the village is one of the few to have survived. The Windermere football team was formed approximately 80 years ago and still field a team today.

The parish church of St Mary has a clock which was electrified in the 1960s, but the chimes have been silenced between the hours of 11pm and 6am because local hoteliers complained the noise was keeping the visitors awake. The Carver Memorial United Reformed church was built by the Carver family and there is a Methodist church situated in the centre of the village.

Just a short walk from the top of the village will take you to Orrest Head where there is a glorious view of the lake and the distant mountains.

Winster ✿

To anybody who knows Winster it conjures up a picture of a churchyard carpeted in spring with wild daffodils and the old post office (Compston House) with its lovely colourful wall of aubretia, alyssum and candytuft. It is named after the river which flows through the centre of the village from its source on Brantfell to its estuary at Grange. The river Winster used to form the Westmorland/Lancashire county boundary along most of its course.

Winster appears in early records in 1170 but it is not until the late 16th century that the church is first mentioned. This church has now gone and the new one was built on an adjacent site and consecrated in 1875.

A notable person in Winster's early history was Jonas Barber, the famous clockmaker. He worked from Bryan Houses from 1682–1720 and was succeeded by his son and grandson Jonas II and III. Jonas Barber III died in 1802 and left all his clockmaking materials to Henry Phillipson, who then moved to Ulverston. Every house of any importance had one or more of his grandfather clocks.

In the 19th century Winster was a busy place with two working corn mills and Low Mill. At Salkeld Tenement the Ellerays carried on the smelly but thriving business of tanning as well as farming. Other trades and professions carried on in the village in 1850 were cobbler, a hoop maker, swiller, weaver, tailor, grocer and of course a publican, schoolmaster and curate. The church and the public house, the Brown Horse, would have been the focal points of village life at this time. The 'Auld Wife's Aik' was one of the village events greatly looked forward to. This was held in the upstairs room of the Brown Horse, as were all the dances and social events at that time. Everyone did a turn, sang, danced and recited – the bar was open all night.

Winster is still an unspoilt village of scattered whitewashed stone cottages, many with a large porch and small orchards of damson trees. Electricity came in 1949 but we are still waiting for mains water, each house depending on piped water from fellside tanks.

Winton ✿

Winton is situated a mile north of Kirkby Stephen off the A685. It contains several buildings of historical interest and in spite of limited development has preserved much of its rural character.

In the centre of the village is the manor house built in 1726, the only three-storeyed building in the village. It was formerly a boys school run on similar lines to that at Bowes. The boys were treated like prisoners and were not allowed to return home until the end of their education in case they told of their life at the school. It was run in conjunction with Winton Hall. This old building is in stone, dated 1665, but its medieval appearance suggests it to be older with its stone buttresses and mullioned windows with iron bars.

Winton elementary school dates from 1659 and stands on the village green. It was rebuilt in 1862 and closed in 1977. Winton Mill was a corn mill which fell into disuse, but Mr R. R. Sowerby converted it into a small power station which gave the village electricity until it was supplied by the National Grid. Recently the mill has been restored and converted into a dwelling.

The green is in middle of Winton. There was once a smithy on it, now demolished. The blacksmith, a Mr Sayer, was also a wheelwright. There is now an agricultural merchant and a dairy, which supplies milk locally. There has always been a joiner's shop. The Bay Horse inn has been extended, keeping abreast with modern social trends.

Winton is a pleasant village and in spite of the many changes over the years a strong community spirit still exists.

Witherslack

Witherslack is a tranquil rural village in the old county of Westmorland, on the east bank of the river Winster five miles north-east of Grange-over-Sands.

St Mary's chapel stood near Witherslack Hall, but was in a ruinous state in 1664 according to the will of John Barwick. Dean Barwick died in 1664 and was buried in St Paul's Cathedral, and he bequeathed monies for repairs to the old chapel and a new burial ground, as previously the dead had to be carried on a dangerous journey across the sands to the

Cottages at Witherslack

mother church of Beetham for burial. St Paul's church was built on ground donated by the Earl of Derby and consecrated by the Bishop of Chester in 1671. Peter Barwick, the executor of the will, further endowed the charitable trust to provide an income for a school, apprenticeships, the advancement of scholars, the 'mayds portion' or dowry, and fuel for the aged and infirm.

Occupations listed in 1786 provide a glimpse of everyday life in 18th century Witherslack. There was a turner, wright, carpenter, glazier, and a waller for construction and six charcoal burners, and four hoopmakers. Three blacksmiths cared for 352 horses, with some using the old pack-horse routes between Ulverston and Kendal, calling at the Black Bull, Rising Sun and Spa inns for refreshment. Millers used the water mill for grinding oats and wheat, and barley for the maltsters to brew ale, and there were 70 orchards to harvest. Farmers provided milk, butter and cheese, and hides for the tanner to make into leather for the cordwainer, clogger and eight shoemakers. Fat was made into tallow for candles used by the candle-box maker. Sheep provided mutton and the wool for four weavers to make into cloth for the tailor. The woodcutter cut willows for the basket-maker and timber for fuel, and peat was dug from the turbaries on the moss.

Woodend 🐝

Situated in what was formerly a busy iron-ore mining area, Woodend was at that time an important junction between the mines and the large railway shunting yard at nearby Moor Row. A row of railway workers' cottages was built in the hamlet, and Woodend Station was a popular passenger and freight link. Excursions to Seascale, just down the West Cumbrian coast, and even as far as Morecambe, are remembered by older residents.

Today, Woodend is a quiet, dormitory hamlet, tucked away between the busy A595 Whitehaven to Egremont road, and the almost equally busy A5086 between Cleator and Egremont. The old station-master's house is still occupied, and the adjoining waiting-rooms have been skilfully converted into a very attractive bungalow with beautifully kept gardens. Next to the old level crossing, the site of the former station yard is now Woodend Timber Centre, with the old engine shed still used as a workshop.

Just around the corner from the old station, a traditional farmstead stands close to the roadside. This is a working dairy and sheep farm, and the surrounding fields are overlooked by mostly modern bungalows, though the original 'big house' still survives, and also a nearby smallhold-ing, now used as horse and pony stables.

Almost hidden away behind the trees, near the centre of Woodend, is Clintz Quarry, now a protected conservation site, where rare species of wild flowers may be seen and kestrels hover overhead. Lower down, the

A5086 road runs close past Woodend Mill, a former corn mill, and near here locals and visitors alike can enjoy a walk round Longlands Lake and Country Park, an unspoilt leisure and picnic area created on the site of former iron ore pits, which had flooded over in 1938.

Woodland 🌿

Where exactly is Woodland? Its name is not on the map and you will find no village, but a broad valley with scattered dwellings, a beautiful place, worthy of the strong loyalties it arouses. The valley is hemmed in by the north-south ridge of the Woodland fells to the east and by an outlying ridge of Broughton Moor to the west; to the south, Wreaks Causeway separates it from the mosses of the Duddon estuary, while on the north the valley's becks emerge from the fells that lead up to Torver High Common.

This is one of Lakeland's richest areas for prehistoric remains. By leaving the road from the east at its highest point, you will find signs of early settlement: Bronze Age field systems and probably a medieval homestead. Nearby is the Giant's Grave, locally reputed to be the last resting place of one of a family of huge men, more likely a Bronze Age barrow.

Down below on a rise of land is the simple church, marked on Saxton's map of Lancashire in 1577, though the present building dates from 1865. Not far from the church, a bridleway, the Monks' Walk, leads north-east to Torver. It was used by the monks of Furness Abbey in the Middle Ages and corpses were brought this way for burial; between Bridgend and Hawes is a ruin, Nether Bolton, said to have been an inn where funeral parties rested.

The valley was not always as quiet as it is today. There was a forge in the 17th century, and above Climb Stile are the remains of a large early bloomery. In Woodland Grove there was a bobbin mill in 1851, employing eleven bobbin turners; later in the same area there were charcoal burners and possibly a blacking factory. Coppice wood was produced and good crops of flax. For a hundred years, there was even a railway; it was opened in 1859 and sadly closed in 1958.

Wreay 🌿

Wreay is a small village five miles south of Carlisle and is thought to derive its name from a Norse word meaning bend in the river – the river in question being the Petteril, half a mile from the village.

Records of Wreay date back to 1319, although it has little of historical interest apart from its Twelve Men. Their meetings are a strange survival of a self-electing body which was responsible for the welfare of the villagers before parish councils came into being. Today the Twelve Men have few powers but still meet once a year in the Plough inn, where they smoke clay pipes whilst conducting what little business they have left. At one time the men were responsible for everything in the village and even built two bridges in the parish. There are minutes of meetings dating back almost 250 years.

The present church stands on a site which is thought to have been occupied by a chapel five centuries ago. The church, the only one of its kind in Cumberland, was provided by Miss Sarah Losh of Woodside and was consecrated in 1842. She also built the school and schoolmaster's house. Sarah sent a Cumberland stonemason to Rome to gain first-hand knowledge before building the church in the Italian style. She was also a great tree-planter and lover of art and nature. Such things as birds, fir cones, butterflies, water lilies and even snakes and alligators are incorporated in the decorations inside the church, which was designed wholly by Miss Losh.

Someone who has disappeared from most villages is the blacksmith. Mr Jim Bulman was the blacksmith at Wreay and was kept extremely busy. Farm machinery was brought for repair and in the days before tractors the farmers had many work horses and these had to be shod. Most of the school children wore clogs and these had to be caulkered quite frequently, especially if their owners tried to make sparks with them on the roads and kicked them off. The blacksmith's shop was a fascinating place with its large fire in the corner and the bellows to brighten it up. When the time came round for playing conkers, Mr Bulman was very popular as he proved the horseshoe nails which were ideal for making the holes through the chestnuts.

Index